LONGMANS' LINGUISTICS LIBRARY

A LINGUISTIC
STUDY OF
THE ENGLISH VERB

LONGMAN LINGUISTICS LIBRARY

THE LINGUISTIC SCIENCES AND LANGUAGE TEACHING
M. A. K. Halliday, Angus McIntosh and Peter Strevens

GENERAL LINGUISTICS
AN INTRODUCTORY SURVEY
R. H. Robins

A LINGUISTIC STUDY OF THE ENGLISH VERB
F. R. Palmer

WHAT *IS* LANGUAGE?
A NEW APPROACH TO LINGUISTIC DESCRIPTION
Robert M. W. Dixon

IN MEMORY OF J. R. FIRTH
Editors: C. E. Bazell, J. C. Catford, M. A. K. Halliday and R. H. Robins

PATTERNS OF LANGUAGE
PAPERS IN GENERAL
DESCRIPTIVE AND APPLIED LINGUISTICS
Angus McIntosh and M. A. K. Halliday

A SHORT HISTORY OF LINGUISTICS
R. H. Robins

SELECTED PAPERS OF J. R. FIRTH 1952-59
Editor: F. R. Palmer

ESSAYS ON ENGLISH
MEDIEVAL AND MODERN
Randolph Quirk

TOWARDS A SEMANTIC DESCRIPTION OF ENGLISH
Geoffrey N. Leech

STUDIES IN ENGLISH ADVERBIAL USAGE
Sidney Greenbaum

ELICITATION EXPERIMENTS IN ENGLISH
LINGUISTIC STUDIES IN USE AND ATTITUDE
Sidney Greenbaum and Randolph Quirk

A Linguistic Study of the English Verb

F. R. PALMER
Professor of Linguistic Science
University of Reading

 LONGMAN

LONGMAN GROUP LIMITED
London

*Associated companies, branches and representatives
throughout the world*

© F. R. Palmer 1965

First published 1965.

Fourth impression 1970

ISBN 0 582 52393 1

*Made and printed in Great Britain by
William Clowes and Sons, Limited, London and Beccles*

Preface

This book is intended for students of Linguistics and for those, especially teachers, who are interested in the description of modern English. It arose out of a course of lectures designed to illustrate to students some of the linguistic problems raised by the description of one part of a language, but the material has been developed to be of use to postgraduate students who are concerned with the teaching of English as a second or foreign language.

It deals in some detail with the English verb, though attention is limited to relation with what in the widest possible sense can be considered the verbal phrase. The syntactic relations between the verbal part and other parts of the sentence would require a separate study. The book is both factual and theoretical (in as far as such a distinction can be made). There is discussion of the problems that arise in the presentation of the material but the scope of the material presented is dictated by its factual usefulness.

The theoretical viewpoint owes a great deal to the views of the late J. R. Firth, and especially to his insistence upon an *ad hoc* approach to the problems of linguistic description.

Bangor   F. R. PALMER

Contents

Preface

1. Introduction   1

1.1. Linguistic background   2
    1.1.1. Speech and writing   2
    1.1.2. Form and meaning   6
    1.1.3. The word   10
    1.1.4. Lexeme and form   11
1.2. Characteristics of the verbal forms   11
    1.2.1. Finite and non-finite forms   12
    1.2.2. Concord   13
    1.2.3. Morphology   14
1.3. Characteristics of the verb phrase   14
    1.3.1. Full verbs and auxiliaries   14
    1.3.2. Syntactic classes   15
    1.3.3. The definition of the verb phrase   16

2. The auxiliary verbs   19

2.1. The forms   19
2.2. Defining characteristics   20
    2.2.1. Negation   21
    2.2.2. Inversion   23
    2.2.3. 'Code'   24
    2.2.4. Emphatic affirmation   25
    2.2.5. DO   26
2.3. Morphology   27
    2.3.1. Positive strong forms   27
    2.3.2. Negative forms   28

2.3.3. 'Weak' forms: summary   29
2.3.4. 'Weak' forms medially   31
2.3.5. 'Weak' forms initially   34
2.4. Classification of the auxiliaries   35
2.4.1. Morphological classes   35
2.4.2. Syntactic classes   36
2.4.3. Primary and secondary auxiliaries   36
2.5. Problematic forms   37
2.5.1. DARE and NEED   37
2.5.2. USED   39
2.5.3. *Better*, *Going to* and *Let's*   40
2.5.4. Semi-negatives, etc.   41
2.5.5. Emphatic *not*   42

3. The full verbs   45
3.1. Morphology of the *-ing* forms   45
3.2. Morphology of the *-s* forms   45
3.3. Morphology of the past tense and past participle forms   46
3.3.1. Alveolar plosive only   47
3.3.2. Alveolar plosive and alveolar nasal   48
3.3.3. Vowel change only   49
3.3.4. Vowel change and alveolar plosive   50
3.3.5. Vowel change and alveolar nasal   51
3.3.6. Loss of final consonant   52
3.3.7. Suppletion   53
3.4. BE, HAVE and DO   53

4. The simple phrase: primary pattern (1)   55
4.1. The paradigms   55
4.1.1. 'Basic' paradigms   55
4.1.2. Infinitivals, participials and imperatives   58
4.1.3. The four categories   59
4.2. Uses of the categories   60
4.2.1. Problems of statement   60
4.2.2. Outline of the uses   61
4.2.3. Time and Tense   62

4.3. Voice   64
    4.3.1. The place of transformation   64
    4.3.2. The function of the passive   65
    4.3.3. Gaps in the pattern   65
    4.3.4. Types of transformation   66
    4.3.5. Transitive/intransitive and voice   68
    4.3.6. Passive versus BE+participle   68
4.4. Tense   69
    4.4.1. Time relations: adverbials   69
    4.4.2. Reported speech   70
    4.4.3. 'Unreality'   71
4.5. Perfect/non-perfect   72
    4.5.1. Time relations: adverbials   72
    4.5.2. Non-progressive forms and 'results'   73
    4.5.3. Progressive forms and 'results'   76
    4.5.4. Past perfect and 'past-past' time   76
4.6. Progressive/non-progressive   77
    4.6.1. Duration: adverbials   77
    4.6.2. Some varieties of use   78

5. The simple phrase: primary pattern (2)   81
5.1. Future and habitual uses   81
    5.1.1. The problem   81
    5.1.2. The simple present   82
    5.1.3. Habitual use   85
    5.1.4. Future use   87
    5.1.5. Future use and adverbials   90
    5.1.6. Combinations of future and habitual   92
5.2. More on the progressive   93
    5.2.1. Limited duration   93
    5.2.2. Sporadic repetition   94
5.3. 'Non-progressive' verbs   95
    5.3.1. 'Private' verbs   95
    5.3.2. Verbs of 'state'   97
    5.3.3. Use in progressive forms   98
    5.3.4. Homonyms   99
5.4. More on the perfect   101
    5.4.1. Special uses   101
    5.4.2. A potential ambiguity   102

6. The simple phrase: secondary pattern (1)   105
6.1. The paradigms   105
6.2. Problems of statement   106
    6.2.1. The function of tense   107
    6.2.2. The formal criteria of the various uses   108
6.3. WILL   108
    6.3.1. Futurity   109
    6.3.2. Volition   110
    6.3.3. Induction   111
    6.3.4. Characteristic   111
    6.3.5. Probability   112
    6.3.6. Insistence   112
6.4. SHALL   113
    6.4.1. Futurity   113
    6.4.2. Promise   113
    6.4.3. *Shall* and *will* together   114
6.5. CAN   115
    6.5.1. Ability   116
    6.5.2. Characteristic   116
    6.5.3. Permission   117
    6.5.4. Possibility   117
    6.5.5. Willingness   117
    6.5.6. Sensation   118
6.6. MAY   118
    6.6.1. Permission   118
    6.6.2. Possibility   118
6.7. MUST   119
    6.7.1. Obligation   119
    6.7.2. Conclusion   119
6.8. OUGHT   120
6.9. DARE and NEED   120
6.10. Summary   120

7. The simple phrase: secondary pattern (2)   122
7.1. Past time reference   122
    7.1.1. Past tense forms   123
    7.1.2. Present tense forms   124
    7.1.3. Forms with *have*   124
    7.1.4. Other forms   125

7.1.5. Reported speech   126
7.1.6. Summary   128
7.2. 'Tentative' use   129
   7.2.1. WILL, CAN and MAY   129
   7.2.2. SHALL   130
   7.2.3. Forms in past time   131
7.3. Conditions and wishes   132
   7.3.1. Real conditions   132
   7.3.2. Unreal conditions   133
   7.3.3. Unreal conditions in past time   136
   7.3.4. Wishes   136
7.4. Future and 'perfect' time reference   137
7.5. Negation   138

8. BE, HAVE and DO   140
8.1. BE   140
   8.1.1. The full verb with anomalous finites   140
   8.1.2. With DO   141
   8.1.3. With to + infinitive   142
8.2. HAVE   143
   8.2.1. The full verb with anomalous finites   143
   8.2.2. With DO   144
   8.2.3. With to + infinitive   145
   8.2.4. With noun phrase + verbal form   146
   8.2.5. Had with infinitive   147
8.3. DO   148
   8.3.1. The full verb   148
   8.3.2. The 'empty' verb   148

9. The complex phrase   150
9.1. Problems of statement   150
   9.1.1. Types of structure   150
   9.1.2. Verbal nouns and adjectives   151
   9.1.3. The structure of the phrase   155
   9.1.4. Analysis of the structures   157
   9.1.5. Negation in the complex phrase   158
9.2. Structures without noun phrase   159
   9.2.1. Model HELP   159

9.2.2. Model AGREE   160
9.2.3. Model KEEP   162
9.2.4. Model LIKE   164
9.2.5. Model REMEMBER   166
9.2.6. Model NEED   167
9.2.7. GET   167
9.3. Structures with noun phrase   168
9.3.1. Model HELP   169
9.3.2. Model LET   169
9.3.3. Model ASK   169
9.3.4. Model SEE   170
9.3.5. Model KEEP   171
9.3.6. Model LIKE   171
9.3.7. Model REMEMBER   173
9.3.8. GET   173
9.4. Contrasting structures   174
9.4.1. Verb+infinitive   174
9.4.2. Verb+*ing* form   177
9.4.3. Verb+past participle   177
9.5. Other structures   178

10. Phrasal verbs and prepositional verbs   180
10.1. Problems of classification   180
10.1.1. Preposition and adverb   181
10.1.2. Idioms   183
10.1.3. The four classes   184
10.2. Phrasal verbs without object   184
10.3. Phrasal verbs with object   187
10.4. Prepositional verbs   188
10.5. Phrasal prepositional verbs   189
10.6. Other verbal combinations   189
10.7. Phrasal verbs as catenatives   190

Verb Index   193

Subject Index   197

Chapter 1

Introduction

The most difficult part of any language is usually the part that deals with the verb. Learning a language is to a very large degree learning how to operate the verbal forms of that language, and, except in the case of those that are related historically, the patterns and structure of the verb in each language seem to differ very considerably from those in every other language. Most of us, as native speakers of a language, are as a result reasonably convinced that our own language has a fairly straightforward way of dealing with the verbs and are rather dismayed and discouraged when faced with something entirely different in a new language.

The verbal patterns of languages differ in two ways, first of all formally, in the way in which the linguistic material is organised, and secondly in the type of information carried.

On the formal side the most obvious distinction is between those languages whose verbal features are expressed almost entirely by inflexion and those which have no inflexional features at all, those which, in traditional terms, used to be distinguished as 'inflexional' and as 'isolating' languages. Extreme examples of these are Latin or Classical Arabic on the one hand and Chinese on the other. English, in this respect, is much closer to Chinese than it is to Latin; or at least this is true as long as we are thinking about *words*. If we ask how many different forms of the verb there are in Latin, the answer will be over a hundred, and the same is true for classical Arabic. For English, on the other hand, there are only five possible forms; if we consider the verb 'to take', we have only *take*, *takes*, *taking*, *took* and *taken*. But this contrast between Chinese and Latin or between English and Latin is rather superficial because it is wholly in terms of the word. For if, when we talk about verb forms in English, we think rather of forms such as *is taking, has been taking, may have taken*, etc., then obviously there are very many more forms in the English verb; in fact there are again well over a hundred. The essential difference between Latin and English is therefore not perhaps so much the matter of the number of verbal forms but rather the way in which the verbal forms are divided up into words.

Perhaps more important, and certainly more difficult for the learner, is the problem of what information is carried by the verbal forms. Speakers of European languages expect that their verbs will always tell them something about time, that there will be a relation between tense and time, and that we shall have at least a future, a present and a past tense referring to a future, a present and a past time. But there is no natural law that says that the verb in any language shall be concerned with time. Indeed there are plenty of languages in which time relations are not marked at all and there are some languages which are concerned with spatial rather than temporal relations. Even in languages where time seems to be dealt with in the verb it is not always a simple matter of present, past and future: indeed, as will be shown later in this work, even English does not handle present, past and future as a trio in the category of tense; we shall not be referring to future tense at all in spite of having past and present tenses. More troublesome is the variety of other features only indirectly associated with time that are dealt with by various languages in their verbal forms. In English, for instance, the verb may indicate that an action took place in a period preceding, but continuing right up to, the present moment, as well as simply in the past. In other languages, such as the Slavonic languages, what is important is whether or not the action has been completed. *I read a book last night* will be translated into Russian in two different ways – depending upon whether or not I finished the book.

In this book an attempt is made to consider both the formal characteristics of the English verb and the way in which the forms function.

1.1. Linguistic background

No detailed *a priori* theoretical framework is postulated for the analysis that follows; the approach is *ad hoc* in the sense that although there are broad general principles the details of the categories and the classification depend on the nature of the material. There are, however, some general points that must first be considered.

1.1.1. *Speech and writing.* Almost all traditional grammars deal mainly with the written language. Indeed they seem to imply very often that only the written language is the *real* language, the spoken language is a rather feeble attempt at reproduction of the written, sometimes to be condemned as mere 'dialect'. Today there are some linguists who have taken precisely the reverse position and who have gone as far as to say that only speech is language. This is an extreme view, though perhaps of some value to redress the balance. What is agreed by almost all linguists is that the spoken and written languages should be kept apart in analysis, that for the purpose of linguistic analysis indeed they are essentially two different languages.

It is very easy to show at the level of the sound and writing systems of the language, the phonology and the graphology, that spoken and written languages are very different. Apart from the fact that they are in different media, one in sound and the other in marks upon paper, there is often no one-to-one correspondence between the units of one and the units of the other, at least in the case of languages that have a long tradition of writing. It is not simply that there are in English such words as *cough*, *tough*, etc., in which there seems to be no relation between the spelling and the pronunciation. The differences go deeper than that. For instance in English there are only five vowels in the writing, but it would be very difficult to analyse the sound system of English in any way that would reduce the number of vowels to less than six. More important is the fact that in speech there are the features of stress, intonation and juncture, which have only to a very limited degree counterparts in the written language. In this respect the reverse of the traditional belief is true. It is writing that is a very poor representation of speech.

Even the grammar of the spoken language is different from the grammar of the written. For instance in the written language the form *has* is irregular – one would expect on the analogy of *have* to find **haves*, while the form *does* is quite regular – we may compare *go*, *goes* and *do*, *does*. But in the spoken language *does* [dʌz] is quite as irregular as *has* [hæz], for we should expect to find, on analogy with the other forms, **[duːz] and **[hævz]. Conversely, the negative form of *am*, which appears in questions only, is so odd for the writing that we are not sure whether we ought to write it at all – *aren't I?* But in the spoken language this is a perfectly normal regular form; it is completely paralleled by *can't I?* and *shan't I?* The negative form differs from the positive in that the vowel is [ɑː] instead of [æ], and that the last consonant of the positive form is missing in the negative form.

can [kæn]   *can't* [kɑːnt]
am [æm]   *aren't* [ɑːnt]
shall [ʃæl]   *shan't* [ʃɑːnt]

We are concerned in this book with the spoken language. None of the examples are taken from literature, as is usually the case in books on grammar. For this reason there might seem to be a very good case for writing all the examples in a phonetic script. This practice, however, we shall not follow for two reasons. First of all it is unhelpful to many readers; there is the simple fact that for many people the orthography is very much easier to read than a phonetic script. Secondly, there is probably very little to be gained in writing the examples in a phonetic script throughout. Only occasionally is a phonetic script useful. The reason is that the orthography is for most purposes as good an indication of what the utterance is as a phonetic script. The phonetic script itself is not an utterance, but merely an indication of an utterance, and the orthography very often will, at least for someone who knows the language, be a good indication of the utterance to which we are referring. Only where the orthography is inadequate will a phonetic script be used. This is not a betrayal of the principle that the spoken and the written languages are distinct, for we are not here attempting to analyse the written form. We are using the written form simply to indicate a spoken form, and, after all, this is one of the functions of writing.

One thing the orthography does not do is show the intonation, and it is not entirely possible from the orthography to judge stress and juncture. Should we then mark the feature either by using a phonetic script or by adding diacritics to the orthography? To answer this question we must look briefly at the nature of intonation. It must be clearly stated that the study of intonation does involve the study of grammar. It involves it in two ways. In the first place features of intonation are very often exponents of grammatical categories of the traditional kind. We may, for instance, make a distinction between the two sentences

> *I didn't do it because it was difficult,*

and   *I didn't do it, because it was difficult.*

In the writing a comma may be used here to show that in the first case the sentence means that I did it but not because it was difficult, but in the second that I didn't do it (because it was difficult), and we could say, and indeed should say, that in the first it is the dependent clause *because it was difficult* that is negated, whereas in the second it is the independent clause *I did it*. The difference will normally be quite easily carried by the intonation. In the first we shall probably have a single tune and a fall-rise. In the second we shall have, very often, two tunes, a rise followed by a fall.

> *I ˅didn't do it·because it was ˅difficult.*
> *I ₋didn't ˌdo it, ₁because it was ˎdifficult.*

Secondly, however, intonation involves us in grammatical statements of a less familiar kind. For if we allow that ˡ*Shall I·come to morrow?* is grammatically different from *I shall come to morrow* on a fall, then presumably so too is *I shall come to´morrow?* on a high rise. The fact that in one case question and statement are distinguished by word order, in the other by intonation, is not very important. If the one is a grammatical distinction, so too is the other. We presumably must go on to say that *I shall come to*ᵛ*morrow*, with a fall-rise, is grammatically different again. It is different in its meaning (it states that I shall come tomorrow but not on some other day), and it is different in its phonetic-phonological shape. We could similarly contrast the complimentary *She's* ˡ*very* `*pretty* on a fall, with the uncomplimentary *She's* `*very* ᵛ*pretty*, which implies that prettiness is the only good characteristic she has. The difference between these seems to be no less grammatical than the difference between *She's very pretty* and *She isn't very pretty*, or *She was very pretty*.

In spite of this we shall, very largely, exclude intonation from our study in this book. Of course, we can add an indication of intonation to the orthography, and this we shall occasionally do as we have already done in the sentences quoted above. But even this is not often necessary or useful. To a very large extent we can ignore intonation in the study of the verbal forms of English. The reason for this is twofold. In the first place, the grammar that belongs to intonation is to a very large extent quite independent of the rest of the grammar of the language. We can, that is to say, deal very largely with most of the characteristics of the verbs of English, we can talk about the tenses, about the other grammatical categories, progressives, perfect, active and passive, the modal auxiliaries, the catenatives, etc., without saying very much at all about the intonation. This point is, however, in itself not a sufficient reason for excluding intonation. The second point is the vital one. It is that it is difficult, if not impossible, to analyse intonation in the kind of framework within which more traditional grammar is handled. The reason for this is that the relation between the intonation tunes that we may recognise and their functions is incredibly complex. For most grammatical features we can talk about specific phonological exponents. For instance, in the case of past tense in English we can with many verbs talk about the addition of an alveolar consonant, comparing *like* [laik] with *liked* [laikt], and *love* [lʌv] with *loved* [lʌvd], and add the rules for the past tense forms of the kind *took*, *bought*, etc. What we do not find is that an alveolar consonant is sometimes the exponent of past tense, sometimes of future, sometimes of negation, sometimes of a modal auxiliary. Yet in the case of intonation we do find

the position is rather like that. A single intonation tune seems to have a
vast variety of different functions; its precise function will depend upon a
number of factors, some of them within the language, some of them
situational and outside the language.

Detailed studies of stress, intonation and juncture are required, but
here in the study of the English verb nothing would be gained and a very
great deal in clarity would be lost if at all times these features were marked
in all the various utterances. In the vast number of cases the intonation,
etc., of an utterance is quite irrelevant for our purpose. *Saw* is a past
tense form in English irrespective of the intonation and juncture in such
sentences as:

> *I saw him.*
> *They saw John yesterday.*

The marking then of one of these features on any utterance is the indication that in this utterance it is specifically associated with the grammatical category or the grammatical element which we are considering.
Indication of them will be made only in those comparatively rare cases
where they are, along with other features, one of the exponents of a
grammatical element.

1.1.2. *Form and meaning.* The analysis presented here is formal, or at
least it is based upon a formal analysis. That is to say, the grammatical
categories are defined in terms of the forms of the language and not upon
meaning, semantics or notions. All linguists today are agreed upon the
necessity for a formal approach to grammatical analysis. The reason for
this is in the first place a purely logical one. In order to describe how
language is used we have first of all to describe what are the forms of the
language and then to describe how they are used. We must keep apart the
forms and the use of the forms of the language. In traditional grammars
the categories are based partly upon form and partly upon meaning, and
this simply leads to confusion. The well-known pair *oats* and *wheat* are
sufficient to illustrate this. If we define plurality in English in terms of
counting then we simply cannot justify the distinction between *oats* and
wheat as plural and singular, for they both refer either to numerous
grains or to a single mass of grain.

In theory it would be possible to start at either end, either to start with
semantics or to start with form. We could set up semantic categories and
see how the forms fitted into them, or alternatively we could set up
formal categories and see how they related to semantic features. In fact
the latter course is the only practical one. The reason is that our semantic

or notional categories are, in the first place, very vague, and, in the second place, very often directly associated with, and dictated by, the formal features of the language. That is to say that what we think are purely semantic, notional or even logical categories are really no more than reflections of formal features of our own language. If, for instance, we were to define plural in English in terms of more than one we should, in the first place, have difficulties sometimes in deciding what was more than one. For instance, is a lawn more than one? It is only one lawn but it is a lot of blades of grass, and the same objection, of course, would hold for *oats* and *wheat*. *Oats* is more than one only if we think of individual grains of oats, and wheat is only one if we think of a single mass or heap of wheat. If, of course, we then appeal to our notions about these concepts and say that we think of wheat as one, and we think of oats as more than one we are merely making matters worse. No one learning English could possibly know that the Englishman (if indeed this is true and I do not think it is) thinks of wheat as a single one and oats as more than one. Similarly we shall get into difficulties if we start with semantics to handle conditionals to find a meaning for *if* before we deal with *if*. Yet a purely notional grammar does need to assume that we have a clear idea of '*if*-ness'. Not only are some notional definitions rather vague, but they are largely subjective. We alone know what concepts we have, and to define a grammatical element notionally is to give it a definition that is accessible in full only to ourselves. There is a logical reason then for keeping our formal and our notional categories apart, and a very practical reason for dealing first, and independently, with the formal categories.

It is important, however, not to move from this formal position to a position that has been adopted by many linguists, that of ignoring meaning altogether, and thinking that the task of the linguist is merely to do the formal analysis. On the contrary it is very important to talk about the way in which the forms are used, to deal with meaning after the formal statement has been made, and in this book we shall talk about the use of the tenses and so on. All those features of use that are not dealt with in the lexicon, those that are not associated with individual lexical items, must be stated somewhere in the grammar.

There is another important, though more theoretical, point. To say an analysis is formal is not to say that meaning has not been used in any sense at all in arriving at the analysis. In linguistic analysis we are faced with a vast variety of choices, we can arrange the material in many different ways, and it is only reasonable to arrange it in a way which will allow a semantic statement to follow most easily. There is nothing dishonest or odd about making a formal statement into which semantic considerations have entered. A formal statement is formal as long as the criteria are formal, the definitions are made in terms of the form. The extent to which semantic considerations have *led to* a particular statement is quite irrelevant.

It follows from this that we shall *expect*, or even *demand*, our grammatical categories and elements to have meaning. The extreme formalists have attacked definitions of, for instance, the morpheme which refer to its meaning. But a morpheme or any other grammatical unit which did not in some sense have a meaning would be of no use at all for linguistic analysis. I say 'in some sense' because it may not be possible (and seldom is possible) to give a simple statement of meaning. But it is surely a requirement of every grammatical (and lexical) item that it shall be possible to relate it directly or indirectly to the contexts in which it is used. It is no accident, no coincidence, then that grammatical elements are so often 'meaningful'; it is a necessary part of their function that they should be. *Oats* and *wheat* and the difficulty of stating the meaning of *if* may warn us against an utterly naive semantic approach to grammar, but they ought not to lead us to the utterly barren concept of a formal grammar that excludes all reference to meaning.

If we do not accept this point of view but insist that a formal statement is somehow based upon the form in the sense that no semantic considerations have, at any time, entered the analysis we are faced with rather an odd situation. We are faced with a situation in which practically all statements are formal to a varying degree, and perhaps in which no statements are utterly and completely formal. Statements will be more or less formal and less or more semantic. This comes out fairly clearly in Chapter 6 of this book, where we talk about the uses of modal auxiliaries such as WILL. We assign six different uses to WILL (6.3.). Are these semantic classes or are these formal classes? It might seem at first sight that they are essentially semantic classes, for they talk about six different ways in which WILL is used. Some formal features are mentioned but perhaps these are just tacked on to the semantic classes. The difficulty is, however, now that we are attempting to weight the semantic against the formal features – to what extent will we be guided by semantic features, to what extent will we be guided by formal features? The answer is probably that we will be guided by both. Sometimes the formal features appear to be incidental. If, for instance, we define a future use in terms of collocation with future adverbials, it may fairly be argued that this is not really a formal test at all, that the future adverbials are only used with the forms that refer to the future because they, too, refer to the future. But, on the other hand, we find with some of these modals that the distinctions of use are more formal than semantic. For instance, if we turn to consider the uses of CAN, one of the uses is with the verbs of perception. We say *I can see my brother over there* as well as *I see my brother over there.* Now this use of CAN is more easily handled in purely formal terms – CAN is used with the verbs SEE, FEEL, HEAR, SMELL and TASTE, which in any case belong to a rather special class (5.3.4.). This use of CAN cannot really be explained in semantic terms although it is sometimes said in grammar books that with verbs of sensation what is stressed is the ability to have the experience – that *I can see my brother* means *I am able to see my brother.* This is a very dubious argument. When we say *I can see my brother* we are not referring to ability, we are referring to the actual fact that we have at this moment the sensation. Even more clearly formal perhaps is the distinction between the two uses of MUST, between *There must be a hundred people here* and *He must do as he is told.* The two uses of MUST may clearly be defined formally, by consideration of the corresponding negative and past time forms (6.7.). It would seem to be reasonable to consider that the distinction between the two uses of MUST is essentially a formal one. But then if we refer once again to the distinction between some of the uses of WILL, we see they can be distinguished, too, in terms of the forms used for past time, and to that extent they, too, are formal. What is clear then is that it never makes sense to say, 'Is this distinction *really* a semantic one?' or '*really* a formal one?' If the distinction is made in terms of formal criteria it is then formal, whatever may have been the semantic considerations that led the analyst to handle his material in the way he has.

Formally definable categories are very often given names that imply their semantic connections. The grammatical category of number, for instance, singular and plural, does suggest that there is some relation to counting, to one and to more than one. This does not make the category any the less formal. It is merely that the semantic feature provides the most convenient label. Similarly when we are distinguishing here between various formally definable distinctions we may sometimes talk about the 'uses' of auxiliaries such as WILL and SHALL, and give these uses semantic labels. Once again this does not imply that the uses are not formally defined. It is perhaps arguable that some of these formal distinctions are not worth making; it may be that the semantic considerations are too vague to warrant categorisation at all. But what is not allowable is to say that some of the distinctions are formal and others are not.

1.1.3. *The word.* The most important unit with which we deal in this book is the word, and for that no apology is to be given. Recently many linguists have been very concerned with how a word can be defined and have indeed doubted very much whether the word is really an important unit in grammar at all. But the justification for using the word as the basis of analysis is a practical one. If we take the word as a basic unit we can, quite conveniently, say most of what needs to be said. The fact that we already have some preconceived idea of what words are is not a serious objection at all. Certainly if we found that our preconceived ideas of what a word is clashed with the convenience of the grammatical statement we should abandon it. In fact the reverse is true. For all practical purposes the word as we know it is a very useful concept indeed.

An alternative as the basic unit of grammar is the morpheme. But the term 'morpheme' is used in a number of senses that may be arranged along a scale of abstraction. At one end it is used, or was used at least, to refer to the smallest, grammatically relevant, but phonologically segmentable element. For instance, the word *dogs* in this sense of morpheme consists of the two morphemes *dog* [dɔg] and *s* [z]. A refinement on this view of the morpheme treats the morpheme rather as a class of such elements (now renamed 'morphs' or 'allomorphs') such that we classify together the [s] of *cats* [kæts] the [z] of *dogs* [dɔgz] and the [iz] of *horses* [hɔːsiz]. But analysis of this kind breaks down very soon in English. For we cannot easily distinguish the morphemes (or morphs) in *feet*. Similarly it is impossible to establish two morphemes, two distinct segments that is, in *took* the part tense of TAKE, in spite of the ease with which we may establish the two morphemes of *liked*. At the other end of the scale we may disassociate the morpheme from specific phonological segments and use it rather in the sense of an abstract grammatical category so that in *dogs* we have two morphemes, one of which is 'plural', not just *s*. Similarly then we can talk about the two morphemes of *feet*. In the case of *dogs* the 'exponent' of plural may indeed simply be the presence of *s*, but in the case of *feet* the exponent of plural is the occurrence of *feet* rather than *foot*. In this sense of morpheme we do not need to segment the elements at all. It is in this second sense only that the morpheme is of any real use, but in this sense the term 'morpheme' is not really needed at all, for then it is synonymous with 'grammatical category' or with 'term in a gram-matical category', and it is not a basic unit, an identifiable unit, a piece of the language in the same sense as the word is. In this second sense of 'morpheme' the word still remains as the basic unit, as the smallest reasonably segmentable unit.

There is a further problem of the elements above the word, larger than the word, and here we would often wish to use the terms 'phrase' and 'clause'. Indeed in this work we shall often talk about the word 'phrase', but a strict theoretical viewpoint which insists that all clauses are divisible into phrases, and that the phrases themselves are all identifiable as nominal, verbal, adjectival, etc., runs into very great difficulty. As with the problem of the word, the solution here is purely a practical one. (See below 1.3.3.)

1.1.4. *Lexeme and form.* One very important point that is very often not made very clear in books on grammar is that when we talk about a 'verb' or a 'noun' we use the term in two different senses. Sometimes it refers to a specific form, and sometimes to a set of forms, all those that belong to one paradigm, that are dealt with under a single heading in the lexicon. For instance, if we talk about the verb 'take' we might mean 'take' as opposed to 'takes', 'taking', 'took' and 'taken', or we might mean to include all these forms. In traditional grammars we very often use the infinitive form with *to* to refer to the set of forms and talk about 'to take'; the verb 'to take' that is, includes 'takes', 'taking', 'took' and 'taken'. The difficulty about this is that 'to take' itself could be considered to be *one* of the forms subsumed under 'to take'. When we talk about the verb 'to take', do we mean all the forms or do we mean specifically this infinitive? Admittedly there would seldom be ambiguity, but there is really no need for the confusion of the terms. What we shall do in this book (and have in fact already done) is to talk about the set of forms as the 'lexeme', and write it in small capital letters, e.g. TAKE, and to write the individual forms in italics, thus, *take, takes, took, taking, taken.* The lexeme TAKE subsumes all these forms. The terms 'verb', 'noun', etc., are used to refer to lexemes. Forms are 'nominal forms', 'verbal forms', etc. Often, however, we need to refer to forms (in examples, for instance) *qua* members of the set, and not as distinct from other forms. It would be pedantic (and sometimes misleading) here to speak of 'the noun form', 'the verb form', etc.; instead we shall talk about 'the noun', 'the verb', etc.

1.2. Characteristics of the verbal forms

In this section we wish to consider briefly some of the characteristics of the verbal forms that will either be assumed in later sections or will not again be mentioned.

1.2.1. *Finite and non-finite forms.* Subsumed under the lexeme TAKE are five distinct forms – *take*, *takes*, *took*, *taking* and *taken*. It would be sufficient for our purpose merely to number these 1 to 5, but this we shall not do for two reasons.

First it is important to make the syntactical distinction between finite and non-finite forms. Finite forms are those that may occur as the only verbal forms in independent clauses, while non-finite forms occur only with finite forms in independent clauses, though some of them may occur alone in dependent clauses (4.1.2.).

There can be no place here for a full analysis of clauses and sentences, but the point is simply illustrated by the occurrence of:

> *I take coffee,*
> *He takes coffee,*
> *I/He took coffee,*

but not

> **I/He taking coffee,*
> **I/He taken coffee.*

Moreover when, in English, finite and non-finite forms occur together the first and the first only is finite:

> *... has been taking ...*
> *... may have taken ...*
> *... keeps wanting to take ...*

We may state then that *take*, *takes* and *took* are finite, *taking* and *taken* are non-finite. But *take* is also non-finite since it occurs non-initially in sequences of verbal forms. If we regard the distinction finite and non-finite as basic, there are six forms, not five, *take* being treated as two forms distinguished by their syntax.

The second reason for not merely numbering the forms is the purely practical one that it may well simply confuse the reader. Instead therefore names will be given to each form. But suitable names are not easily to be found. Names based upon the form itself are preferable, and for that reason we shall call *takes* the '-*s* form' and *taking* the '-*ing* form'. The finite form *take* is referred to as the 'simple form'. It might be possible to refer to *took* as the '-*ed* form', but this would confuse since many forms, like *took* itself, do not end in -*ed*, and moreover some forms that do end in-*ed* are syntactically equivalent to *taken* as well as *took* (e.g. *liked*). Instead the form will be referred to as the 'past tense form'; similarly the simple form *take* and the -*s* form *takes* may sometimes be referred to, jointly, as the 'present tense forms'. (But N.B. from Chapter 4 onwards the term 'present' and 'past time forms' are used in a related but different sense – see 4.1.3.) For the non-finite *take* and *taken* the traditional terms 'infinitive' and 'past participle' are available; the use of the name 'present participle' for the *-ing* form would have been perfectly possible in this book but is avoided because traditional grammars distinguish two kinds of *-ing* forms – 'gerunds' and present participles (see 9.1.2.). This distinction is not made here, but the use of one of the terms might lead to confusion. The forms are then:

take	simple form
takes	-s form
took	past time form
take	infinitive
taking	-ing form
taken	past participle

We shall briefly have to consider in 4.1.2. some verbal pieces that contain no finite forms at all. These involve the use of the infinitives and the *-ing* form only and are dealt with under the heading of Infinitivals and Participials. Examples are *having said, to have made* in such sentences as:

> *Having said that, he walked away.*
> *He cannot be said to have made a success.*

These sequences occur either in dependent clauses (there is no place here for the analysis of dependent clauses) or as part of a complex phrase (Chapter 9). Also considered in 4.1.2. are the imperatives (the forms used in requests and commands). The simple form *take* is used as the imperative, but the imperatives do not follow, in the phrase, the entire pattern of the other verbal forms.

1.2.2. *Concord.* There is no place here for the traditional paradigm of the type *I take, Thou takest, He takes*, etc. All that need be noted is that there are certain very limited features of concord of agreement of the verbal form with the subject of the sentence. There are, in fact, three kinds of concord of which only the first is at all generalised.

(i) All the verbs of the language with the exception of the modal auxiliaries (below 1.3.1. and 2.4.3.) have two distinct present tense forms. One of them is used with the pronouns *he, she* and *it*, and a noun phrase whose head-word is singular. This is the *-s* form. The other form, the simple form, is used with all other pronouns, *I, you, we* and *they*, and with noun phrases whose head-word is plural. We cannot here, of course, define the two verbal forms as singular and plural, respectively, unless we wish to treat the first person singular pronoun *I* as plural also, since it is found only with the simple form and not with the *-s* form.

(ii) The verb BE alone has two distinct past tense forms, *was* and *were*.

These can in fact be regarded as singular and plural, respectively, since the first is found with the pronoun *I* as well as the pronouns *he, she* and *it* and singular nouns. The other is found only with the plural pronouns and with plural nouns.

(iii) The verb BE alone in the language has a special form for the first person singular of the present tense – *am.*

1.2.3. *Morphology.* The details of the morphology of the verbs are dealt with in later chapters. It is enough here to mention what is involved in the morphological statement.

(a) For the auxiliary verbs alone we must deal with morphology associated with negation. This is in fact one of the defining characteristics of the auxiliary verb (see below 2.2.1. and 2.3.2.).

(b) For the full verbs of the language we can recognise five forms as described in **1.2.1.**, a simple form, an *-s* form, a past tense form, an *-ing* form and a past participle. These are not, however, always distinct in their phonological shape. With some verbs either the past tense form or the past participle or both have the same shape as the simple form (see Chapter 3).

(c) The auxiliaries differ considerably in their morphology from the full verbs. None of them have what might be considered a 'regular' *-s* form, though this form is always quite regular for the full verbs with the exception of BE, HAVE and DO when they occur as full verbs and SAY (3.2.). The verb BE, moreover, has a whole set of quite idiosyncratic forms.

1.3. Characteristics of the verb phrase

The analysis of the verb phrase in English depends first and most importantly on the recognition of different kinds of verbs (lexemes). We have to distinguish first of all between full verbs and auxiliaries, and then further sub-classify. Secondly, some of the verbs at least are to be classified in terms of the verbal form by which they are followed. This syntactical classification is mainly relevant for Chapter 9 and to a much lesser degree for Chapter 2. Finally in this section we must consider what is meant by a verb phrase and what are the divisions within the verb phrase.

1.3.1. *Full verbs and auxiliaries.* We may classify the verbs first of all in terms of full verbs and auxiliaries; the defining criteria are dealt with in Chapter 2. Further sub-classification is possible, the auxiliaries being divided into primary auxiliaries and secondary or modal auxiliaries.

This, too, is dealt with in Chapter 2. The full verbs may be classified in terms of the catenatives and those that are not catenatives. The distinction is made in Chapter 9. We have then:

1. Auxiliary verbs.
   (a) Primary.   BE, HAVE, DO.
   (b) Secondary or modal.   WILL, SHALL, CAN, MAY, MUST, OUGHT
                         DARE, NEED (and possibly USED).
2. Full verbs.
   (a) Catenatives.   WANT, KEEP, and many others.
   (b) Non-catenatives.   All the remaining verbs of the language.

Basically the criteria are that the auxiliary verbs occur with negation, inversion, 'code' and emphatic affirmation (2.2.) while the full verbs do not. The primary auxiliaries occur in the 'primary' pattern of the verb and with the exception of DO are not followed by the infinitive, while the secondary or modal auxiliaries occur in the 'secondary' pattern of the verb and are followed by the infinitive only (2.4.3.). The catenatives are those full verbs that are followed by other verbal forms with regular rules of co-occurrence (9.1.).

The classification is to a small degree arbitrary since varying criteria are used and they do not all give exactly the same answer. In terms of negation, for instance, MAY is, it could be said, not an auxiliary verb at all, but in terms of inversion it certainly is. Similarly in view of the fact that OUGHT alone is followed by to + the infinitive we could possibly exclude OUGHT from the auxiliaries. In theory perhaps a detailed statement of these verbs should be 'poly-classificatory', but for convenience of statement a single classification system is preferred.

I.3.2. *Syntactic classes.* The verbs of English may be classified in terms of the form of the verb by which they are followed. Some of them are followed by the infinitive without *to*, some by the infinitive and *to*, some of them by the *-ing* form, and others by the past participle. We may then talk about the verbs that enter into the syntactic structures:

1. infinitive alone e.g. CAN
2. *to* + infinitive   OUGHT, WANT
3. *-ing* form   KEEP, BE
4. past participle   GET, BE

This classification clearly cuts right across the classification in the previous section, and is not a very important one in itself. It is of great importance only when we come to deal with the sub-classification of the catenatives (9.1.4. but see also 2.4.2.).

1.3.3. *The definition of the verb phrase.* The term 'phrase' is here used deliberately in a sense which does not necessarily imply that it is a specific element within a clause. A wholly hierarchical approach to the analysis of the English sentence in which sentences are composed of clauses, clauses are composed of phrases, phrases of words, and in which decisions must be taken as to the status in terms of phrases, etc., of any individual piece, is avoided in this book. This decision is taken for both practical and theoretical reasons. For practical purposes we need not be concerned with what exactly a phrase really is since we do not go on to consider sentence analysis. But there are also theoretical objections to this wholly segmental approach towards language. Many of the problems are shown fairly clearly in Chapter 9, but it is worthwhile briefly stating some of them here.

It is reasonable to divide *The little boy lost his dog* into three sections: *The little boy*, *lost* and *his dog*, and to regard these as a noun phrase, a verb phrase and another noun phrase. Noun phrases, indeed, are fairly easily definable, and a striking characteristic of them is that they may occur in the position either of *the little boy* here as subject or in the position of *his dog* as object, as well as in other definable positions within the clause. But there are difficulties once we turn to such sentences as:

> *John is swimming.*
> *John can swim.*
> *John kept swimming.*

If we must segment into phrases, what in each of these is the verb phrase? It could well be argued that only the finite form *is*, *can* and *kept* form verb phrases here, and *swimming* and *swim* are distinct phrases.

For the first we should compare *John is happy*, where clearly *happy* is reasonably to be regarded as an adjectival phrase, a complement with the verb BE. Is *swimming* similarly the complement, similarly an adjectival phrase? In fact, as we shall see in Chapter 4, there is very good reason for not analysing *is swimming* into two elements in this way but to treat it as a single verbal form, and therefore as a single verbal phrase. If we do not, we shall have great difficulties with *has swum*, since we do not find anything like **John has happy*.

In the case of *can swim* there might seem to be a strong case for regarding this as a single verbal unit and, therefore, a single verbal phrase, since *can* is not followed by any other type of word than a verbal form. We do not find, for instance, **John can cricket*. In spite of this, however, Jespersen argued that the infinitive form after *can* was its object. The reason for this, of course, is that the infinitive is often used as a nominal.

If it is here interpreted as a nominal then it presumably is the object of the verb. But here again we should not wish to follow Jespersen.

With *John kept swimming* we should be able to compare *John kept happy*. Is *swimming* once again adjectival, the complement of the verb? Perhaps a rather stronger case for this interpretation could be made here than was possible with *John is swimming*. But even here there are great objections to this interpretation. These are dealt with in very much greater detail in Chapter 9, but it may briefly be stated that the objections are: (a) There are very close associations between the verb in the finite form and the following form. We do not, for instance, find *John keeps to swim*, in spite of *John began to swim*. This 'selection' of the corresponding form is not at all typical in English of the relation between the verb and its complement or object.

(b) In many cases it would be difficult to decide, especially in the case of the -*ing* form, whether it is a nominal or an adjectival, and in fact the traditional grammars have fallen into great difficulties in talking sometimes about 'participles' and sometimes about 'gerunds'. All that we do in this book, and indeed all that we need to do, is to state what are the possibilities of co-occurrence of particular verbs and verbal forms. The term 'phrase' will be used to cover those pieces of language within which we wish to state relations of this kind.

Within the phrase we shall distinguish between simple phrases and complex phrases. The simple phrases are those that contain only one (form of a) full verb, though they may contain a number of (forms of) auxiliaries. The complex phrases contain more than one (form of a) full verb. Complex phrases are, in fact, those that involve catenatives. Thus *can be swimming* is a simple phrase, but *began swimming* is a complex phrase. Even within the simple phrase we shall distinguish between those phrases that contain (forms of) modal auxiliaries and those that do not. Those that do not contain (forms of) modals we refer to as phrases of the *primary* pattern, and those that do, as phrases of the *secondary* or *modal* pattern.

References

Page   4   **Phonetic script.** Cf. H. E. Palmer and F. G. Blandford, *A grammar of spoken English*, W. Heffer and Sons, Ltd., Cambridge 1939 (2nd Edn.). The script used here is that of Daniel Jones, *An outline of English phonetics*, W. Heffer and Sons, Ltd., Cambridge 1956 (8th Edn.).

Intonation. For works using similar systems of marking intonation see W. R. Lee, *An English intonation reader*, Macmillan and Co. Ltd., London 1960; M. Schubiger, *English intonation*, Max Niemeyer Verlag, Tübingen 1952; and J. D. O'Connor and G. F. Arnold, *Intonation of colloquial English*, Longmans, Green and Co. Ltd, London 1961.

Morpheme. Cf. C. F. Hockett, 'Two models of grammatical description', *Word*, 10, 210–31; and F. R. Palmer, 'Grammatical categories and their phonetic exponents', *Proceedings of the IXth International Congress of Linguists*, 338–45.

Page   **6** **Formal analysis.** For a statement of the strictly formal approach see R. H. Robins, 'Some considerations of the status of grammar in linguistics', *Archivum Linguisticum*, 11.2, 91–114; cf. also D. W. Bolinger, 'Linguistic science and linguistic engineering', *Word*, 16, 374–89; N. Chomsky, 'Some methodological remarks on generative grammar', *Word*, 17, 218–39; and C. E. Bazell, 'Meaning and the morpheme', *Word*, 18, 132–42.

Page **11** **Lexeme.** Cf. J. Lyons, *Structural semantics*, Basil Blackwell, Oxford (Publications of the Philological Society XX), 1963, 12.

Page **15** **Catenative.** Cf. W. F. Twaddell, *The English verb auxiliaries*, Brown University Press, Providence (R.I.) 1960.

Page **16** **Hierarchy.** Cf. M. A. K. Halliday, 'Categories of the theory of grammar', *Word*, 17, 241–92.

O. Jespersen, *A modern English grammar*, Allen and Unwin, London, (reprinted) 1954, Part V, 171.

Chapter 2

The auxiliary verbs

A simple phrase was defined in the previous chapter as one containing only one (form of a) full verb; all other (forms of) verbs within the simple phrase must, by definition, be (forms of) auxiliaries. This chapter is concerned with establishing the auxiliary verbs and stating their chief characteristics.

2.1. The forms

There are eleven or possibly twelve auxiliaries, with twenty-eight distinct forms in all, or thirty if those that function both as finites and non-finites are counted twice:

		finite	non-finite
(i)	BE	*is, are, am, was, were*	*be, being, been*
(ii)	HAVE	*has, have, had*	*have, having*
(iii)	DO	*do, does, did*	
(iv)	WILL	*will, would*	
(v)	SHALL	*shall, should*	
(vi)	CAN	*can, could*	
(vii)	MAY	*may, might*	
(viii)	MUST	*must*	
(ix)	OUGHT	*ought*	
(x)	DARE	*dare*	
(xi)	NEED	*need*	
(xii)	USED	*used*	

USED is the doubtful auxiliary. It does not fit into the full pattern of the auxiliaries and cannot be handled together with them in any detail. But it does in the speech of some people have some of the characteristics that are used as criteria of the auxiliaries. It is considered apart in 2.5.2.

The non-finite forms do not concern us in detail until we deal with the sequences that occur in the primary pattern (in later chapters). But there are two points that may be noted here.

First, only two of the verbs, BE and HAVE, have infinitive forms; indeed, they alone have any non-finite forms. The use of the infinitive as the label for the verb (the lexeme) is, thus, not always feasible. Reference to the auxiliary verbs 'to will' and 'to shall' is now a linguistic joke; the latter, of course, is non-existent, and the former, though historically related to the auxiliary verb, is synchronically to be considered as a different, and full, verb. Errors of this nature are, unfortunately, still made. Even in a recent grammar there is reference to the auxiliary verb 'to do'; yet the auxiliary verb has no infinitive form (in spite of *does go* there is no **to do go*). There are also infinitives 'to can' and 'to must' and the dictionary quotes 'to may', but these are unconnected with the auxiliaries. 'To dare' and 'to need' are certainly closely associated with the auxiliary verbs, but, as we shall see later, we must distinguish between the auxiliary verbs and the full verbs which share the forms *dare* and *need*; the infinitive forms belong to the full verbs. The use of small capital letters to indicate lexemes makes it unnecessary to recognise an infinitive in every case, though where one is available, it is the form so used; elsewhere the present tense form is used (in all such cases there is only one such form – *can*, *will*, etc.).

Secondly, there is no place for *had* among the non-finite forms. The auxiliary HAVE has a finite past tense form *had*; while the full verb HAVE has both a finite form and a non-finite (past participle) *had*. But *had* does not occur among those forms of the auxiliary that occur as non-finites in either the primary or the secondary pattern. We may attest, then:

> *He's had his lunch,*

but not   **He's had had gone.*

Having and *being* similarly do not occur, except in initial position in the phrase; here they mark subordinate 'participial' clauses that are dealt with separately in 4.1.2., e.g.:

> *Having said that, he left.*
> *Being caught, he admitted his guilt.*

2.2. Defining characteristics

It is not their use in the expression of futurity, potentiality, obligation, etc., that makes the auxiliary verbs a class apart from the full verbs of the language, though relying on such notional categories some traditional grammars have treated some of the forms we are now considering as 'tense auxiliaries', others as 'modal auxiliaries' and yet others as 'full verbs'. On the contrary there are four clearly statable formal characteristics of the auxiliary verbs, their use in what I shall call 'negation', 'inversion', 'code' and 'emphatic affirmation'. The first two of these are the most easily applied as a test and give almost the same results. They are, therefore, to be treated as the essential criteria of an auxiliary verb. But the other two lead also to almost the same classification (but see on DARE and NEED – 2.5.1.).

2.2.1. *Negation.* The first test of an auxiliary is whether it is used in negation, that is to say, whether it occurs with the negative particle NOT, or more strictly, whether it has a negative form (2.3.2.). Examples of sentences with auxiliaries used for negation are:

> *I don't like it.*
> *We aren't coming*
> *You can't do that.*
> *He mustn't ask them.*
> *They mightn't think so.*

Positive sentences may or may not contain an auxiliary form:

> *I can come.*
> *We must go.*
> *I like it.*
> *We saw him.*

An auxiliary verb may then be defined as one whose forms are used together with the negative particle – or, to put it a better way, one which has paired positive and negative forms. The difference between an auxiliary and a full verb in this respect is seen clearly if we consider the negative sentences corresponding to the four given above. The first two, are:

> *I can't come.*
> *We mustn't go.*

But there are no similar formations corresponding to the last two. The following are not possible English utterances:

> **I liken't it.*
> **We sawn't him.*

In modern English it is not even possible to say:

> *I like not it.*
> *We saw not him.*

Instead the corresponding negative sentences, like all negative sentences, contain an auxiliary form – one of the forms of DO:

> *I don't like it.*
> *We didn't see him.*

More striking is the fact that other verbs which notionally might seem to be 'auxiliary' – verbs like WANT and BEGIN – are shown clearly not to be auxiliaries in the formal sense in which the term is defined here by the fact that they too are found only with the forms of DO in negative sentences, as illustrated by:

> *I want to ask you,*
> *I don't want to ask you,*
>
not   **I wantn't to ask you.*
> *He began to cry,*
> *He didn't begin to cry,*
>
not   **He begann't to cry.*

These verbs are catenatives, the subject of Chapter 9.

There are some verbs that have not been included in the list of auxiliaries that may seem to be used with the negative particle. Examples of sentences containing such verbs are:

> *I prefer not to ask him.*
> *I hate not to win.*

These can be excluded if, as suggested early in this section, an auxiliary is defined not in terms of the occurrence of its forms with the negative particle, but as one which has negative as well as positive forms. For certainly we shall not attest:

> **I prefern't to ask him.*
> **I haten't to win.*

In fact the two sentences must be regarded as positive sentences, the form *not* being associated not with *prefer* and *hate* but with *to ask* and *to win*. For there are corresponding negative sentences that do contain an auxiliary:

> *I don't prefer not to ask him.*
> *I don't hate not to win.*

The problem is dealt with in greater detail later (2.5.5. and 9.1.5.).

A more difficult problem is that of MAY. For we shall not attest, for many speakers, a negative form **mayn't*. Instead of

> **He mayn't come,*
>
we find   *He may not come.*

Mightn't occurs, certainly in my own speech, though it is not used by

many speakers of American English. Although in this respect MAY does not fully satisfy the criteria of an auxiliary it must be included. For
(a) it satisfies the other criteria;
(b) it has the characteristics of the modal auxiliaries that are stated in Chapters 6 and 7.

Usedn't similarly is a rare form, but the problem of USED is dealt with separately in **2.5.2.** There is also no negative form of *am* except with inversion (see **2.3.2.**).

2.2.2. *Inversion.* The second test of an auxiliary is whether it can come before the subject in certain types of sentence, the order being auxiliary, subject and full verb. The most common type of sentence of this kind is the interrogative. Examples are:

> *Is the boy coming?*
> *Will they be there?*
> *Have you seen them yet?*
> *Ought we to ask them?*

In these the auxiliary comes first, before the subject. The verbal phrase is discontinuous, divided by a nominal phrase, the subject of the clause. The examples given are all questions, but the definition of an auxiliary cannot be in terms of question. For in the first place, a question may be asked without the use of inversion at all, but merely by using the appropriate intonation, commonly (though not necessarily) a rising intonation:

> *He's ʹcoming?*
> *They'll ʹbe there?*
> *You've ʹseen them?*

Secondly, inversion is found in sentences that are not questions, especially with *seldom* and *hardly*, and in certain types of conditional sentence:

> *Seldom had they seen such a sight.*
> *Hardly had I left the room, when they began talking about me.*
> *Had I known he was coming, I'd have waited.*

There is another kind of inversion that does not require an auxiliary verb, as illustrated by:

> *Down came a blackbird.*
> *There are elephants in Africa.*
> *Into the room walked John.*
> *In the corner stood an armchair.*

The essential feature of these (which, of course, must be excluded) is the adverbial of place in initial position.

We must restrict inversion, then, as the test of an auxiliary to questions and sentences with initial *hardly, seldom, scarcely, never, nowhere* – adverbs that we later shall consider as 'semi-negatives' (2.5.4.).

If we go back to the four sentences that were considered in the previous section, the test of inversion and its parallelism with negation becomes clear. We find:

> *I can come*   *Can I come?*
> *We must go.*   *Must we go?*

But we will not find:

> *I like it.*   **Like I it?*
> *We saw them.*   **Saw we them?*

Instead once again the forms of DO are used:

> *Do I like it?*
> *Did we see them?*

The test shows again that WANT and BEGIN are not auxiliary verbs:

> *Do I want to ask you?*   **not**   **Want I to ask you?*
> *Did he begin to cry?*   **not**   **Began he to cry?*

A rare exception to this, in colloquial speech only, is the verb GO, but only in sentences beginning with *how*:

> *How goes it?*
> *How goes work?*

Alternative forms with little or no difference of meaning are:

> *How's it going?*
> *How's work going?*

These sentences are used as part of a conventional formula for greeting. Sentences using DO – *How does it go?* are not used in this context.

2.2.3. '*Code.*' The third characteristic of an auxiliary is its use in what H. E. Palmer called 'avoidance of repetition' and J. R. Firth called 'code'. There are sentences in English in which a full verb is later 'picked up' by an auxiliary. The position is very similar to that of a noun being 'picked up' by a pronoun. There are several kinds of sentence in which this feature is found. A type that illustrates it most clearly is one that contains ... *and so* ...:

> *I can come and so can John.*
> *We must go and so must you.*
> *I like it and so do they.*
> *We saw them and so did he.*

In none of these examples is the whole verbal phrase repeated in the second part. In all of them the only verbal form after ... *and so* is an auxiliary. Where the first part contains an auxiliary, it is the auxiliary alone that re-occurs. Where the first part contains no auxiliary, once again one of the forms of DO is used. By the same test WANT and BEGIN are excluded from the class of auxiliary verbs:

> *I want to ask you and so does Bill.*
> *He began to cry and so did she.*

There are other types of sentence in which the auxiliary is used in this way. A common use is in question and answer:

> *Can I come?*   *You can.*
> *Must they go?*   *They must.*
> *You saw them?*   *I did.*

Very commonly, of course, there will already be an auxiliary in the question sentence since inversion is so common in asking questions. But, as the last pair of sentences shows, if a question is asked without inversion and without an auxiliary (being marked only by the intonation) a form of DO is used in the reply.

It is possible to invent quite a long conversation using only auxiliary verbs. If the initial sentence, which contains the main verb, is not heard, all the remainder is unintelligible; it is, in fact, truly in code. The following example is from Firth:

> *Do you think he will?*
> *I don't know. He might.*
> *I suppose he ought to, but perhaps he feels he can't.*
> *Well, his brothers have. They perhaps think he needn't.*
> *Perhaps eventually he may. I think he should, and I very
> much hope he will.*

The 'key to the code' is *join the army.*

2.2.4. *Emphatic affirmation.* Finally, a characteristic of the auxiliaries is their use in emphatic affirmation with nuclear stress upon the auxiliary. Examples are:

> *You ˋmust see him.*
> *I ˋcan do it.*
> *We ˋwill come.*
> *He ˋhas finished it.*

This use of the auxiliaries is not easy to define formally. For any verbal form may have nuclear stress. We may find, for instance:

> *I ˋlike it.*   *I can ˋcome.*
> *We ˋsaw them.*   *We must ˋgo.*
> *I ˋwant to ask you.*
> *He beˋgan to cry.*

What is essential about the use of the auxiliaries is that they are used as emphatic affirmation of a doubtful statement, or as the denial of the negative. In such contexts we should find:

> I ˋcan come.   (you are wrong to think I cannot)
> You ˋmust go.   (you do not want to)
> We ˋdid see them. (you thought we did not)

Once again, it may be seen, forms of DO occur. Very often these forms would have occurred in the previous utterance which would be a question or a negation, *I ˋdo like it* being the emphatic affirmative reply to either *Do you like it?* or *You don't like it.* But this is not necessarily so; the previous sentence might well be *You like it?* or *Perhaps you like it.*

2.2.5. DO. Finally, we must collate the uses of DO. It is a special type of auxiliary, in that it is used *only* under conditions under which an auxiliary is used. It occurs only, that is to say, with negation or inversion or code or emphatic affirmation. If none of these conditions apply it does not occur. It is thus the 'neutral' or 'empty' auxiliary used only where the grammatical rules of English require an auxiliary, but where an auxiliary is not established by the general context. It follows therefore that we shall find:

> I don't like it.
> Do I like it?
> I like it and so does Bill.
> I ˋdo ₁like it.

There is, however, one further possibility. Any of the auxiliaries may be stressed without having *nuclear* stress; the stress focuses attention upon the auxiliaries. We may thus attest:

> He ˈwill ˋcome,
> He ˈhas ˋcome,

and, no less,   He ˈdoes ˋcome,
> He ˈdid ˋask,

or, and perhaps more commonly, with the stress/intonation pattern

> He ˋdoes ᵛcome.
> He ˋdid ᵛask.

With stressed DO attention is drawn to the fact that a simple form (not a progressive or perfect, or a form with a modal) is being used. What does not occur is unstressed DO except in negation, inversion or code (it is always stressed, of course, in emphatic affirmation). We shall not find:

> *I do ˋlike it   (with *do* unstressed)

except in certain English dialects (e.g. West of England, especially Bristol, and South Wales). The simple form without DO occurs instead.

Not only, however, is DO required for negation, inversion, etc., where there is no other auxiliary, but also it does *not* occur where there is an auxiliary. There are no such forms as:

> *He doesn't can go.*
> *Does he will come?*
> *I may go and so does he.*
> *He ˋdoes must.*

The only exception is of the pattern of:

> *Do be quick.*

On this see 4.1.2. and 8.1.2.

2.3. Morphology

The auxiliary verbs differ morphologically from the full verbs in several ways. First, none of them have a present third person singular form that differs from other present forms *only* by having a final *-s* [s], [z] or [iz] (3.2.). Most of them have no distinct third person form (*I can*, *he can*) at all, while the forms *is*, *has* and *does* [dʌz] cannot (in the spoken form) be interpreted phonologically as *am* (or *are*), *have* and *do* [duː], respectively plus *-s*. The verb BE has other idiosyncratic forms too. Secondly, most of them have negative forms; there is indeed a good case for talking about 'a negative conjugation' since negation is essentially morphological; though *not* occurs commonly in writing, the form [nɔt] rarely follows an auxiliary form in speech. Thirdly, most of the auxiliary verbs have forms that are always completely unstressed, containing either the vowel [ə] or no vowel at all – the so-called 'weak' forms, as well as 'strong' forms that may (or may not) be stressed.

2.3.1. *Positive, 'strong' forms.* Apart from the negative and 'weak' forms the auxiliary verbs have a number of forms that do not follow the pattern of the full verbs (which are considered in later sections). A feature shared by them all is that none has a third person singular present tense form that follows the full verb pattern of having simply a final *-s*. In detail we find:

(a) The verb BE has five wholly irregular finite forms.

(i) In the present tense there is a distinct form, *am* [æm], for the first person singular; for all other verbs the form is identical with the plural form.

(ii) The third person singular and plural form of the present tense are wholly idiosyncratic – *is* [iz] and *are* [ɑː].

(iii) There are two past tense forms *was* [wɔz] (in my own speech [wʌz]) and *were* [wəː], which are again idiosyncratic, not only in their form but also in that in no other verb are there distinct past tense forms for singular and plural. A further peculiarity is that the first person singular form is identical with the third singular; both are *was*. In all other paradigms, apart from the present tense of BE, the first person singular form is identical with the plural forms; it is the third person singular that stands alone – *I love, they love*, but *he loves*.

(b) The third person singular present tense form of HAVE is *has* [hæz], not **haves* (the past tense form *had* too is irregular, but so too are many such forms of full verbs).

(c) The third person singular present tense form of DO is *does* [dʌz] not **[duːz]*, in spite of *do* [duː]. It is worth noting here that even as a full verb DO has the irregular form (see **3.2.** and **8.3.1.**) and that the only other full verb with a similar form is SAY – [sez] not **[seiz]*.

(d) Apart from BE, HAVE and DO, none of the auxiliaries have a distinct form for the third person singular of the present – no form in *-s*. (*Dares* and *needs* are not to be regarded as forms of the auxiliary, see **2.5.1.**).

2.3.2. *Negative forms.* The auxiliaries have negative forms ending in orthographic *n't*, phonetically [nt], but the relations between the positive and the negative forms are of several kinds:

(a) The negative form differs only in the addition of [nt] in the case of *is, are, was, were, has, have, had, does, did, would, should, could, might, ought, dare* and *need*.

(b) The negative form lacks the final consonant of the positive form in the case of *must* and *used* [mʌst] [mʌsnt], [juːst] [juːsnt].

(c) The negative form has a different vowel from that of the positive form in the case of *do* [duː] [dount].

(d) The negative form has a different vowel from that of the positive form and lacks final consonant in the case of *will* [wil] [wount], *shall* [ʃæl] [ʃɑːnt], *can* [kæn] [kɑːnt]. With these three the differences are paralleled by differences in the orthography too – *won't, shan't* and *can't* (not **cann't*).

(e) *Am* has no negative form in statements; the negative form of a sentence containing *am* contains the form *not* [nɔt]:

> *I'm going.* [aim gouiŋ]   *I'm not going.* [aim nɔt gouiŋ]

In questions with inversion, however, there is a negative form [ɑːnt]:

   Am I? [æm ai]   [ɑːnt ai]

The only possible orthographic form of this is *Aren't I?*, but in a formal style this is avoided presumably because it is felt to be the negative of *are* and not of *am*, and *Am I not?* is written in its place. But the form is no stranger than *can't, won't* or *shan't* either in transcription or in orthography. Similarly as was noted in 2.3.2. there is, for many speakers, no negative form corresponding to *may* – no **mayn't* while *usedn't* is at least uncommon.

There is no negative form corresponding to *be*, though on the analogy of the imperative forms *do, don't*, one might expect *be* and **ben't*; but no such form exists (see 4.1.2.).

It would be entirely reasonable to talk about a 'negative conjugation' in English since the negative forms must be handled in the morphology. Indeed we may consider that there is one 'regular' formation with the addition of *n't* [nt] and five irregular ones.

Finally we may note one further feature – that in the case at least of orthographic *can't, won't, shan't* and *don't* the final nasal and stop may be homorganic with the following consonant – these forms that is to say have final nasality and non-nasal 'obstruence' (a plosive, an affricate or a fricative), but the place of the articulation is wholly determined by the initial consonant of the following word. This may be shown by using transcriptions such as [kɑːmp], [kɑːŋk]:

   [ai kɑːmp biː ðɛə]   *I can't be there.*
   [ʃi wouŋk kɛə]   *She won't care.*
   [ai ʃɑːmp pei]   *I shan't pay.*
   [wi douŋk gou ðɛə]   *We don't go there.*

In many cases, however, there is nothing to justify the writing of non-nasal obstruents – one at the end of the auxiliary and the other at the beginning of the following verb. There is simply homorganic nasality and obstruence as a feature of the whole complex. This is true of alveolar articulation as well as bilabial and velar:

   [ai doun θiŋk sou]   *I don't think so.*
   [ai kɑːm bi ðɛə]   *I can't be there.*
   [ʃi wouŋ kɛə]   *She won't care.*

2.3.3. *'Weak' forms: summary.* Most of the auxiliaries have forms that occur only in unstressed positions. These are the so-called 'weak' forms. Some of these are non-syllabic; the others are syllabic but contain

vowels of the kind that are associated with absence of stress in English
– most commonly [ə], but also [i] ([u] does not occur in the weak forms
of the verbs), or a syllabic consonant:

[ail kʌm]	*I'll come.*	Cf. [ai wil kʌm]
[dʒɔn kən kʌm]	*John can come*	Cf. [dʒɔn kæn kʌm]

It must not, however, be supposed that strong forms may not occur in
unstressed position. Indeed strong forms often occur initially, even without stress (though this raises fundamental problems regarding the nature
of stress – it could be argued that the occurrence of a strong form in an
environment where a weak form is possible is itself an exponent of
stress):

[hæv juː ´siːn him]	*Have you seen him?*
[kæn ´ai kʌm]	*Can I come?*

Moreover, in clause-final position, when the verb is acting in 'code' function, the weak form does not occur at all; though the form is unstressed
the form is always the 'strong' one:

He's bigger than I am.	[´ai æm]
She can't do it but he can.	[´hiː kæn]

The weak forms are difficult to describe because 'weakness' is not, so to
speak, a 'yes or no' characteristic but a 'more or less' one. There are, that
is to say, many degrees, and a whole gradation of forms. For instance,
there are a number of forms corresponding to orthographic *we are* that
differ phonetically between [wiː ɑː] and [wə]. Only some of the gradation
may be represented phonetically – [wiː ə*] [wiə*] [wi*] and [wə*].
Even when it is important to contrast two forms phonetically, it is not
certain that the contrast will always be observable. For instance we would
usually distinguish the vowel sequences of orthographic *key will* and *he
will*:

He'll be there,	[hiːl] or [hil]
The key'll be there,	[kiːəl] or [kiəl]

but it would be rash to maintain that the difference is always maintained.
An accurate statement could be made only in statistical terms based
upon experimental phonetics. The statements that follow are thus only
brief approximations. Not only is the number of distinctions that are
made based on an arbitrary (though now traditional) choice, but it is not
supposed that distinctions that are shown are always maintained.

One important classification of the forms, however, is into those that
are syllabic and those that are not. The forms are set out, and this distinction made in the following table. The asterisk indicates, as is now
traditional, that there is a 'linking r' before vowels:

Orthographic	Strong	Weak syllabic	Weak non-syllabic
am	æm	əm	m
is	iz		z, s
are	ɑː*	ə*	*
was	wɔz	wəz	wz
were	wəː*	wə*	w*
have	hæv	həv, əv	v
has	hæz	həz, əz	z, s
had	hæd	həd, əd	d
shall	ʃæl	ʃəl, ʃl̩	ʃl
should	ʃud	ʃəd	ʃd
will	wil	əl, l̩	l
would	wud	wəd, əd	d
can	kæn	kən, kn̩, kŋ	kn
could	kud	kəd	kd
must	mʌst	məst, məs	ms
do	duː	du, də	d
does	dʌz	dəz	dz
did	did		dd, d
be	biː	bi	
been	biːn	bin	

The basic problem is simply to state the conditions under which the non-syllabic form occurs. This depends on no less than five factors:
(i) position of the form in the sentence;
(ii) the verbal form itself (they do not all function in the same way);
(iii) whether the preceding word is (a form of) a noun or a pronoun;
(iv) whether the preceding form ends in a consonant or a vowel;
(v) if the preceding form (noun forms only) ends in a consonant, the place of articulation of that consonant.

The types of weak form that occur medially in the clause are different from those that occur initially. The two types are therefore dealt with separately in the two sections that follow.

2.3.4. *'Weak' forms medially.* In terms of the patterns of weak forms in medial position the auxiliaries fall into three main classes.
(i) The forms corresponding to orthographic *is* and *has* may be non-syllabic, except where the final element of the preceding word is a sibilant or palatal consonant. Where this condition does not apply the auxiliary form is 'fused' with the preceding noun or pronoun form, the whole piece having the phonological characteristics of a single word.

The most important feature concerns the presence or absence of voice of the final element. For we write [s] or [z]:

  [ðə kæts hiə]   *The cat's here,*
  [ðə dɔgz hiə]   *The dog's here,*

but the absence or presence of voice is shared by both the sibilant and the preceding element – the final element (consonant or vowel, though all vowels are voiced) of the noun or pronoun form. The auxiliary is here phonetically identical with the -*s* of plurality and the possessive -*'s* (though these occur, of course, with nouns only, and not with pronouns). In all cases the final element of the piece is a sibilant accompanied by voice or voicelessness, but this final voice or voicelessness is essentially a characteristic of the noun (the lexeme) in all its forms. This is shown by the following:

[dɔgz]	*dog's (dog is, dog has)*	*dogs*	*dog's, dogs'*
[kæts]	*cat's (cat is, cat has)*	*cats*	*cat's, cats'*
[biːz]	*bee's (bee is, bee has)*	*bees*	*bee's, bees'*

With pronouns we find only:

[hiːz]	*he's (he is, he has)*
[ʃiːz]	*she's (she is, she has)*
[its]	*it's (it is, it has)*

The element with which the auxiliary is 'fused' need not be head of the noun phrase that is the subject of the verb, as shown by:

  The girl with the ticket is waiting for you.   ([tikits])

If the noun ends in a sibilant or a palatal the auxiliary must have a syllabic form. With *is* this can only be [iz] (the strong form), while with *has* it is commonly [əz], e.g.:

[tʃəːtʃ iz]	*church is,*
[tʃəːtʃ əz]	*church has,*
[fens iz]	*fence is,*
[fens əz]	*fence has.*

Yet it is misleading to write the forms in phonetic script as two words (with a space between them, as I have done here, in accordance with traditional practice), if it suggests that there is any feature other than that indicated by the vowels [i] and [ə]. For the pattern is still the same as that of the forms with *s* plural and *'s* possessive except that the *has* form has a central vowel (and even this point is not very important since the vowel qualities of both forms show considerable variation). We may then add to the table above if we omit the space between the noun and auxiliary forms:

[hɔːsiz]	*horse's (horse is)*	*horses*	*horse's, horses'*
[hɔːsəz]	*horse's (horse has)*		

(ii) For the forms corresponding to orthographic *am, are, will* and *have* there is a similar feature when preceded by pronoun forms ending in a vowel. The pronoun and verb forms again make a single piece, with the phonological characteristics of one word. The forms are best set out paradigmatically; indeed there is a strong case for treating them as if they were comparable to the paradigms of the so-called 'inflected' languages. For completeness the table that follows includes *he* and *she* with *is* and *has*, which were dealt with under (i):

am/(is)/are	*had* or *would*	*will*	*have/(has)*
aim	aid	ail	aiv
(hiːz)	hiːd	hiːl	(hiːz)
(ʃiːz)	ʃiːd	ʃiːl	(ʃiːz)
wiə*, wi*, wə*	wiːd	wiːl	wiːv
juə*, jɔː*, jə*	juːd	juːl	juːv
ðeiə*, ðɛə*, ðə*	ðeid	ðeil	ðeiv

Two things to be noticed are, first, the degrees of 'weakness' (not all of them shown) that may be indicated for some of the forms, and secondly the vowels of [jɔː*] and [ðɛə*].

An important point to be noted here is that this feature is restricted to pronoun and verbal forms in the grammatical construction now being considered. It does not follow at all that all sequences of pronoun form plus *have*, etc., will have this characteristic. We shall not usually find [aiv] for instance in:

Should I have gone. ([ai əv])

Here *have* is an infinitive and not the finite form with *I* as the subject. The auxiliary forms now being considered are normally syllabic when preceded by forms of nouns or the pronoun form *it*, the 'weakest' forms being [ə*], [l̩], [əv] and [əd], though *would* is usually [wəd] and so distinct from *had*.

In spite of [mænz] (*man is, man has*) we do not find [*mænd] (*man had, man would*), though it is phonologically perfectly possible, but only [mæn əd] or [mæn wəd]. Similarly a contrast can be made with *she* and the diminutive of Sheila which I shall write *Shei*:

[ʃiː əl bi ðɛə]	*Shei'll be there.*
[ʃiːl bi ðɛə]	*She'll be there.*
[ʃiː wəd bi ðɛə]	*Shei'd be there.*
[ʃiːd bi ðɛə]	*She'd be there.*

But there is no difference between *She's* and *Shei's* (except in the quite different feature that the former may be unstressed).

(iii) Nothing yet has been said about the forms with two consonants – those of *can, could, shall, should* and *must*. After a final consonant these will always be syllabic. But we must perhaps recognise non-syllabic forms that occur after a vowel – especially when following pronoun forms (thus patterning with the forms considered under (ii)). A set of contrasts between *Shei* and *she* can again be made. But the differences are not absolute, and an accurate statement could only be statistical. We are again faced here with degrees of weakness. For although we might wish to write [kd] in

[ai kd ɑːsk]   *I could ask,*

this would not imply, except in very fast speech, that the [k] was un-released. It would be different from the (unreleased) [k] of:

[laik dɑːts]   *Like darts.*

The release of the [k] may here then be treated as a mark of a syllable – and in that case the problem is not one of syllabic versus non-syllabic forms, but of degrees of syllabicity. A further point to be noted is that *can* may occur as [kŋ] with a velar nasal. Yet in this case it must be obvious from the fact of the homorganic nasality that there is no release of the [k] before the [ŋ]. But that does not now exclude syllabicity. On the contrary [ŋ] is probably always syllabic after [k]:

[ai kŋ ɑːsk im]   *I can ask him.*
[juː kŋ teik wʌn]   *You can take one.*

There are a few other small points to be noted. First in the case of the syllabic forms of *can* we ought perhaps also to note [kəm] and [kəŋ] to show the possibility of nasality that is homorganic with the following consonant:

[ai kəm pei]   *I can pay.*
[ai kəŋ gou]   *I can go.*

But statements of this kind ought not to be considered as special state-ments about certain of the forms; they are rather statements about the limits of our phonetic description and transcription. There are similar features with all the forms, but they are more difficult to describe and transcribe. Secondly, nothing has been yet said about the non-finite forms *be, been* and *being*. In unstressed position *be* and *been* have weak forms. It is usually stated that *being* has no weak form, and it is always written [biːiŋ]. But this is misleading; we are probably justified at times in writing [biːŋ] and even perhaps [biŋ].

2.3.5. '*Weak*' *forms initially*. With the exception of forms of DO, syllabic forms are much more common at the beginning of a sentence:

[kən ai kʌm]   *Can I come?*   (*not* *knai)

[wəd juː gou]   *Would you go?*   (*not* *dju:)

The forms of HAVE, moreover, are commonly those with initial [h]:

[həv juː siːn im]   *Have you seen him?*

[həz iː gɔn]   *Has he gone?*

In medial position these forms would be much less common in normal quick speech.

A non-syllabic form of *do* is very common, often linked to the following consonant in some way:

[dwiː nou ðəm]   *Do we know them?*

[dʒə wɔnt tu]   *Do you want to?*   (Palatal affricate)

[dðei sei sou]   *Do they say so?*   (Interdental [d])

A similar feature may be noted for *does* especially when followed by *she:*

[dzʃi wɔnt tu]   *Does she want to?*

Did may be represented only by an initial voiced alveolar stop; its duration may often, but not always, justify the transcription [dd]:

[dd ai sei sou]   *Did I say so?*

or   [dai sei sou]

In this example there can be no confusion with *Do I* which must always have rounding – a rounded vowel or [w] – [du ai], [dwai]. But there is the possibility of ambiguity in:

[dðei sei sou]   *Do they say so?*   or   *Did they say so?*

This is not to say that the two are never distinct, but simply that they are not always.

The forms of *can* that have homorganic nasality with the following consonant occur initially too:

[kəm bɔb kʌm]   *Can Bob come?*

[kəŋ keit kʌm] *Can Kate come?*

2.4. Classification of the auxiliaries

The auxiliaries could be classified either morphologically or syntactically. In fact, however, neither a purely morphological nor a purely syntactical classification is very useful. What matters is the place of the auxiliaries in the primary and secondary systems of the simple phrase.

2.4.1. *Morphological classes.* In terms of morphology the verbs fall into five classes.

(i) BE is the only verb in English that has five finite forms (distinct forms for first person singular of the present and for the singular forms of the past) as well as an infinitive, an *-ing* form and a past participle.

(ii) HAVE has three finite forms (one, *has*, is idiosyncratic morphologically) and two non-finite forms (infinitive and *-ing* form, but no past
participle).

(iii) DO has three finite forms (*does* is idiosyncratic in the spoken form –
[dʌz]) and no non-finite forms. (Only the full verb DO has non-finite
forms, see **3.4.**).

(iv) WILL, CAN, SHALL, MAY each have two finite forms, but no non-
finite forms, and no distinct form in *-s* for the third person singular of
the present.

(v) MUST, OUGHT, DARE, NEED and USED, have one finite form only.

If we take one morphological feature only – the presence or absence of
an *-s* form the verbs fall into two types. They correspond to the 'primary'
and 'secondary' auxiliaries of **2.4.3**.

2.4.2. *Syntactic classes.* The auxiliaries may be classified in terms of
the structures suggested in **1.3.2**.

The four structures suggested are:

1. *take* (infinitive)
2. *to take* (to+infinitive)
3. *taking* (*-ing* form)
4. *taken* (past participle)

In terms of these the auxiliaries fall into four classes:

   (i) structure 1 only – DO, WILL, SHALL, MAY, MUST, DARE, NEED,
     CAN;

  (ii) structure 2 only – OUGHT, USED;

(iii) structure 3 and 4 – BE;

(iv) structure 4 only – HAVE.

Dare and *need* are also found with structure 2, but are then to be regarded as forms of the main verbs DARE and NEED.

But the fact that the auxiliaries fall into these classes depends almost
entirely on their place in the primary and secondary patterns of the
verb. If we leave out DO (which has a very special function) there are two
main classes that correspond to the primary and secondary auxiliaries of
the next sub-section – those that do not occur with infinitives (structures
3 and 4), and those that do (structures 1 and 2).

2.4.3. *Primary and secondary auxiliaries.* Of paramount importance is the
classification of the auxiliaries into class I, the primary auxiliaries, and
class II, the secondary or modal auxiliaries. Class I is subdivided.

I (a) BE and HAVE,
   (b) DO;
II   All the other auxiliaries.

The importance of this classification and the chief justification for it is found in the analysis of the simple verb phrase in terms of the two patterns, the primary and the secondary pattern. The primary pattern uses only class I auxiliaries (I (b) only with negation, inversion, 'code' or emphatic affirmation). The secondary pattern makes use of the class II auxiliaries and is essentially an extension of the primary system with the addition of the modal auxiliaries. The two patterns are set out and dealt with in 4.1. and 6.1., respectively. As has already been indicated in the two previous sub-sections, the primary and secondary auxiliaries differ considerably both in their morphology and in the structures with which they are associated.

2.5. Problematic forms

There are a number of forms, both single words and sequences, which raise problems concerning their relation to the auxiliary verbs.

2.5.1. DARE *and* NEED. These provide some difficulty because:
(a) if we use the criteria we have established, it is clear that some of their forms are forms of auxiliaries, but others of full verbs;
(b) there is considerable overlap between the auxiliary and full verb forms but the distribution of the auxiliary form is defective.

DARE and NEED are clearly shown to be auxiliary verbs in their use in negation and inversion, e.g.:

> *He daren't go.*
> *You needn't ask.*
> *Dare we come?*
> *Need they look?*

Moreover, not only are these verbs used here in negation and inversion, but they also have the characteristic of modal auxiliaries in not having an -s form to be used with the third singular. There are no forms **daresn't* or **needsn't*; nor do we say **Dares he ...* ? or **Needs he ...* ?

At the same time we must recognise that the full verbs DARE and NEED are used in the following:

> *He doesn't dare to go.*
> *You don't need to ask.*
> *Do we dare to come?*
> *Do they need to look?*

4

That they are here full verbs and not auxiliaries is, of course, clear by the presence of one of the forms of DO in the negative and inverted form.

An important difference between the auxiliary and the full verb is the structure with which it is associated. The auxiliary is associated with structure 1 – it is followed by the infinitive form alone, while the full verb is associated with structure 2 – it is followed by *to*+the infinitive.

With inversion and negation, then, both the auxiliaries and the full verbs may be used (the latter, of course, with DO). In all other cases only the full verb occurs. This is especially to be noted for the positive non-inverted forms:

He dares to ask me that!   You dare to come now!
He needs to have a wash.   They need to get a new car.

The reasons for stating that these are full verbs and not auxiliaries are:
(a) the forms have a final -*s* for the third person singular;
(b) the structure is 2 (infinitive with *to*) – that associated with the full verb, and not 1 – that associated with the auxiliary.

These reasons would not in themselves be sufficient criteria for excluding the forms from the auxiliaries since the primary auxiliaries have -*s* forms and since the modal OUGHT is associated with structure 2, but since a distinction between full verbs and auxiliaries has been made they are sufficient to link the forms to the full verbs DARE and NEED, rather than the auxiliaries whose characteristics (no -*s* and structure 1) are shown in the negative and inverted forms.

In the other types of sentence in which auxiliaries may occur without DO – 'code' and emphatic affirmation, the full verbs DARE and NEED occur, but the auxiliaries do not (or if they do, very rarely):

You dare to ask me that! I do.   **not**   **I dare.*
I need to see her and so does he.   **not**   **and so needs he.*
He ˋdoes dare to come.
They ˋdo need to ask.

The functions of the auxiliaries and the full verbs are shown in the following diagram (using only NEED, though a similar statement could be made for DARE):

	Auxiliary	Full verb
Positive		*He needs to come.*
Negative	*He needn't come.*	*He doesn't need to come.*
Inverted	*Need he come?*	*Does he need to come?*
'Code'		*He needs to come and so do I.*
Emphatic		
Affirmative		*He ˋdoes need to come.*

There are, however, reservations to be made. First, the auxiliaries do occur with the 'semi-negative' adverbs *never*, *hardly* and *scarcely*; this point is dealt with in **2.5.4.** Secondly, even when the full verb DARE occurs in negative or inverted sentences (with DO) the structure may be 1 (infinitive alone), the pattern elsewhere associated with the auxiliary:

> I don't dare ask.   **as well as**   I don't dare to ask.
>
> Does he dare ask?   **as well as**   Does he dare to ask?

The same is true of NEED; but much less commonly are forms of the full verbs to be found with structure 1. The following are at least rarer than forms with structure 2:

> I don't need ask.   (more commonly ... to ask)
>
> Does he need ask?   (almost always ... to ask)

2.5.2. USED. It was stated at the beginning of the chapter that USED is a doubtful member of the class of auxiliary verbs. For we may attest both

> He usedn't to do that.
>
> Used he to do that?
>
> I used to do it and so used he.
>
> He ˋused to do it.

and

> He didn't use to do that.
>
> Did he use to do that?
>
> I used to do it and so did he.
>
> He ˋdid use to do it.

The latter (in which the verb is a full verb and not an auxiliary by our criteria) is certainly common in colloquial speech, but most speakers probably use forms from both types. For negation a form which belongs to neither set is possibly the commonest – with *not* ([nɔt]):

> He used not to do that.

This pattern is found with both full verbs and auxiliaries (cf. **2.2.1.,** **2.5.5., 9.1.5.**) as shown by:

> I prefer not to go.
>
> I ought not to go.

In my own speech I find that I would normally use the *used not* form for negation, though I may also have *usedn't*, but would feel *didn't use* to be a little sub-standard. With inversion, however, I find *did ... use* much more likely than *used ...*, and with 'code' and the emphatic affirmative would always use forms with *did*. It is clear that, in my own speech at least, USED largely patterns like a full verb. But if it is a full verb it is a defective one. It has no present tense forms and one non-finite form – *use*.

Finally it must be noted that *used* is phonetically [juːst] with final voicelessness, or simply [juːs] in [juːs tu] (*used to*). This distinguishes it quite clearly from the past tense form of the full verb USE, which is always [juːzd].

2.5.3. Better, Going to *and* Let's. Quite common in English are utterances of the type [juː betə gou]. The normal written form would be:

You'd better go.

There is no doubt, however, that often the orthographic 'd has no counterpart in the spoken utterance. To deal with this type of utterance one of three statements may be made:

(i) that this is a verbless sentence,

(ii) that the weak form which is written 'd has here a nil phonetic exponent,

(iii) there is a verb BETTER.

The third solution, though perhaps the most surprising, has much to be said for it. BETTER might, moreover, be stated to be a modal auxiliary since:

(a) it has no -s form,

(b) it is associated with structure 1 (infinitive only).

But its function is limited to positive, non-inverted sentences. In all other types of sentence it occurs only with *had* or its weak forms (see **8.2.5.**).

In children's speech I have attested:

[betnt hi]

Such a form is based on the assumption that BETTER is not only an auxiliary verb but also one which has a negative as well as a positive form (which is, of course, not true of adult speech).

Going to is commonly used to refer to future time (cf. **4.2.3.**), and in this use has weak forms, the 'weakest' being [gnə] and [gənə]:

I'm going to do that.   ([aim gənə duː ðæt])

This would be quite different from what is orthographically the same – I'm going (to London) to (in order to) do that. But it does not fit into the auxiliary pattern at all.

Similarly *let's* is not to be identified with *let us* in:

Let's go.   (I suggest we go)

Let us go.   (Don't stop us going)

But while like *going to* it is a special form it too is idiosyncratic and does not fit into a wider pattern. Its negative is either *Don't let's* or *Let's not*:

Don't let's do that.

Let's not do that.

2.5.4. *Semi-negatives, etc.* Although 'negation' was defined earlier in terms of the negative forms of the auxiliaries, there are several forms which are notionally negative and which may even in formal terms be regarded as closely connected with negation. There are two kinds of sentence in which 'semi-negatives', such as *never, scarcely, hardly* and *no one* function as negatives.

First we may note the use with DARE and NEED. The forms *dare* and *need* with no -*s* and with verb pattern 1 (forms of the auxiliaries not the full verbs) occur, we have seen, only with negation and inversion. Yet we find:

> *No one need know.*   Cf. *John needs to know.*
> *He hardly dare ask.*   Cf. *He even dares to ask.*
> *He need never know.*   Cf. *He needs to know.*

The occurrence here of *dare* and *need* not *dares* and *needs*, suggests that *no one, hardly* and *never* are here negative *formally* as well as semantically.

Secondly, we may note sentences with question 'tags':

> *He's tried, hasn't he?*
> *He hasn't tried, has he?*

Intonationally they are of two main kinds – with a rise or a fall on the tag. The rise asks for confirmation of the suggestion though leaving it open for a denial to be given, while the fall demands confirmation and does not expect a denial. What is important is that a positive initial sentence is followed by a negative 'tag' and vice versa. When words such as *never* occur in the first part, the tag is positive:

> *He's never tried, has he?*

This again suggests that *never* is a negative (formally).

It must be admitted, however, that we may attest:

> *He's* ₪*never* `tried, ´*hasn't he?*

But this is not comparable to (the positive-negative)

> *He's* `tried, ´*hasn't he?*

but to another type of sentence which is positive-positive or negative-negative:

> *He's* `tried, ´*has he?*
> *He* ₪*hasn't* `tried, ´*hasn't he?*

These utterances are almost threats – implying that the speaker is incredulous and intends to react to what has been done, or not done. Here again *never* functions as a negative; the pattern is negative-negative. Other intonation tunes are possible, though less likely. With all of them *never* functions with the negatives.

Sentences with *never*, then, pattern with the negative sentences. This is shown in the following table:

(i) Expecting confirmation (denial possible)

He's ‖*always* ˋ*tried,* ´*hasn't he?*   *He* ‖*hasn't* ˋ*tried,* ´*has he?*

He's ‖*never* ˋ*tried,* ´*has he?*

(ii) Expecting confirmation (denial not expected)

He's ‖*always* ˋ*tried,* ˋ*hasn't he?*   *He* ‖*hasn't* ˋ*tried,* ˋ*has he?*

He's ‖*never* ˋ*tried,* ˋ*has he?*

(iii) Expressing disbelief (threatening)

He's ‖*always* ˋ*tried,* ´*has he?*   *He* ‖*hasn't* ˋ*tried,* ´*hasn't he?*

He's ‖*never* ˋ*tried,* ´*hasn't he?*

There is the same kind of picture with *hardly, no one, nowhere, at no time,* etc.:

> *He's hardly time, has he?*
> *No one's come yet, have they?*
> *It's nowhere to be found, is it?*

It may be briefly noted (though a detailed statement is beyond the scope of this work) that there are pairs of words such as *some* and a *lot, any* and *many,* that are linked to positive and negative (though the patterns are very complex):

> *He has some.*
> *He hasn't any.*
> *He has a lot.*
> *He hasn't many.*

With these too, the 'semi-negatives' function as negatives:

> *He never has any.*
> *I've hardly any.*

2.5.5. *Emphatic* not. In addition to *I won't come, mustn't come,* we may attest *I will not come, I must not come,* with the full form [nɔt]. *Prima facie* there does not seem to be any good reason for treating these as different except in respect of the emphasis on *not* – in both cases we have a negative form of the auxiliary. We have already noted the use of *not* with *am, may* and *used.*

Not follows full verbs, however, as in:

> *I prefer not to come.*

but for reasons already given (**2.2.1.**) it is obviously best to associate *not* with *to come* rather than with *prefer.*

A difficulty arises from the fact that it is possible to say:

> *You can* ´*come, or you can* ˋ*not* ₁*come.*

We may even note:

        I can't not come,

or   *I won't not come.*

From these examples it is clear that we must allow for the possibility of negating both the auxiliary and the non-finite form that follows it. *Not come* must then be treated as a single unit in both *You can't not come* and *You can not come.* In both these examples there would be nuclear stress on *not.*

Similarly we must perhaps treat *not come* as a single unit (so that the auxiliary is not negative) in:

        I ‖will ˋnot come.

        I ‖must ˋnot come.

        He ‖ought ˋnot to come,   etc.

Semantically, however, these do not differ from *I won't come,* etc., in the way that *You can't come* differs from *You can not come.* (The first says that it is not possible for you to come, the second that it is possible for you not to come.) But the problem of these auxiliaries and negation is a difficult one. As we shall see later (**7.5**), *You needn't come* is in one sense the negative of *You must come.* These problems are best left until later; at the moment we ought to be concerned only with the formal criteria for establishing the association of *not* with the auxiliary or the following non-finite form. At least we may say that *not* with nuclear stress is to be associated with the following form. Where there is no nuclear stress the problem is more difficult; it is probably best to handle the negative particle together with the auxiliary in such cases, as in:

        He ‖cannot ˋcome.

        He ‖will not ˋcome.

These are, perhaps, to be related to the forms *can't* and *won't* in exactly the same way as the strong forms of *can* and *will* [kæn], [wil] are to be related to the weak forms [kən], [l]. These are used, that is to say, in a slower, more deliberate kind of speech (though the terms 'strong' and 'weak' would not be applicable as 'weak' is defined in terms of absence of stress, and the negative forms always have full stress).

References

Page 19 **Auxiliaries.** For a rather different analysis of the auxiliaries cf. W. F. Twaddell, *The English verb auxiliaries* (op. cit.).

Page 20 **'To will'** and **'to shall'.** Cf. J. Vendryes, *Le Langage*, La renaissance du livre, Paris 1921, 29 (but corrected in the English version).

'To do'. R. W. Zandvoort, *A handbook of
English grammar*, Longmans, Green and Co. Ltd., London
1957, 78.

Page 24 **H. E. Palmer** and F. G. Blandford, *Grammar of spoken
English* (op. cit.), 124–5.

Page 27 **Weak forms.** Cf. Daniel Jones, *An outline of English
phonetics* (op. cit.).

Chapter 3

The full verbs

This chapter deals, very briefly, with the morphology of the full verbs in English. The syntactical characteristics of some of them, the catenatives, are dealt with in a later chapter.

The morphology of these verbs involves up to five distinct forms, e.g. for TAKE we have *take*, *takes*, *taking*, *took* and *taken*. The simplest way to handle the morphology of these verbs is first of all to regard the first form, the simple form, as basic, and to deal briefly with the *-ing* form and the *-s* forms, and then to deal with the past tense and the past participle forms together.

A separate brief section deals with BE, HAVE and DO as full verbs.

3.1. Morphology of the *-ing* forms

We may dispose quickly of the morphology of the *-ing* form. In all cases it differs from the simple form only by the addition of [iŋ]:

   cut [kʌt]   *cutting* [kʌtiŋ]

In rapid conversational style the final nasal is often alveolar ([n]) instead of velar ([ŋ]). Forms with the alveolar nasal are often regarded as sub-standard, but they certainly occur in my speech and in that of others.

3.2. Morphology of the *-s* forms

The *-s* form differs from the simple form by the addition of an alveolar fricative (a sibilant). Phonetically there are three possibilities:

(i) a voiceless sibilant ([s]) where the final element of the simple form is voiceless and is not sibilant or palatal,

(ii) a voiced sibilant ([z]) where the final element of the simple form is voiced and is not sibilant or palatal,

(iii) a voiced sibilant ([z]) preceded by the vowel [i] where the final element of the simple form is sibilant or palatal.

These features are entirely determined by phonetic characteristics; their differences are not to be regarded as grammatical. The phonological exponent of the -s form is simply 'sibilance', and the English orthography, which does not make a distinction but merely writes a final -s, is grammatically more appropriate than phonetic notation which writes each of the three phonetically different forms in three different ways. We have then:

(i)   *hate* [heit]   *hates* [heits]
(ii)   *love* [lʌv]   *loves* [lʌvz]
       stay [stei]   *stays* [steiz]
(iii) *miss* [mis]   *misses* [misiz]

Apart from BE, HAVE and DO there is only one verb in English which is irregular in respect of its -s form; this is the verb SAY, whose -s form, though spelt *says*, is nevertheless [sez] not *[seiz].

3.3. Morphology of the past tense and past participle forms

To deal with the morphology of the past tense and past participle forms we must take note of four kinds of 'formation' involving:

(a)   an alveolar plosive ([t] or [d]) in final position,
(b)   an alveolar nasal ([n]) in final position,
(c)   vowel change,
(d)   loss of final consonant.

The picture is complicated by two facts, first, that with some verbs the two forms are identical but with others they are different, and secondly, that with some of the forms the features occur alone and with others in combination. As a result many ways of classifying the verbs are possible. Here we shall set up six classes in terms of the occurrence of:

(i)   an alveolar plosive only,
(ii)   an alveolar plosive and an alveolar nasal,
(iii) vowel change only,
(iv)   vowel change and an alveolar plosive,
(v)   vowel change and an alveolar nasal (plus, for one verb only, an alveolar plosive),
(vi)   loss of final consonant (always accompanied by an alveolar plosive and, with one exception, vowel change.).

There are, however, a number of sub-classes for each of these classes, and even in some cases sub-sub-classes. A seventh class involves suppletion.

3.3.1. *Alveolar plosive only.* Where an alveolar plosive alone is involved in the formation, the two forms, past tense and past participle, are in all cases identical. There are four sub-sections.

(a) The vast majority of the verbs in the English language are, of course, those whose past tense and past participle forms differ from the simple form only by the addition of a final *-d* or *-ed* in the orthography. In the spoken language the difference is in the addition of a final alveolar plosive which, like the final sibilant of the *-s* form, is either voiceless, voiced, or preceded by the vowel [i], depending upon the characteristics of the preceding sound. An essential difference is that the alveolar plosive is preceded by this vowel when the preceding consonant is another alveolar plosive (and not as in the case of the *-s* form, a sibilant or a palatal). This is, however, to be expected; there is here a feature similar to 'dissimilation' – the non-occurrence of two consonants of the same type together. The final alveolar plosive is then:

(i) voiceless ([t]) when the final element of the simple form is a voiceless consonant that is not an alveolar plosive, e.g.:

   like [laik]   *liked* [laikt]

(ii) voiced ([d]) when the final element of the simple form is a voiced consonant that is not an alveolar plosive or is a vowel, e.g.:

   love [lʌv]   *loved* [lʌvd]
   stay [stei]   *stayed* [steid]

(iii) a voiced consonant ([d]) preceded by the vowel [i] when the final element of the simple form is an alveolar plosive ([t] or [d]), e.g.:

   hate [heit]   *hated* ([heitid]

(b) There is a small number of verbs in English in which the past tense and past participle forms again differ from the simple form in having an additional alveolar plosive, but a *voiceless* plosive though the preceding consonant is voiced. In all cases this previous consonant is a voiced lateral or a voiced nasal. e.g.:

   smell [smel]   *smelt* or *smelled* [smelt]

The verbs that belong to this class are BURN, LEARN, SPELL, SMELL, SPILL, SPOIL, and DWELL if it is ever used. In the orthography the ending is either *-t* or *-ed*.

(c) There are some verbs whose simple forms end in a voiced alveolar plosive while the past tense and the past participle forms end in a voiceless alveolar plosive. In all cases the preceding consonant is a voiced lateral or a voiced alveolar nasal (see the previous sub-class), e.g.:

   bend [bend]   *bent* [bent]

Verbs that belong to this class are BEND, BUILD, LEND, SEND, SPEND and (if they are ever used) REND, and GIRD.

(d) There are many verbs in English in which the past tense and past participle forms are exactly the same as the simple forms. But in *all* cases the final consonant of the form is an alveolar plosive. These are usually treated in works on linguistics as having zero suffixes. This fails to make clear what is the important feature – their final alveolar plosive, e.g.:

> *hit* [hit]   *hit* [hit]
>
> *spread* [spred]   *spread* [spred]

To handle these forms in terms of zeros suggests that it is the past tense and past participle forms that are 'irregular', yet they share, with all the other forms that are dealt with in this sub-section, the fact that they have a final alveolar plosive, and are to that extent perfectly 'regular'. Verbs that belong to this class are (with final voiceless alveolar plosive) BET, BURST, CAST, COST, CUT, HIT, HURT, LET, PUT, QUIT, SET, SHUT, SLIT, SPLIT, THRUST, UPSET and (with final voiced alveolar plosive) RID, SHED and SPREAD. WET belongs to both this sub-class and sub-class (a).

The whole of the section may be briefly stated in terms of sandhi rules, treating the suffix as t. We have then (noting the forms with no change as well as those with change):

  (i) -Ct → -Ct   where -C is voiceless,

 (ii) -Ct → -Cd   where -C is voiced,

except that always

(iii) -Ct → -C   or   -Cid   where -C is alveolar,

and for some verbs

(iv) -Ct → -Ct ⎫
(v) -Cdt → -Ct ⎭ where -C is a nasal or lateral.

3.3.2. *Alveolar plosive and alveolar nasal.* The occurrence of the alveolar nasal is confined to the past participle. It is a feature, therefore, that always occurs in combination with one of the other features (in the past tense form).

(a) There is only a very small number of verbs in English for which the past tense form has a final alveolar plosive and the past participle a final alveolar nasal, as in:

> *sew* [sou]   *sewed* [soud]   *sewn* [soun]

The verbs in this sub-class are SEW, SOW, SHOW. HEW, if it is ever used, also belongs here.

(b) One verb only belongs to this class but follows the pattern of (d) of the previous section in regard to the past tense form. That is to say the past tense form ends in an alveolar plosive but is identical with the simple form, while the past participle has an additional final alveolar nasal. This is BEAT:

> *beat* [biːt]   *beat* [biːt]   *beaten* [biːtn]

3.3.3. *Vowel change only.*

Verbs in which the morphology of the past tense and past participle forms involves only vowel change may be divided into three sub-classes: first, those in which all three forms are different; secondly, those in which the past tense and the past participles are the same but differ from the simple form; thirdly, those in which only the past tense form differs from the other two, the past participle being identical with the simple form.

(a) Verbs in which all three forms are different follow a single pattern. The vowel of the simple form is [i], the vowel of the past tense form is [æ], the vowel of the past participle is [ʌ], e.g.:

> *drink* [driŋk]   *drank* [dræŋk]   *drunk* [drʌŋk]

Verbs that belong to this class are BEGIN, DRINK, RING, SHRINK, SING, SINK, SPRING, STINK, SWIM. All the verbs in this class have a final nasal or a final nasal + a homorganic plosive.

(b) There are many verbs whose past tense and past participle forms are identical but differ from the simple forms. The vowel changes involved are as many as twelve different kinds, leading to twelve sub-sub-classes. The patterns involved and the verbs belonging to these are:

(i) *win* [win]   *won* [wʌn]
   CLING, DIG, FLING, SLING, SPIN, STICK, STING, STRING, SWING, WIN, WRING

(ii) *sit* [sit]   *sat* [sæt]
   SIT, SPIT

(iii) *bleed* [bliːd]   *bled* [bled]
   BLEED, BREED, FEED, LEAD, MEET, READ, SPEED
(A feature that all these have in common is a final alveolar plosive.)

(iv) *get* [get]   *got* [gɔt]
   GET

(v) *hang* [hæŋ]   *hung* [hʌŋ]
   HANG (*hanged* is used where reference is to capital punishment)

(vi) *find* [faind]   *found* [faund]
   BIND, FIND, GRIND, WIND

(vii) *light* [lait]   *lit* [lit]
   LIGHT, SLIDE

(viii) *shine* [ʃain]   *shone* [ʃɔn]
    SHINE
 (ix) *fight* [fait]   *fought* [fɔːt]
    FIGHT
  (x) *strike* [straik]   *struck* [strʌk]
    STRIKE
 (xi) *hold* [hould]   *held* [held]
    HOLD
(xii) *shoot* [ʃuːt]   *shot* [ʃɔt]
    SHOOT

(c) There are only a few verbs in English in which the past participle is the same as the simple form but the past tense form is different. They are two sub-sub-classes:

 (i) *come* [kʌm]   *came* [keim]   (*come* [kʌm])
    COME, BECOME
(ii) *run* [rʌn]   *ran* [ræn]   (*run* [rʌn])
    RUN

3.3.4. *Vowel change and alveolar plosive.* For all the verbs in which both vowel change and an alveolar plosive are involved the past tense and the past participle forms are identical. They can be sub-classified in terms of features involving the alveolar plosives as were the verbs of the first class we considered (**3.3.1.**). Further classification is in terms of the type of vowel change.

(a) There are a few verbs in which there is vowel change with the alveolar plosive in the pattern of the 'regular' verbs of the English language in that there is an alveolar consonant that is voiced or voiceless according to the voice or voicelessness of the final element of the simple form. There are six sub-sub-classes; only the first two have more than one member:

 (i) *keep* [kiːp]   *kept* [kept]
    CREEP, KEEP, LEAP, SWEEP, SLEEP, WEEP
 (ii) *sell* [sel]   *sold* [sould]
    SELL, TELL
(iii) *flee* [fliː]   *fled* [fled]
    FLEE
(iv) *hear* [hiə]   *heard* [həːd]
    HEAR
 (v) *say* [sei]   *said* [sed]
    SAY
(vi) *shoe* [ʃuː]   *shod* [ʃɔd]
    SHOE

(b) There are a few verbs in which the final alveolar plosive is voiceless although the final consonant of the simple form is voiced. In all cases once again (see 3.3.1.) this final consonant is a lateral or a nasal (the sandhi rules apply):

> *mean* [miːn]   *meant* [ment]
> DEAL, DREAM, FEEL, KNEEL, LEAN, MEAN

We might also perhaps include here (but cf. the forms in 3.3.6.(b) – the sandhi rules do not apply):

> *buy* [bai]   *bought* [bɔːt]
> BOUGHT

(c) There are two verbs in which the final consonant of the simple form is voiced but the corresponding consonant of the past tense and participle forms is voiceless; the following alveolar plosive is also voiceless. These belong to two separate sub-sub-classes:

(i) *leave* [liːv]   *left* [left]
> LEAVE, and BEREAVE if used

(ii) *lose* [luːz]   *lost* [lɔst]
> LOSE

3.3.5. *Vowel change and alveolar nasal.* As in 3.3.3. there are three sub-classes here depending on whether there are three different vowels or two vowels, and whether, in the latter case, the vowels of the past tense and of the past participle forms are identical but different from that of the simple form or whether the vowel of the past tense form alone is different from the other two.

(a) There are not very many verbs in which three distinct vowels are involved. There are two sub-classes but all except one of the verbs belong to the first:

(i) *ride* [raid]   *rode* [roud]   *ridden* [ridn]
> DRIVE, RIDE, RISE, STRIVE, WRITE, and if it is used SMITE. We should perhaps add STRIDE, with past tense *strode*, but without a past participle (there is no *stridden).

(ii) *fly* [flai]   *flew* [fluː]   *flown* [floun]
> FLY

(b) There are seven sub-sub-classes of verbs for which the vowels of the past tense forms and the past participles are identical but differ from those of the simple forms:

(i) *steal* [stiːl]   *stole* [stoul]   *stolen* [stouln]
> FREEZE, SPEAK, STEAL, WEAVE

(ii) *break* [breik]   *broke* [brouk]   *broken* [broukn]
> BREAK, WAKE

  (iii) *forget* [fəget] *forgot* [fəgɔt] *forgotten* [fəgɔtn]
     FORGET, TREAD
  (iv) *bear* [bɛə] *bore* [bɔː] *borne* [bɔːn]
     BEAR, TEAR, SWEAR
  (v) *lie* [lai] *lay* [lei] *lain* [lein]
     LIE (=LIE DOWN)
  (vi) *bite* [bait] *bit* [bit] *bitten* [bitn]
     BITE, HIDE
  (vii) *choose* [tʃuːz] *chose* [tʃouz] *chosen* [tʃouzn]
     CHOOSE

(c) There are a few verbs in which the vowel of the past participle is the same as that of the simple form, but different from that of the past tense form. There are seven sub-sub-classes:

  (i) *see* [siː] *saw* [sɔː] *seen* [siːn]
     SEE
  (ii) *eat* [iːt] *ate* [et] *eaten* [iːtn]
     EAT
  (iii) *forbid* [fəbid] *forbade* [fəbeid] *forbidden* [fəbidn]
     FORBID, FORGIVE, GIVE, and BID if it is used
  (iv) *take* [teik] *took* [tuk] *taken* [teikn]
     FORSAKE, SHAKE, TAKE
  (v) *fall* [fɔːl] *fell* [fel] *fallen* [fɔːln]
     FALL
  (vi) *draw* [drɔː] *drew* [druː] *drawn* [drɔːn]
     DRAW
  (vii) *grow* [grou] *grew* [gruː] *grown* [groun]
     BLOW, GROW, KNOW, THROW

(The past tense form of KNOW is [njuː]; the palatal semivowel is a common feature in the sequence [n]+[u].) A further sub-class would be provided by SLAY, if it is used.

    slay [slei] *slew* [sluː] *slain* [slein]

(d) One verb alone has the feature of vowel change and alveolar nasal in the past participle, but an alveolar plosive alone as the mark of the past tense:

    swell [swel] *swelled* [sweld] *swollen* [swouln]
    SWELL

3.3.6. *Loss of final consonant.* Loss of final consonant is always associated with the occurrence of an alveolar plosive and, except for one verb, vowel change.

(a) There is only one verb in which there is no vowel change – MAKE:

   make [meik]   *made* [meid]

The alveolar plosive is voiced (following a (voiced) vowel).

(b) Where there is vowel change the alveolar plosive is voiceless, although the preceding element is a vowel. There are three sub-classes:

  (i) *bring* [briŋ]   *brought* [brɔːt]

   BRING, THINK

 (ii) *teach* [tiːtʃ]   *taught* [tɔːt]

   TEACH, and if they are used, BESEECH and SEEK

(iii) *catch* [kætʃ]   *caught* [kɔːt]

   CATCH

(c) A problematic pattern is that of:

   stand [stænd]   *stood* [stud]

   STAND, UNDERSTAND

This pattern can be treated here (differing from (b) only in the voicing of the alveolar plosive) or in 3.3.3. (b) (vowel change only) with a special statement to account for the absence of the nasal in the past tense and past participle forms.

3.3.7. *Suppletion.* The only verb in English in which there is suppletion is GO. The past tense form is *went*, the past participle has a final nasal with vowel change:

   go [gou]   *went* [went]   *gone* [gɔn]

3.4. BE, HAVE and DO

The full verbs BE, HAVE and DO have the same form as the auxiliaries except that the auxiliaries HAVE and DO do not have the full range of possible forms.

The full verb BE has the same number of forms as the auxiliary and the same forms. It is completely irregular except for its *-ing* form, *being*, and the past participle which fits the alveolar nasal pattern without vowel change (cf. 3.3.2.).

The full verb HAVE has a past participle lacking in the auxiliary – *had*. It follows, in respect of past tense and past participle forms, the pattern of MAKE (3.3.6. (a)).

The full verb DO has an *-ing* form and a past participle that are absent in the auxiliary. The *-ing* form follows the regular pattern. The pattern of the past participle and the past tense forms is that of 3.3.5. (a), though in a new sub-sub-class.

   do [duː]   *did* [did]   *done* [dʌn]

The *-s* forms of HAVE and DO are both irregular – [hæz] and [dʌz].

References

Page 45 **Verb morphology.** B. Bloch, 'English verb inflexion', *Language*, 23, 399–418; and H. R. Gleason, *An introduction to descriptive linguistics*, Holt, Rinehart and Winston, New York, 1961 (Rev. Edn.), Chap. 8.

Chapter 4

The simple phrase: primary pattern (1)

In a simple phrase there may be a number of auxiliaries, though in fact the number is not unlimited; the maximum is four, or possibly five. In contrast, there is no theoretical limit to the number of full verbs that may occur in a complex phrase.

Even within the simple phrase two further types of phrase must be recognised; these are distinguished in terms of a primary and a secondary pattern. Phrases of the primary pattern contain forms of the primary auxiliaries only (BE, HAVE, DO), and include phrases consisting of a single (full verb) form. Phrases of the secondary pattern are essentially extensions of primary pattern phrases, but contain, in addition, one form of a secondary (modal) auxiliary (WILL, SHALL, CAN, MAY, MUST, OUGHT, DARE or NEED). This chapter and the next are concerned only with the primary pattern.

4.1. The paradigms

With most full verbs 'basic' paradigms of fourteen (or possibly sixteen) forms are to be established. These take into account only finite phrases and exclude phrases containing imperatives. Paradigms containing fewer forms are required for the non-finite participials and infinitivals (see **1.2.1.**) and for phrases that contain imperatives.

4.1.1. *'Basic' paradigms.* A basic paradigm in the primary pattern of the simple phrase is set out below. The paradigm stated is one of several; further paradigms may be set up by taking into account:
(i) the different forms associated with number and person, the paradigm here being for the third person singular (for the first person singular

replace *takes* by *take*, *is* by *am*, and *has* by *have*, and for all other forms replace *takes* by *take*, *is* by *are*, *was* by *were*, and *has* by *have*);

(ii) the forms used in negation, inversion, etc. (replace *takes* by *does take* or *do take* and *took* by *did take*).

For TAKE the paradigm is:

(1) *takes*
(2) *took*
(3) *is*   *taking*
(4) *was*   *taking*
(5) *has*   *taken*
(6) *had*   *taken*
(7) *has*   *been*   *taking*
(8) *had*   *been*   *taking*
(9) *is*   *taken*
(10) *was*   *taken*
(11) *is*   *being*   *taken*
(12) *was*   *being*   *taken*
(13) *has*   *been*   *taken*
(14) *had*   *been*   *taken*
(15) *has*   *been*   *being* *taken* (?)
(16) *had*   *been*   *being* *taken* (?)

The columning is deliberate, and is explained in 4.1.3. Numbers 15 and 16 are marked with a question mark; their validity is discussed later in this section.

There are two important characteristics of the forms that justify their treatment in this paradigmatic fashion. First they are a closed class: there are no other forms that will fit. This does, of course, depend on defining the primary pattern in terms of the occurrence of primary auxiliaries only, but this is wholly justified formally by the difference in the primary and secondary patterns as well as the morphological differences between the primary and the secondary auxiliaries (2.4.1), and the fact that except with DO, which has a very special function and is quite unlike the secondary auxiliaries, the forms in the primary pattern contain no infinitives (cf. 2.4.2). This permits the exclusion of both *He is to take* and *He has to take* from the primary pattern (see 8.1.3 and 8.2.3.).

The second point is that each form in the paradigm is essentially a whole. They cannot be analysed either formally or semantically in terms of the individual (word) forms of which they are composed, except in the morphological description of these (word) forms. Analysis in terms of selection classes, the syntactical structures with which they are associated (that BE is followed by the -*ing* form and by the past participle and that HAVE is followed by the past participle only), is insufficient, since this will not rule out the following, which are not attested:

*is been taking
*is being been taken
*was had taken
*was having taken
*is being had been having taken   etc.

Moreover, the grammatical categories in terms of which the forms of the paradigm are to be analysed (4.1.3.) and the semantic features associated with these categories (4.2.) cut right across word division in these forms. The position is very different from that in the complex phrase where the analysis of, e.g., *He kept asking her to help him get it finished* may be handled entirely in terms of the semantic and syntactic characteristics of the verbs KEEP, ASK, HELP and GET.

Forms number 15 and 16 are marked with a question mark, because there is some doubt whether they can be attested. I have considerable doubts whether I ever use them myself, and they are marked by H. E. Palmer as 'wanting'. On the other hand A. A. Hill quotes as an example:

John had been being scolded by Mary for a long time when the neighbors came in.

This problem raises two linguistic questions. The first is whether we ought to base the analysis strictly upon an already existing text. This is the usual practice of traditional grammars, their text being often the whole of English literature. But these are written texts; if our attention is confined to the spoken language it will be almost impossible to obtain sufficient material for a detailed analysis and we shall be forced to draw examples not from already recorded texts, but from texts that are provided *ad hoc* by ourselves, i.e., from what we consider to be 'possible'. The second point is how, if we accept the inevitability of the second alternative, we decide what is possible. For there is no doubt that there is both formally and semantically a place for 15 and 16, and if they ever do occur we should understand perfectly well how they are being used. The only answer here is that the linguist must attempt to be strictly honest and accept (or reject) only those forms that he is certain he actually does (or does not) use, irrespective of arguments based upon analogy, logic or anything else. For myself I am clear that I can and do use forms 13 and 14 where 15 and 16 might be expected on semantic grounds. In the example quoted above I would say *John had been scolded* ....

4.1.2. *Infinitivals, participials and imperatives.* The paradigms required for non-finite verbal pieces (the infinitivals and participials) and for phrases containing imperatives have fewer forms.

The paradigm of infinitival forms contains exactly half the number found in the basic paradigms, one form corresponding to each consecutive pair (there being no tense distinction – see **4.1.3.**). For the participials the number is further reduced in that there are no forms containing two consecutive *-ing* forms. The possibilities are, then:

	Infinitivals	Participials
(1/2)	*to take*	*taking*
(3/4)	*to be taking*	(**no** **being taking*)
(5/6)	*to have taken*	*having taken*
(7/8)	*to have been taking*	*having been taking*
(9/10)	*to be taken*	*being taken*
(11/12)	*to be being taken*	(**no** **being being taken*)
(13/14)	*to have been taken*	*having been taken*
(15/16)	*to have been being taken* (?)	*having been being taken* (?)

Phrases containing imperatives are still further limited in number in that there are none containing HAVE forms. Semantically there seems no reason to exclude **Have taken*, **Have been taking*, etc., but in fact these forms do not exist. But the four other possible forms are to be found – *Take*, *Be taking*, *Be taken* and (possibly) *Be being taken*. It might, admittedly, be difficult to attest all the forms with TAKE which is here chosen solely as a model, particularly the last two, but there is nothing odd about *Be dressed* and (though with less certainty) *Be being dressed*.

The infinitival and participials may all be preceded by *not* – these are the negative forms. But the negative and emphatic forms of the phrases with imperatives require special treatment. The fact that there is no negative form of *be* has been noted (**2.3.2.**); *don't* is the only negative imperative form. All the negative forms of the paradigm contain *don't* – *don't take*, *don't be taking*, *don't be taken* and *don't be being taken*. The last three break the rule that is valid for all other types of phrase, that DO does not occur with another auxiliary verb. In addition, there are emphatic forms `do take`, `do be taking`, `do be taken` and (?) `do be being taken`. Apart from the first, which follows the regular pattern, these might appear more surprising since it might be expected that the emphatic form would be marked simply by nuclear stress on *be*. On the other hand, it is not surprising that the emphatic forms should (as elsewhere) have the same

characteristic (occurrence of DO) as the negatives. A set of examples to
illustrate the negative and emphatic forms is:

> *Be reading when I come in!*
> *Don't be reading when I come in!*
> *Do be reading when I come in!*

4.1.3. *The four categories.* The sixteen forms in the basic paradigm of the
primary pattern can be divided into two sets of eight in four different ways,
each division being in terms of a formal feature (which is later linked to a
semantic one). Each form is thus characterised in four different ways, and
distinguished from all the others in these terms. If sixteen forms are
admitted there are no 'gaps' – all the possibilities occur; but, as we have
seen, only fourteen of them can be positively accepted.

First, the forms may be classified in terms of tense, past and present.
Present tense (phrase) forms are defined as those containing present tense
(word) forms. The word forms are, of course, defined morphologically,
takes, *is* and *has* being present and *took*, *was* and *had* past. In the paradigm
the odd-numbered forms are present and the even-numbered ones past;
the difference of tense is marked in the first column of the diagram (p. 56).

Secondly, a distinction in terms of progressive and non-progressive may
be made, progressive forms being those that contain both a form of BE
and an -*ing* form (occurring in column three). Every second pair in the
paradigm (beginning with 3 and 4) is progressive. There is no obvious
name for this category, the term 'tense' being best confined to the present/
past distinction, while 'aspect', if used at all, is more suitable to the category considered in the next paragraph. The terms 'continuous' and 'non-
continuous' are sometimes used. So too are 'habitual' and 'non-habitual'
(habitual = non-progressive) but these are to be rejected as quite misleading (see 5.1.1.).

Thirdly, the forms are to be classified as either perfect or non-perfect,
the perfect forms being those that contain a form of HAVE, which is
always followed by a past participle (in column two). The first four and
the third set of four (9 to 12) are non-perfect, and the others perfect. The
term 'aspect' could be used to designate this category.

Finally, the traditional category of voice, active and passive, distinguishes
those forms that contain both a form of BE and a past participle (passive)
from those that do not (active). The first eight are active and the last
eight passive. There is some superficial resemblance between the passive
and the perfect since both are defined in terms of one of the two auxiliaries
plus a past participle. But the place of the participles in the phrase is

different, as is shown by the columning of the paradigm. The participle associated with the perfect is always second while that associated with the passive is always last (in column four), with in each case the relevant form of the auxiliary preceding it. Structurally, then, the two are quite different.

This analysis provides a basis, indeed the only satisfactory basis, for more detailed analysis of the forms. In particular it should be noted that there is no place for a 'future tense' (cf. 4.2.3.).

4.2. Uses of the categories

The remainder of this chapter and the whole of the following one are concerned with the ways in which the categories are used. Use in this sense includes both formal and semantic features. Indeed, as was stated in the first chapter, it is felt that no useful purpose is achieved by a deliberate separation of the two. In fact all the categorisation is formal in the sense that formal criteria are given, a formal definition is achieved and indeed priority is given to these formal criteria. But there is, and can be, no suggestion that the analysis makes no use of semantic criteria; a great deal of it could be justified ultimately only by reference to some kind of meaning, and part of it rests almost wholly upon semantic considerations.

The next four sections of this chapter deal with the main uses of the four categories. But before these it is necessary to point out some of the difficulties and problems, to give an outline statement of the uses of the categories, since they are interrelated to some degree, and a brief statement of the general picture is needed before a separate and detailed analysis of each category, and finally to make some remarks about tense and time, especially with regard to the future.

4.2.1. *Problems of statement.* The difficulties are of three kinds.

First there is the fact that many of the forms have (at least) three different uses. They may be used in what may be called a 'basic' use, but in addition may refer to both future and to habitual activity, the 'basic' use being defined negatively as the one that has neither future nor habitual reference. Examples are:

> *I'm working at the moment.*   ('basic')
> *I'm working tomorrow.*   (future)
> *I'm always working.*   (habitual)

A whole section is devoted to the examination of the future and habitual uses (5.1.). Previous sections exclude them. Failure to make clear these distinctions, which are formally marked only by collocation with adverbs, has been a cause of great confusion.

Secondly the progressive forms create difficulty because although we may generally keep apart the uses of the four categories and the special uses (habitual and future) noted above, the progressive forms have a special function (or rather two functions) where there is reference to habitual activity. These are dealt with in 5.2.

Thirdly the use of the progressive forms depends to some degree upon the full verb in the phrase. Most striking is the fact that progressive forms only rarely occur with certain verbs (5.3.).

4.2.2. *Outline of the uses.* (i) The progressive indicates activity continuing through a period of time – activity with duration. The non-progressive merely reports activity, without indicating that it has duration. This is shown by comparison of:

> *He walked to the station.*
> *He was walking to the station.*

The first sentence simply gives the information that he walked to the station; the second indicates that the walking had duration. There is, of course, no suggestion that there are two kinds of activity one without and one with duration, but simply that attention is drawn in the one case to its durational aspect. The reasons for drawing attention to this are various; a common one is to show that the period of time during which the activity took place overlapped a briefer period or a point in time:

> *When I met him, he was walking to the station.*
> *He was walking to the station at ten this morning.*

(ii) Tense and perfect/non-perfect are initially best handled together, in order to make the point, not usually made, that both are essentially concerned with time relations. The time features are most simply illustrated by considering progressive forms that indicate activity continuing *throughout* a period of time (they do not always do this – see 4.5.3.):

> *I'm reading at the moment.*
> *I've been reading for an hour.*
> *I was reading when he came.*
> *I'd been reading for an hour when he came.*

The present non-perfect refers to a period of time in the present – a vague period that includes both past and future time but overlaps the present moment. The past non-perfect refers to a similar time in the past, which may overlap an indicated point of time in the past; it does not extend to the present. The perfect forms indicate periods of time that began before and continued up to a point of time, the present moment in the case of the present tense, and a point of time in the past in the case of the past tense. The four possibilities may be shown diagrammatically:

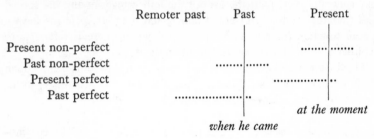

With the perfect the initial point of the period may be indicated, e.g., by *for an hour*, or *since Tuesday*, as well as the final point.

(iii) Voice differs from other categories in that a difference in voice involves changes in the syntactical relations between elements of the clause other than the verbal phrase, relations of the kind that are usually handled in terms of transformation. We shall relate:

The wind blew the tree down,

with   *The tree was blown down by the wind,*

not   **The wind was blown the tree down.*

No specific semantic feature distinguishes the paired active and passive forms, other than those directly related to the formal feature that the object of the active verb is the subject of the passive while the subject of the active is the 'agent' of the passive. If any semantic features may be assigned to the subject and object of the active ('actor', 'person/thing acted upon') these may be assigned to the 'agent' and the subject of the passive, respectively. But in a given situation the choice of active or passive is governed by features that are not easily categorised.

4.2.3. *Time and tense.* The traditional statement of tense in terms of present, past and future, exemplified by *I take, I took* and *I shall take*, has no place in the analysis presented here.

The main reason for this is quite simply that while *I take* and *I took* are comparables within the analysis, in that they exemplify the formal category of tense as established in the primary pattern, *I shall take* belongs to the secondary pattern and ought not, therefore, to be handled together with the other two.

There are other characteristics of the verb that support the decision to separate future time reference from reference to past and present. First there is the fact that we have already noted, and will examine later in more detail, that many of the verbal forms of the primary pattern may refer to the future. What is important is that past tense forms, no less than present tense forms, may refer to the future. As a result future/non-future cuts across past/present, giving us four possibilities, not three. This is shown by:

Present non-future	*I'm reading* (at the moment).
Present future	*I'm reading a paper tomorrow.*
Past non-future	*I was reading when he arrived.*
Past future	*I was reading a paper tomorrow.*

The second point is that there is really very little justification for the selection of WILL and SHALL as the markers of future tense in English, even if we rely heavily upon time reference. For, in the first place, WILL and SHALL are not the only ways of referring to future time; in fact there are four quite common constructions – as illustrated by:

  (i) *I'm reading a paper next Wednesday.*
 (ii) *I read my paper next Wednesday.*
(iii) *I'm going to read a paper next Wednesday.*
(iv) *I shall read a paper next Wednesday.*

The first two are examples of the primary pattern forms used with future reference (the subject of the first point made). But the third type—with *going to* – is very common, indeed, probably more common than sentences with WILL and SHALL in ordinary conversation.

A second difficulty about WILL (though not SHALL) is that it often does not refer to the future at all. It may, for instance, indicate probability

     That'll be the postman,

or it may refer to habitual activity,

     She'll sit for hours watching the television.

Even when it does refer to the future it may suggest not merely futurity but willingness as in:

     Will you come?

(which is different from *Are you coming?* see **6.3.2.**).
It is, moreover, characteristic of the other modal auxiliaries that they may refer to the future (though with additional reference to ability, probability, etc.) as in:

     I can/may/must/ought to come tomorrow.

There is clearly an over-riding case for handling WILL and SHALL with the other modal auxiliaries in the secondary pattern and not together with the past and present distinction of tense that belongs to the primary pattern.

4.3. Voice

Voice is considered first because it is so different from the other categories that it can be handled entirely separately from them. The reader may, indeed, omit this section, or return to it after reading the remainder of the chapter and Chapter 5.

4.3.1. *The place of transformation.* As we have already seen voice involves relations of the kind that are exemplified by:

> *The wind blew the tree down.*
> *The tree was blown down by the wind.*

Transformational relations of this kind have only recently been accepted in some kinds of grammatical analysis, yet a moment's reflection will show that they are not something novel at all, and that fundamentally they are no different from the relations involved in tense, etc. The point is that the recognition of *took* as the past tense of TAKE and equally of *is taken* as the passive of TAKE depends upon relating large numbers of sentences and specifically upon a statement of collocations between nouns and verbs in the sentences. For it is not enough to base the analysis simply upon the verbal forms. This would certainly not establish *went* as the past tense form of GO, and would not even permit the recognition of *fought* as the past tense form of FIGHT, rather than FIX (or for that matter any other verb). *Take* and *took* can be brought together only if it may be shown that the classes of nouns collocated with these verbal forms in the functions of both subject and object are the same. We need to pair numerous sentences of the patterns:

> *John takes a book,*   (or *a bath, a look,* etc.).
> *John took a book.*

Sentences must be similarly paired to establish active-passive relations. The only difference is that the nouns collocated with the verbs differ in their sentence functions in each paired sentence. Those that function as subject in the active, function as 'agent' in the passive (preceded by *by*) and those that function as object in the active, function as subject in the passive.

The point to be stressed is that the transformational relations (or, if one prefers, the relations in terms of classes of collocation) are not an additional feature that may or may not be added to the analysis. They are an integral part of it. The description of voice differs, however, in the need for a statement about the related parts of the sentence, where that of the other categories does not. The transformational relations for voice may be symbolised as:

$$N_1 \ V_{act.} \ N_2 \rightarrow N_2 \ V_{pass.} \ by \ N_1$$

The term 'transformation' is best restricted to relations of this kind **provided** it is realised that it does not involve any fundamental **difference** in the approach to the analysis.

4.3.2. *The function of the passive.* The most difficult question to be **asked** about the passive is why it is used rather than the active. There is **only** one obvious and clear reason – that it may be used where the 'actor' **is not** specified, e.g.:

> *He's been killed.*
> *He was hurt in the crash.*

With the active form there must be an indication of the 'actor', **this** being the function of the subject. This does not imply any suggestion about the 'meaning' of the subject. It merely states that whatever information is carried by the subject of the active verb may be omitted by the use of the passive. In the active forms corresponding to the passive above we must specify who did the killing or the hurting or specify that we do not know by using *someone*:

> *John (Someone) killed him,*

or there may be no actor. We shall not normally find:

> *John (Someone) hurt him in the crash.*

This point may be noted in the transformational statement by bracketing *by* N_1:

$$N_1 \; V_{act.} \; N_2 \to N_2 \; V_{pass.} \; (by \; N_1)$$

Apart from this there is little that can be said. There is perhaps **a** tendency to make nouns that refer to animate beings the subject, and **to** select the active or passive on that basis:

> *Mr. Smith was killed by a car.*

is a little more likely than:

> *A car killed Mr. Smith,*

and   *The birds have eaten the strawberries,*

than   *The strawberries have been eaten by the birds.*

It might be thought that the main 'topic' is indicated by the subject. But this does not appear to be so. In our examples it is true that we are interested in Mr. Smith's fate and not what the car did, but in contrast we are surely more interested in what has happened to the strawberries than what actions the birds have performed.

4.3.3. *Gaps in the pattern.* Not every active form has a corresponding passive form. There are two types of non-correspondence.

First, as we have already noted (4.1.1.) perfect progressive passive forms rarely occur. Where a progressive would be expected, the corresponding non-progressive is used. This means that the active forms 7 and 8 (perfect progressive) have (except rarely) no corresponding passive forms (no 15 and 16). The correspondence in terms of voices is between 7 and 8 and 13 and 14 (the non-progressives), though 5 and 6 too correspond with 13 and 14. This is illustrated by:

(5) *The doctors have examined him,*

(13) *He has been examined by the doctors.*

(7) *The doctors have been examining him all morning*

(13) *He has been examined all morning by the doctors.*

The analogously expected form is, of course, *He has been being examined,* but this is unlikely to occur in normal speech.

Secondly, there are verbs which in their active forms occur with an object, yet still have no passive forms. Examples are RESEMBLE and HAVE (POSSESS) as shown by:

He resembles his father,

but not   **His father is resembled by him.*

He has lots of money,

but not   **Lots of money are had by him.*

There are also some verbs which occur with objects in the active, but have passive forms in one meaning, but not in another – e.g., MARRY and EQUAL:

The Rev. Smith married them,

They were married by the Rev. Smith,

Jack married Jill,

but not   **Jill was married by Jack.*

No one equals him in strength,

He is equalled by no one in strength,

Two and two equal four,

but not   **Four is equalled by two and two.*

4.3.4. *Types of transformation.* The 'regular' transformation is symbolised:

$$N_1 \; V_{act.} \; N_2 \rightarrow N_2 \; V_{pass.} \; (by \; N_1)$$

But there are many pairs of sentences which do not fit this pattern, or at least can only be fitted with a fair amount of manœuvring.

(i) There are many combinations of verb plus preposition that occur in both active and passive sentences and in which the transformational relations are of the type:

$$N_1 \; V_{act.} \; prep. \; N_2 \to N_2 \; V_{pass.} \; prep. \; (by \; N_1)$$

He looked after his father.

His father was looked after by him.

We'll have to go into that.

That'll have to be gone into by us.

Most of these are prepositional verbs. These and the problem of their passives are dealt with in **10.4.** There is a similar problem with the 'phrasal' prepositional verbs (**10.5.**):

I can't put up with it,

It can't be put up with,

and with such combinations as TAKE CARE (**10.**6.):

I took care of it,

It was taken care of (by me).

(ii) A more familiar problem is that posed by:

He was given a book (by the teacher).

The child was told a story (by his mother).

The transformational relations are

$$N_1 \; V_{act.} \; N_2 \; N_3 \to N_2 \; V_{pass.} \; N_3 \; (by \; N_1)$$

though another (rarer) passive is

$$N_3 \; V_{pass.} \; prep. \; N_2 \; (by \; N_1)$$

(*A book was given to the child by the teacher.*)

(iii) Rather more difficult to handle is:

Bannister first ran a mile in four minutes.

A mile was first run in four minutes by Bannister.

This could well be treated as an example of the 'regular' pattern in which N_2 is the object of the active and subject of the passive verb. Yet in spite of:

I ran a mile to work,

we shall not attest

**A mile to work was run by me.*

There are two ways of dealing with this. Either we say that RUN is like RESEMBLE and MARRY – that there are no passive forms corresponding to the active ones (with rare exceptions, as exemplified by the first pair of sentences). Or we insist that the transformation relations are statable not simply in terms of numbered N's (N_1 and N_2) but in terms of N's with specific sentence functions – subject, object, etc., and that *a mile* does not function as the object of the verb. The case for treating N_1 as the subject is clear, in that there are features of concord that establish it in that function – *The boy is ... The boys are ...* Unfortunately it is not the status of N_1 but of N_2 that is in doubt, and the question of whether or not N_2 is the object of the verb will depend upon transformational relations.

4.3.5. *Transitive/intransitive and voice.* It will be clear from the previous sections that there is no one-to-one relation between voice and the categorising of verbs as transitive and intransitive. There are transitive verbs such as RESEMBLE that do not occur in passive forms, while intransitive verbs such as LOOK and GO do occur in passive forms (unless we make them transitive by calling them prepositional verbs). But there are many verbs that have both transitive and intransitive forms (occurring with and without an object) in which the intransitive functions like the passive in that the relation of the subject to the verb is transformationally similar to that of the object of the transitive, e.g., SOUND, RING, BLOW:

> *They rang the bell.*
> *The bell rang.*
> *The bell was rung (by them).*
> *The wind blew the tree down.*
> *The tree blew down.*
> *The tree was blown down (by the wind).*

But, as the bracketed elements show, a passive and not an intransitive form is required when the 'actor' is indicated. There are no forms:

> **The bell rang by them.*
> **The tree blew down by the wind.*

4.3.6. *Passive versus* BE+*past participle.* A distinction can be made between *were married* in:

> *They were married last year,*

and in   *They were married when I last saw them.*

In the first *were married* is a passive form (number 10); in the second *were married* is a form of BE as a full verb plus a past participle functioning as an adjectival complement. There is no contradiction, therefore, in:

> *They were married when I saw them in June; they had been married the month before.*

As an adjective *married* has the meaning of 'having been married'. Someone who is married (participle as adjective), has been married (present perfect). A non-perfect form of BE plus the adjectival past participle has almost exactly the same meaning as the perfect form of the verb. Other examples are:

> *They are divorced.*   (Cf. *They have been divorced.*)
> *My bags are packed.*   (Cf. *My bags have been packed.*)
> *It's broken.*   (Cf. *It's been broken.*)

One formal distinguishing feature is that, with a non-perfect form of the verb, the adjective alone may be preceded by *already*:

They were already divorced.
My bags were already packed.
It was already broken.

4.4. Tense

Tense has three functions, first to mark purely temporal relations of past
and present time, secondly (and closely related to the first) in the sequence
of tenses of reported speech, and thirdly to mark 'unreality' in conditional
clauses and in wishes.

4.4.1. *Time relations: adverbials.* The most important function of tense
is to indicate past and present time. The distinction is very clear in:
> *He's reading the paper at this moment.*
> *He was reading the paper when I saw him this morning.*
But there are three reservations to make.
(i) Present time must be understood to mean any period of time that
includes the present moment. It includes, therefore, 'all time' as in:
> *The sun rises in the East.*
> *Water boils at 100° Centigrade.*
Past time excludes the present moment. Past time may seem to be the
'marked member' of the pair, in that it specifically excludes the present
moment. Present time is any period of time, short, long or eternal that
includes the present moment.
(ii) There is one exception only to the statement in (i) – the so-called
historic present. There are many examples of this in literary English, but
it is also to be found in speech, e.g.:
> *He just walks into the room and sits down in front of the*
> *fire without saying a word to anyone.*
The traditional explanation of this usage – that it recalls or recounts the
past as vividly as if it were present, is adequate. It seems highly probable
that it is not specifically English but a characteristic of many if not all
languages that make time distinctions in the verb.
(iii) The use of tense is complicated by its relation to the temporal
characteristics of perfect/non-perfect and by the habitual and future uses
of the forms (which are dealt with in later sections).

The adverbials that are used with tense are of four kinds. First, there
are those that may be used with past tense only, *last week*, *yesterday*, *last
year*, *a long time ago*. Secondly, there are those that may be used with
present tense only; *now*, *at this moment*, appear to be the only ones.
Thirdly, there are those that may be used with either, though the period

of time to which they refer does include the present moment. These are *today, this week, this year, etc.*, as in

> *He was working today,*
> *He's working today.*

These are more commonly used with the present; where they are used with the past, it is because the activity is shown as taking place within the period indicated by the adverbial, but before the present moment. Fourthly, there are adverbials that indicate past or present time according to the time at which the utterance is made, and for this reason may be used with past or present forms. Examples are *this morning, this afternoon* and *this summer*. *This morning* is present if it is still morning, but past if the morning is over. In the afternoon *this morning* will occur with past tense forms. In the morning it may occur with present tense forms, or (as *today*) with past tense forms.

4.4.2. *Reported speech.* With reported speech the verb in the subordinate clause is usually in the past tense if the verb of reporting is also in the past tense:

> *He says he likes it,*
but > *He said he liked it.*

The actual words are/were 'I like it'. A present tense form is, that is to say, reported by a past tense form if the verb of reporting is past. Similarly 'I'm reading' is reported in:

> *He says he's reading.*
> *He said he was reading.*

But present tense verbs of reporting may occur with past tense forms of the verb in the words reported, where the actual words contained a past tense form:

> *He says he was reading.*

The words were 'I was reading'.

The use of the past tense forms here is very close to the use we considered in the previous section – that of indicating past time. The original utterance was made in the past, and if it then referred to present time, when reported it obviously refers to past time. 'I'm reading' uttered yesterday is in the past if reported today. The normal pattern is, then:

> *I'm reading.*   *He says he's reading.*
>   *He said he was reading.*
> *I was reading.*   *He says he was reading.*
>   *He said he was reading.*

There are, however, two exceptions to this 'normal' pattern. First, we may not exclude:

> *He said he likes it.*

But such examples as these merely emphasise the temporal characteristic of tense even with reported speech. For this utterance specifically indicates that 'he likes it' is still true – that it refers to the present. It is virtually equivalent to:

> *He likes it – he said so.*

This use is rare, naturally enough because the reporter usually merely reports – what was said was true, or supposedly true, in the past, and a past tense form is used. The use of the present indicates not merely the validity of the original statement when it was made, but its continuing relevance into the present.

Secondly, a non-perfect past tense form may be reported by a perfect past form, which thus has the function of a 'past-past'. We may attest:

> *He said he'd seen him the day before.*

The actual words were:

> *I saw him yesterday,*

but (a) equally possible in this situation is a non-perfect past form,

> *He said he saw him the day before,*

and (b) the past perfect also reports a present perfect or even a past perfect. Both

> *I've seen him already*

and

> *I'd seen him already*

are reported by: *He said he'd seen him already.*

It will be apparent, then, that there are only two forms used for past time reporting, and that these may report four different forms in the original. The pattern is:

Original	Reported
I see ⎫	… he saw
I saw ⎬	
I have seen ⎬	… he had seen
I had seen ⎭	

4.4.3. '*Unreality.*' The use of the past tense to refer to 'unreality' is very common with forms of the secondary pattern (7.2. and 7.3.).

But it is also found with primary pattern forms:

(i) It is used, though rarely, to express a tentative or polite attitude in questions and requests:

> *I wanted to ask you about that.*
> *Did you want to speak to me?*

These are a little more tentative or polite than:

> *I want to ask you about that.*
>
> *Do you want to speak to me?*

(ii) It is always used in the *if* clause of 'unreal' conditions (the main clause must contain a secondary auxiliary):

> *If he came he would find out.*

The 'real' condition is:

> *If he comes he will find out.*

Similar to this are clauses introduced by *supposing* and some relative clauses that must be regarded as also being part of 'unreal' conditions:

> *Supposing we asked him, what would he do?*
>
> *Anyone who said that would be crazy.*

Belonging to this pattern is the almost fossilised *If I were you.* Only in this form is *were* used regularly with *I* in spoken English. *If I was you* would be regarded as sub-standard English, but in other cases *was* or *were* are both possible. There is choice between:

> *If I were rich ...*   *If I were to ask him ...*
>
> *If I was rich ...*   *If I was to ask him ...*

(iii) It is found in wishes and statements of the type *It is time ...*:

> *I wish I knew.*
>
> *It's time we went.*

Sentences beginning *If only* are perhaps to be handled here, though they might equally be treated as unreal conditions:

> *If only I understood what you are saying.*

The feature of 'unreality' is much more important with the modal auxiliaries and is dealt with in detail in **7.2.** and **7.3.**

4.5. Perfect/non-perfect

As has already been suggested, the perfect is used to indicate a period of time that began before, but continued right up to, a point of time (either present or past, according to the tense).

4.5.1. *Time relations: adverbials.* There is no problem as long as we are concerned only with activity going on throughout the period of time as in:

> *I've been reading for an hour.*
>
> *I'd been reading for an hour when he came.*

With the first (present tense) the activity began an hour before, and continued right up to, the present; in the second (past tense) it began an hour before, and continued right up to, the past point of time indicated by the adverbial clause.

The adverbials associated with tense are the same with the perfect forms as with the non-perfect. That is to say *last week*, *yesterday* occur with past (perfect) tense forms, *now*, *at this moment* only with present (perfect) tense forms, *today*, *this week* with either, while the use of *this morning*, *this afternoon* etc. depends upon the actual time of speaking. What is important here is that the adverbials that are collocated only with past tense forms are collocated only with the past perfect and never with the present perfect, even though the present perfect appears to have reference to the past – at least it refers to activity that began in the past. But we cannot say:

> **I've been reading yesterday.*

In addition to the adverbials collocated with tense, there are some that are specifically associated with the perfect. These are the adverbial clauses and phrases beginning with *since* – *since Tuesday*, *since we met*. They indicate the starting point of the period of time.

The adverbials beginning with *since* are collocated only with perfect forms (except rarely with progressive forms used for limited duration – 5.2.1.):

> *I've been reading since three,*
> *I'd been reading since three o'clock,*

but not

> **I'm reading since three o'clock,*
> **I was reading since three o'clock.*

Adverbials beginning with *for* (*for an hour*, etc.) are often used with perfect forms, but they are not restricted to them. The restrictions on adverbials of this kind are in terms of the progressive/non-progressive.

4.5.2. *Non-progressive forms and 'results'.* In spite of the simple picture set out in the previous section there is a problem where it is clear that the activity does *not* continue throughout the relevant period of time. This is necessarily always so with non-progressive forms, since activity is without marked duration:

> *I've cut my finger.*
> *He's painted his house.*
> *Have you seen him?*

A common explanation of such examples is that the perfect is used where the activity has results in the present. This is, however, rather misleading unless we interpret results to include 'nil results' as is shown by:

> *I've hit it twice, but it's still standing up.*
> *I've written, but they haven't replied.*

A more accurate explanation is in terms of 'current relevance' – that in some way or other (not necessarily in its results) the action is relevant to something observable at the present. The past perfect may be treated in a similar way – activity occurring before, but relevant to, a point of time in the past.

But examples such as these in no way refute the suggestion made earlier that the perfect/non-perfect category refers, like tense, to features of time, and that the perfect indicates a period of time preceding but continuing up to a later period of time (present or past). To make this point, we will again consider only the present perfect; but similar considerations hold for the past perfect too. Examples of present perfect (non-progressive) forms are:

> *I've seen John this morning.*
> *I've mended it three times today.*
> *He's written the letter.*

In all three cases, the activity took place in the past. The same actions could have been reported by past tense forms:

> *I saw John this morning.*
> *I mended it three times today.*
> *He wrote the letter.*

What this proves is that the periods of time indicated by the present perfect and the past (non-perfect) overlap, and that an action performed in the past may be included in either of them. The interpretation in terms of time reference that accounts for *I've been reading* equally accounts for the perfect forms exemplified here; the actions all took place in a period of time that began in the past and continued right up to the present.

The problem that remains is to establish what determines the choice of the present perfect rather than the past in these cases, but the question is best asked in the form, 'Why is the activity placed in the period of time indicated by the present perfect rather than the period indicated by the simple past, since it occurred within them both?' It is here that we must refer to current relevance. A period of time that includes the present is chosen precisely because there are features of the present that directly link it to the past activity. The temporal situation being envisaged by the speaker is one that includes the present; the present perfect, is, therefore, used. Examples are:

> *I've bought a new suit.*
> *I've finished my homework.*
> *They've left the district.*

In all of these there are features of the present which form part of the whole relevant situation set out in time. The new suit may be displayed at the time of speaking, or the implication may be 'I shan't be untidy any more'. The child who says 'I've finished my homework' is probably asking to be allowed to go out to play now. The information 'They've left the district' tells us that we shan't find them, that it's no use calling on them any more. Other examples, with comments, are:

> *I've cut my finger.*   (It's still bleeding.)
> *He's broken the window.*   (It hasn't been mended.)
> *I've told you already.*
> 　　　　(You are stupid *or* I won't tell you again.)
> *They've fallen in the river.*
> 　　　　(They need help *or* Their clothes are wet.)
> *You've had an accident.*   (I can see the bruises.)

The insistence on the interpretation of the perfect/non-perfect category in terms of periods of time is partly justified by the fact that it makes possible a single statement for all the perfect forms, and does not need to handle current relevance as a special meaning of the perfect, unrelated to its other uses. But it is wholly confirmed by a consideration of the adverbials that are collocated with the present perfect and past tense forms, for an adverbial that indicates purely past time is never used with a present perfect. We cannot say *They've come last Monday*, though an adverbial that indicates a period that includes the present is possible – *They've come this week*. An explanation simply in terms of results or current relevance cannot account for this, for that would not exclude *They've come last Monday*, meaning that they came on Monday and are still here. English would be the richer if this were possible, for as it is we cannot in a single phrase combine the two pieces of information about (i) their arrival at a specific time in the past and (ii) the current relevance of this. Current relevance may be indicated only if the period of time that is stated is one that includes the present. It is because the present perfect indicates such a period of time that it is not possible further to specify by an adverbial a past time at which the activity took place.

Indeed, often it is only the choice of the adverbial that determines the choice between present perfect and past. There is no question of current relevance, but only whether the period of time being indicated includes the present moment or not. Thus we may say *I've seen him three times today*, but *I saw him three times yesterday* and not *I've seen him three times yesterday*. Similarly *I've seen him this morning* is a possible utterance only if it is still morning; if the morning is over, the period of time indicated is wholly in the past and a present perfect form cannot be used.

4.5.3. *Progressive forms and 'results'.* Where progressive forms are used, they often, as we have seen, refer to activity going on throughout the period of time. But this is not always so. There is a problem with such sentences as:

> *Someone's been moving my books.*
> *Who's been eating my porridge?*

The position is exactly the same as with the non-progressive forms, provided only that it is accepted that the use of the progressive does not necessarily imply that the activity continues *throughout* the relevant period of time, but merely that it has duration *within* the period. Someone had been moving my books (continuing activity) within a period of time that began in the past and continued up to the present; this period of time rather than a wholly past period is chosen because the present disorderly state of the books is linked to the past activity. So, too, the three bears ask, 'Who's been eating my porridge?' because they can see that some of it has gone. Other examples are:

> *I've been working in the garden all day.*
> *I've been cleaning the car.*

Both activities continued for some time and both are to be related to the present (even if they did not continue up to the present). The man who has been working suggests that he is tired and has a right to be, while the man who has been cleaning his car is probably apologising for the state of his hands and clothes. It would be an error to regard these examples as essentially different from those in which the activity is clearly shown to continue right up to the present, usually by the adverbials *since* ... and *for* ... The period of time is the same; it is the adverbials, not the progressive form itself, that show that the activity continued throughout. Other examples are:

> *You've been working too hard.* ('You need a rest' – to someone now in bed, certainly not still working.)
> *You've been playing with fire.* (I can smell it.)
> *I've been drinking tea.* (That's why I'm late.)
> *He's been talking about you.* (I know something now.)

4.5.4. *Past perfect and 'past-past' time.* Similar statements may be made for the past perfect, but there is one further point to be made about these forms. The past perfect is occasionally used merely as a 'past-past' to indicate an activity preceding one already in the past. The normal use of the past perfect is of course merely to place the activity in a period of time preceding, but going up to, a past point of time as in:

> *I had already seen him, when you arrived.*

During the period before, and up to, your arrival, I saw him. Quite different, however, is:

> *I had seen him an hour before you arrived.*

The period indicated by *an hour before* clearly does *not* include the time of arrival. A similar sentence with a present time reference requires not a present perfect but a past tense form:

> *I saw him an hour ago,*

not   **I've seen him an hour ago.*

We have already noted similar uses of the past perfect as 'past-past' in reported speech (4.4.2.). It functions in the same kind of way in 'unreal' past time conditional (7.3.2.).

4.6. Progressive/non-progressive

It has already been suggested that the progressive indicates duration. There are, however, some rather special uses of the progressive that are linked either to its habitual use (5.2.) or to particular verb classes (the non-progressive – 5.3.). These are dealt with in a later section.

4.6.1. *Duration: adverbials.* Adverbials that indicate extent of time or continuity are collocated with progressive forms – *all morning, continually, for a long time:*

> *I was reading all morning.*
> *He's been working for a long time.*

But there are three points to note:

(i) Adverbials that indicate duration may be used with the non-progressive forms of verbs of two kinds. First they are used with those that indicate an activity that is not momentary in the sense that it indicates a single action – verbs such as READ, WORK, SLEEP. We shall attest such sentences as:

> *I read all day yesterday.*
> *I worked in the garden for three hours.*
> *He slept all night.*

Secondly they are used with verbs that indicate distinct actions where it is clear that the action is repeated:

> *He hit him for a long time.*
> *He jumped up and down for several hours.*

(ii) Adverbials with *for* are very common with negative non-progressive forms – indicating that a period of time was devoid of the activity referred to:

> *I haven't met him for years.*
> *I didn't touch it for a week.*

The corresponding positive forms would be much less common and would usually refer only to habitual activity (5.1.3.):

> *I've met him every lunch time for years.*
> *I've touched it every morning for a week.*

(iii) We must note the use of the progressive with such adverbials and adjectivals as *more and more, faster and faster:*

> *It's getting bigger and bigger.*
> *More and more people are buying television sets.*
> *He's working less and less.*

The comparative adverbs and adverbials indicate an increase or decrease in the activity or some aspect of the activity, and therefore imply duration. But perhaps this is 'limited duration' – see 5.2.1.

4.6.2. *Some varieties of use.* Although in general we may point to duration as the feature marked by the progressive, there are several points to make:

(i) The use of the non-progressive does not necessarily indicate a single action. This is shown by:

> *He hit him three times.*

Equally, of course, the progressive does not imply a single action with duration:

> *He was hitting him for several minutes.*

The number of distinct actions is irrelevant. What matters is that there is activity which is either merely reported, or stated to have duration.

(ii) Where a point of time is indicated by an adverbial, the progressive and non-progressive differ in their temporal relations to that point of time. The progressive always indicates activity continuing both before and after the time indicated. The non-progressive indicates either simultaneity or, more commonly, immediate succession. A contrast may be made between:

> *When I saw him, he was running away.*
> *When I saw him, he ran away.*

In the second clearly the act of running away was preceded by (and probably an effect of) my seeing him. Simultaneity is possible, however, as in:

> *As the clock struck, he died.*
> *He died at ten o'clock.*

The non-progressive specifically excludes overlap, as is shown where a number of actions are reported:

> *When I arrived, he shouted three times.*

All three shouts followed my arrival here. In fact, English has no simple way of showing that there were three shouts and that the shouting both preceded and followed my arrival. There is no logical reason why the non-progressive should always indicate successive activity rather than, for instance, immediately preceding activity; it is merely a fact of English that it does.

(iii) As we have already seen the progressive does not necessarily indicate that the activity continues throughout the period of time indicated. This remark cannot apply to the non-perfect since there are no indicated limits to the period of time, but it does apply to the perfect (where the period of time specifically continues up to a present or past point of time). But, as we have already seen in dealing with the perfect, the activity itself does not necessarily continue *throughout* the period (4.5.3.); indeed if it does, this fact is indicated by an adverbial.

(iv) The use of the progressive does not necessarily imply unbroken activity. The following sentence is ambiguous:

I'm reading 'The Mayor of Casterbridge'.

This may mean either that I am at this moment sitting with a book in front of me, or it may mean that I have read part of the book, and intend to read some more, but that at the moment I am not actually reading it. We may similarly compare:

I'm writing a letter.

I'm writing a book.

It is at least likely that the letter is actually being written at the time of speaking, whereas the book has merely been begun.

(v) The progressive often suggests that the activity was unfinished, while the non-progressive normally suggests its completion. We may compare:

I painted the table this morning.

I was painting the table this morning.

It is more likely that in the first case the painting of the table has been completed. This is not a completely clear distinction. It is possible to say:

I painted the house this morning,

without meaning that I completed the painting, but simply to report the activity. But such a statement might imply the completion of the activity and invite the reply:

What? The whole of it?

Where the present progressive is used, the activity is not complete, since it indicates activity continuing into the future. If I say 'I'm reading a book', it follows that I have not finished it.

References

Page 55 **Auxiliaries.** Cf. W. F. Twaddell, *The English verb auxiliaries* (op. cit.), for a similar though different treatment.

Page 57 **H. E. Palmer** and F. G. Blandford, *A grammar of spoken English* (op. cit.), 131;
A. A. Hill. *Introduction to linguistic structures*, Harcourt, Brace and Co. Inc., New York 1958, 220.

Page 59 **Aspect.** The term 'aspect' might, perhaps, be used for progressive/non-progressive. For perfect/non-perfect the term 'phase' has been suggested. Cf. M. Joos, *The English verb*, Wisconsin University Press, Madison, 1964.

Page 64 **Transformation.** Cf. N. Chomsky, *Syntactic structures*, Mouton and Co., The Hague 1957, 21.

Page 72 **Perfect.** Cf. R. A. Close, *English as a foreign language*, Allen and Unwin Ltd., London 1962.

Chapter 5

The simple phrase: primary pattern (2)

This chapter deals, first, with the future and habitual uses of the forms, and secondly, with some further characteristics of the progressive/non-progressive and perfect/non-perfect categories.

5.1. Future and habitual uses

The fact that many of the forms are used to refer to the future or to habitual activity is a source of great confusion. All too often comparison is made between forms in their basic uses and forms in their habitual or future uses. Up until now we have been concerned only with the basic uses.

5.1.1. *The problem.* We have already seen that a single form, e.g., the present progressive non-perfect may be used to refer to an action in the future, or an action that is habitual, as well as to an action going on at the present time:

> *He's reading at the moment.*
> *He's reading a paper tomorrow.*
> *He's reading, whenever I see him.*

The future and habitual uses are normally marked by adverbials (*tomorrow, next week*, etc., and *always, whenever* ...) while the basic use is normally not marked in this way.

A common and misleading statement of the uses of the forms is one that treats the non-progressive non-perfect present form (henceforth to be called the 'simple' present) as 'habitual' and the present progressive as referring to action taking place at the present moment – making the distinction between habitual and non-habitual present action:

> *He reads the paper every day.*
> *He's reading the paper at the moment.*

But this is merely to compare incomparables. For the progressive as well as the simple form may be used in a habitual sense:

> *He's always reading at meals.*
> *He always reads at meals.*

The difference between the two is, as usual, one of duration (or statable in terms of one of the other features associated with the progressive that are still to be described). But in *both* cases the activity is habitual. The contrast habitual/actual present is a false one.

Another, slightly less misleading, interpretation is that the present tense form is timeless – that it may be used to refer to the future, the past, the present or to timeless situations, while the past tense alone specifies time – past time. But if this is to be taken to imply (as it must) that only present tense forms may refer to habitual actions or to the future, while past tense forms refer to actions in the past, it is false. For we may certainly attest habitual actions in the past:

> *I saw him every day,*
> *I was seeing him every day,*

and, more surprisingly, there is the possibility of referring to the future, too:

> *I was seeing him tomorrow,*   (but now I can't).

These examples show that the present is not very different from the past in respect of reference to habitual or future activity.

It is clear that future and habitual reference must be treated separately, and not as characteristics of any one of the forms or of any one of the terms in the four grammatical categories.

5.1.2. *The simple present.* One of the reasons why the simple present is often designated 'habitual' is that it is rarely used in its basic, non-habitual, non-future use. But this fact ought not to obscure the overall pattern, especially since there are reasons for its rarity in its basic use.

There are two reasons why the simple present is rarely used in its non-habitual sense. First, a non-progressive form merely reports an activity, but it is rarely that we need to report a present activity, for the simple, but non-linguistic, reason that if the speaker can observe it (at the present time) so too in most circumstances can the hearer. Past activity on the contrary is often reported by a speaker who observed it (or heard about it) to a hearer who did not. With the past tense, therefore, unlike the present, non-habitual activity is commonly referred to, as well as habitual activity:

> *I saw my mother yesterday.*
> *I saw my mother every day.*

A second point is that present activity is usually incomplete and therefore even when there is no specific reference to the duration of the activity, its incompleteness implies the use of the progressive. In, for instance, *What are you doing?* the speaker avoids the suggestion that the activity is complete.

The progressive is, thus, the commoner form for reference to present activity. We can, indeed, treat it as the norm, and say that unless there are obvious reasons to the contrary the progressive is used. (With the 'non-progressive' verbs, as we shall see (5.3.), the reverse is true.) But there are a number of situations in which the non-progressive, the simple present, is used.

First, it is the form normally used in a commentary, especially on the radio where the commentator is reporting something that the listeners cannot see. This use is exactly parallel to the use of the simple past to report past activity:

> *... and he passes the ball to Smith, and Smith scores!*
> *He bowls, and he just misses the wicket.*
> *He hits him again, right on the jaw.*

Secondly, it is used in demonstrations, where the audience can see what is happening, but the demonstrator reports it as well to make sure there is no misunderstanding. Once again he is merely reporting the activity, he is not indicating its duration; the simple present is the only appropriate form:

(Conjuror)   *I place the rabbit in the box and close the lid.*
(Cookery demonstration)

> *I take three eggs and beat them in this basin. Then I add sugar ...*

A third use is where the words themselves form part of the activity they report. Again they merely state the occurrence of the activity:

> *I name this ship ...*
> *I pronounce you man and wife.*
> *I declare the meeting closed.*

A rather similar use is of verbs of statement which are used merely to reinforce the fact that the speaker makes his statement:

> *I say he should go.*
> *I call it an outrage.*

These utterances imply not 'I am saying ...' or 'I am calling ...' but '... that's my opinion' and '... that's my name for it.'

Less easy to explain are:

> *He talks like an expert.*
> *Look at the way he walks!*
> *Why do you say that?*

The common characteristic of all these utterances is that they contain an adverbial to indicate either the manner or the cause of the activity. It is in the manner or cause that the speaker is interested; the duration of the activity is not in question. Again the simple present is appropriate. In some cases it might be argued that we are concerned with habitual activity:

> *Why do you cut it like that?*

But it is equally clear that in many cases the activity is not habitual, that the speaker is concerned only with a single present activity. There can be contrast between a present and a past activity, neither of them apparently habitual, as in:

> *Yesterday he talked nonsense. Today he talks like an expert.*
> *He walked all the morning. Look at the way he walks now.*
> *You said something different a few minutes ago. Why do you say that now?*

Similar considerations hold for:

(Stage directions)

> *John enters through the window.*
> *It says in the Bible ...*

The stage directions are similar to a commentary; the play simulates present activity. The words in the Bible are simply statements; we are concerned only with the fact of statement and there is no indication of any duration. It must be admitted that the present is timeless in some cases but only in so far as present *time* is timeless, in that it extends without limit on both sides of 'now'. This may partly account for the use of the simple present in stage directions and in the report of written statements. More will be said on this point in dealing with the habitual. But what has been shown here is that most of the non-habitual uses of the simple present fit quite normally into the pattern, and ought not to be treated as 'special' uses of the form. On the contrary there is more plausibility in treating habitual usage as secondary to the basic use, in spite of its much greater frequency with this particular form.

The simple present does, however, cause difficulty to the teacher of English, at least if he tries to illustrate the verb forms situationally; for in order to illustrate the use of the present progressive, he is likely to perform actions and describe them:

> *Now I am opening the door.*
> *Now I am writing on the blackboard.*

The natural reaction of a native speaker in these situations would be to use the simple form, not the progressive, but teachers are warned not to use this form, as it will confuse the pupils. What is wrong here is not the form – but the situation. For the teacher *is* demonstrating and ought to use the simple form; but he is pretending not to be demonstrating, but acting in a 'normal' non-demonstrating type of situation. The classroom unfortunately creates a situation (that of demonstration) in which the progressive would not normally be used, and, therefore, cannot be taught naturally. It is obviously necessary to use artificial situations in teaching, but in this case the difference in the forms used in the pretended situation and those likely to be used in the actual situation (in the classroom) can only create confusion.

5.1.3. *Habitual use.* Every one of the forms may be used in a habitual (as well as a non-habitual sense). Examples of all of them (active only) are:

1. *He bowls, and ...*
   He always bowls well.
2. *He's writing a book.*
   He's always writing a book.
3. *He went to work yesterday.*
   He always went by bus.
4. *He was reading when I arrived.*
   He was reading, whenever I saw him.
5. *He has come to see me.*
   He has come to see me every day.
6. *He had called on them, when I saw him.*
   He had called on them every week, when they died.
7. *He's been reading since three.*
   Whenever I've seen him, he's been reading.
8. *He had been reading all day.*
   Whenever I'd seen him, he'd been playing golf.

As the examples show, the distinction made by progressive/non-progressive are valid for the habitual use no less than the non-habitual – the activity may or may not be durational. The points made in 4.6.2. are still valid too, though there are some complications with the perfect that are considered separately in a later section (5.4.2.). Especially to be noted is the distinction made by the progressive/non-progressive with respect to simultaneity and successivity where a point of time (or in the case of the habitual a series of points of time) is indicated:

> *Whenever I see him, he runs away.*
> *Whenever I see him, he's running away.*

On each occasion the activity of running follows (non-progressive) or overlaps (progressive) my sight of him.

The simple present is often used to refer to what are called 'eternal truths':

> *Cows eat grass.*
> *Oil floats on water.*

These can be subsumed under the use of the non-progressive forms to refer to habitual, though non-durational, activity. Yet it must be admitted that these sentences are not wholly similar to the obviously habitual:

> *I go to work every Saturday.*

One difference, of course, is that the eternal truths are true for all time whereas other habitual statements (about my own activity for instance) are not. But this is a fact about our treatment of present time. It extends without stated limits on both sides of 'now' and may, therefore, refer to a few minutes, a few years, or eternity.

It is difficult to draw any dividing lines between statements of habitual activity and eternal truths. This may be shown by the following list, graded, as far as possible, in varying approximations to completely eternal truths:

> *I always take sugar in tea.*
> *The milkman calls on Sundays.*
> *The Chinese grow a lot of rice.*
> *Cows eat grass.*
> *Birds fly.*
> *The Severn flows into the Atlantic.*
> *The sun rises in the east.*
> *Oil floats on water.*
> *Water boils at 100°.*

The last three might seem eternal truths (or perhaps the last two only). But what about the Severn? Did it always flow into the Atlantic? (Did the sun always rise in the east?)

It might, however, be feasible to distinguish:

(i) habitual, iterative, activities,

> *I go to work every day,*

(ii) inductively known facts,

> *Oil floats on water,*

(iii) 'general' truths,

> *The Severn flows into the Atlantic.*

A distinguishing feature of (i) is regular collocation with adverbials such as *every day*, while (ii) is to be compared with (and is replaceable by) a form with *will* (cf. **6.3.3.**).

What is important is to contrast these simple present forms in their habitual/eternal truth usage with the progressives. With the removal or addition of relevant adverbials and with progressive forms the sentences refer to activity going on (with duration) at present:

> *I'm going to work.*
> *The oil is floating on the water.*
> *The Severn is flowing into the Atlantic.* (I can see it moving.)

An interesting trio is (the third refers to habitual activity with duration):

> *The bucket leaks.* (It has a hole.)
> *The bucket's leaking.* (You can see the water coming out.)
> *The bucket's always leaking.* (In spite of countless repairs.)

Among the adverbials used with the habitual use are *every day*, *always*, *whenever*. There are some, such as *continually* and *for ever*, which occur almost exclusively with progressive forms, but with these the progressive usually indicates not duration but sporadic repetition (5.2.2.).

5.1.4. *Future use.* Future time reference cannot be dealt with in terms of a three-term system of present, past and future if any attention at all is paid to the formal patterning. Instead it must be recognised that the distinction of future and non-future cuts across the present/past distinction and that there are not three possibilities but four:

> Present non-future   *I'm reading* (at the moment).
> Present future   *I'm reading a paper tomorrow.*
> Past non-future   *I was reading* (when he called).
> Past future   *I was reading a paper tomorrow,* (but am now not going to).

But there are five points to note:

(i) By 'future' is meant the future relative to the period of time indicated by the verbal form. In the case of a past tense form, that is, future may be in relation to the present, past or future time. This is clearly shown by:

> *I was reading a paper yesterday,*   (but didn't).
> *I was reading a paper today,*   (but am not now).
> *I was reading a paper tomorrow,*   (but shan't now).

(ii) When a past progressive form occurs as in the examples quoted above to refer to 'future in the past' it is often associated with a fall-rise intonation with nuclear stresses on the auxiliary and often with nuclear stress on the adverbial too:

> *I* ˅*was* ˌ*reading a* ˌ*paper* ˌ*tomorrow,*
or
> *I* ˅*was* ˌ*reading a* ˌ*paper* ˋ*tomorrow.*

The fall-rise tune is the tune that suggests *but* ... and is appropriate here since there is reference to unfulfilled intention – there was (intended) future activity, but it did not in fact take place. Without this intonation there would often be ambiguity, at least where the time of the intended activity is past (relative to the present time). *I was reading a paper yesterday* would more often be interpreted as referring to actual activity yesterday, than to an activity intended yesterday. But the intonation is not wholly necessary if it is clear from the context that reference is to an unfulfilled intention:

> *Oh dear! I was writing him a letter this morning and forgot all about it.*

Conversely, the fall-rise intonation alone does not necessarily imply future in the past. It merely says *but* and leaves the hearer to judge what the reservation is:

> *He* ˅*was* ₗ*writing a* ₗ*book,*   (but he didn't finish it).

(For another kind of ambiguity see 5.1.5.)

(iii) Especially with the progressives, reference to the future is very largely restricted to verbs of motion or verbs which at least imply motion:

> *I was meeting him tomorrow.*
> *I'm coming to see you.*
> *They were taking the children,*   (but left them).
> *He was sending it on,*   (but probably hasn't).
> *He's joining the army next week.*

But other verbs may be used:

> *I'm watching television this evening.* (It is now afternoon.)
> *We're having turkey for lunch tomorrow.*

(iv) The future use is not found with all the forms. It is, as we have already seen, common with the non-perfect (present and past) progressives. It is also found with the perfect progressives:

> *I've been coming to see you for ages.*
> *He's been going abroad for years.*
> *I'd been coming to see him the next day,*   (but he died).
> *We'd been going to Paris for years,*   (but never went).

Except where there is an adverbial to mark futurity such as *the next day* utterances of this kind are ambiguous. They may refer to actual as well as intended activity, though the context will usually decide. The fall-rise intonation is possible, with nuclear stress on the *-ing* form:

> *I'd been* ˅*coming to* ₗ*see him the* ˈ*next* ˋ*day.*

Verbs of motion or implying motion are those most commonly used in this sense, but in the right contexts other verbs may also be found:

> *He'd been writing a new book for ages.*

The non-progressives are not all used with future reference. The simple present certainly is:

> *I start work tomorrow.*
> *He goes to Paris next week.*
> *Exams begin on Monday.*

There is again a restriction on the type of verb most commonly used – verbs of motion and those indicating commencement. But in the right context other verbs may again be used. Certainly we may find:

> *I read my paper tomorrow.*
> *He gets his reward on Tuesday.*

The perfect forms are never used to refer to the future. We shall not find:

> **I've read my paper tomorrow.*
> **I'd read my paper the next day.*

But a more problematic case is that of the simple past. It appears to be used in a future sense in:

> *They had to leave early as they started work the next day.*

This is, however, ambiguous. It might mean that they actually did start the next day. An example without such ambiguity, but which may not be wholly acceptable to all English speakers is:

> *They appointed me on the spot. I started work the next day, but then found a better job and didn't come.*

But it must be admitted that such a use is rare.

(v) The difference between progressives and non-progressives with this future use is that the non-progressives refer to a decision or fixed plan, the progressives to an intention. This is the main distinction between:

> *I start work tomorrow.*
> *I'm starting work tomorrow.*

The second of these suggests that the speaker now intends to start (he may, for example, have been ill), while the first suggests that tomorrow is the day fixed for starting (by the firm, or after illness by the doctor). There is a contrast, though not a wholly clear one, between a general intention and a fixed decision. Certainly we should normally expect:

> *Exams begin on Thursday,*

rather than   *Exams are beginning on Thursday.*

The beginning of examinations is fixed by a firm decision. Quite clearly verbs which refer to activities that are commonly fixed by firm decisions are more likely to occur with the non-progressives with the future sense. This accounts for the high probability of the occurrence of BEGIN, END, START and similarly FINISH.

The fact that the progressives are used to suggest a general intention is to be associated with the fact that the progressives imply duration and intentions may have such duration. This is quite clearly shown where a perfect form is used:

I've been coming to see you for a long time.

The intention has lasted over a long time, and, as the perfect shows, began in the past and extended right up to the present moment. But the present non-perfect is often used where there is reference to the duration of the future action (not the duration of the intention):

I'm working all day tomorrow.

He's supervising the examinations tomorrow.

In the first example the duration of the activity is shown by the adverbial. In the second there is, one could assume, a fixed decision; it is the intended activity that has duration. In some cases it is difficult to decide whether it is the intention of the proposed activity that is marked as having duration.

With verbs such as READ, or WORK, which refer to non-momentary activity (see 4.6.1.) the progressive would usually suggest duration of the activity itself, especially if a point of time is indicated (the activity extending over, both before and after, the point):

(Don't call on me) I'm working at twelve.

In contrast, the activity has no duration in:

I'm leaving at twelve.

If this differs at all from

I leave at twelve,

it is in terms of intention versus fixed plan or decision.

5.1.5. *Future use and adverbials.* Adverbials of future time are commonly found with the present forms, especially the non-perfect forms – adverbials such as *tomorrow, next week, soon,* etc.:

He's coming to see me tomorrow.

He starts work next week.

With past tense forms adverbials with any time reference are possible since the future as seen from the past time may be (in relation to the present moment) either past, present or future. So we may find:

He was coming to see me yesterday,

today,

tomorrow, etc.

With the perfect forms, adverbs referring in the same way to the time of the proposed activity are possible, but certainly less common. We might say for instance:

> *He's been coming to see me tomorrow for a long time.*
> *He'd been coming to see me yesterday/today/tomorrow.*

But there is a problem concerned especially with the simple past tense forms, in that we may have two kinds of time adverbs, the one indicating the period of time (past) and the other the time at which it was proposed to carry out the activity. Since adverbs may indicate both the time period (during which activity was proposed) and the particular usage (activity proposed for the future), ambiguity would appear possible in a sentence such as:

> *He was coming to see me yesterday.*

In actual fact, such ambiguity will seldom arise, since it is resolved by intonation or by the position of the adverb. With a fall-rise and nuclear stress on the auxiliary (and possibly also nuclear stress on the adverb) the adverb always refers to the time of the intended activity:

> *He ᵛwas ₁coming to ₁see me ˋyesterday,* (but he didn't come).

(Yesterday was the time of his intended visit.)

With a separate intonation tune on *yesterday* or with *yesterday* at the beginning of the sentence, the adverb will almost certainly indicate the time of the intention and not the proposed activity:

> *He was ‖coming to ˋsee me, ⁄yesterday.*
> *Yesterday he was coming to see me.*

(Yesterday was the time of the statement of intention.)

It would even be possible to have two adverbials, the one referring to the time of the intention and the other to the time of the proposed activity. In such cases, the most probable pattern is one in which the former of these adverbials occurs at the beginning of the sentence:

> *Yesterday he was coming to see me today.*

Even the following sentence cannot be completely ruled out theoretically, but it would sound comic:

> *He was coming to see me today, yesterday.*

With the corresponding present tense forms *now* commonly occurs as the adverbial of the (present) period of time, either initially or, with the appropriate intonation, finally:

> *Now he's coming to see me tomorrow.*
> *He's ‖coming to ‖see me ˋtomorrow, ⁄now.*

Similar sentences are possible also with the non-progressive present:

> *Now he starts work tomorrow.*
> *He ‖starts ‖work ˋtomorrow, ⁄now.*

With the perfect forms, adverbials marking both the time of the intended action and the duration of the intention are possible:

> *They've been coming to see us tomorrow for a long time.*

But adverbials marking both the time of the intention and the time of the intended activity are unlikely. A sentence such as the following might seem theoretically possible, but it is not likely to be attested:

> **They've been ‖coming to ‖see us to͜morrow, ⸝this year.*

5.1.6. *Combinations of future and habitual.* There are two ways in which future and habitual uses may be combined.

(i) The simple present is used to refer to a future event that is part of a habitual pattern:

> *You get tea at five tonight.*
> *The baker calls on Saturday.*

This use is not very different from the one we have already considered except that there is reference not to a decision but to a regular pattern. In the second example *on Saturdays* (plural) would have indicated habitual activity. The singular *Saturday* may be taken to indicate the application of the habitual pattern to a single future date.

(ii) The progressives may be used to refer to habitual intended activity. This is a combination of the habitual and future uses. Examples in the present non-perfect are:

> *He's always coming to see me,*   (but never does).
> *She's usually writing in a few days.*
> *He's always taking them on holiday,*   (but hasn't yet).

The other progressive forms may be similarly used, though this usage is not common and the following examples are admittedly rather artificial:

> *Whenever I wanted to visit him, he was going away the next day.*
> *Whenever I've wanted to visit him, he's been going away the next day.*
> *Whenever I'd wanted to visit him, he'd been going away the next day.*

With the first of these two kinds of habitual-futures the adverbials used are of the type that refer to the future – *The baker calls tomorrow.* With the second, the adverbials are mainly of the type that indicates the habitual nature – *He's always coming to see us,* though adverbials that refer to the future, such as *the next day,* are also possible.

5.2. More on the progressive

There are two uses of the progressive that, though related to its use to indicate duration, do not directly follow from it. Except with the 'non-progressive verbs' (considered in the next section) both are habitual uses referring to (i) habitual activity over a *limited* period of time, and (ii) habitually repeated but *sporadic* activity.

5.2.1. *Limited duration.* The progressive is used to indicate habitual activity in a limited period of time in:

> *He's going to work by bus.*
> *We're eating a lot more meat now.*
> *We've been getting up early this week.*
> *I'd been visiting him every day.*

The activity is habitual, but it is over a limited period. In the first example the inference is probably that the man's car has broken down, and that he is now forced (temporarily) to take the bus. If he always went by bus, the non-progressive would be normal:

> *He goes to work by bus.*

The period of time is often shown to be limited by adverbials, especially *these days* or *in those days*. We may contrast:

> *We eat a lot of meat,*   (and always have).
> *We're eating a lot of meat these days.*
> *I went to work by bus,*   (all my life).
> *I was going to work by bus in those days.*   (Now I have a car).

The simple present often differs very little in its use from the present perfect, and may even be used with *since*, in spite of the fact that adverbials of this kind mark a period of time characteristic of the perfect:

> *We're eating more meat since the war.*
> *He's going to work by bus since his car broke down.*

In both cases a perfect would equally be possible – *we've been eating, he's been going*. With the perfect the period of time is, of course, often limited; *since* marks the limitation. But one important difference is that the present progressive implies the continuance of the activity, even though for a limited period, through present time into the future. The perfect does not.

In the case of the man whose car has broken down then, if the car is now back at his disposal we will expect *He's been going* rather than *He's going*. The latter suggests that the activity, though limited in its duration, is both future and past.

A special use that can, perhaps, be treated under the heading of limited duration is that of showing increasing or decreasing activity, or increase or decrease of some feature of the activity; this has already been mentioned (4.6.1.):

> *More and more people are buying television sets.*
> *They are visiting us more and more often.*
> *They were stealing more and more of his money.*
> *I've been giving him less and less every week.*

Non-progressives could be used in all these sentences, but they are far less likely. Adverbials such as *more and more* suggest limited duration.

5.2.2. *Sporadic repetition.* The progressive is also used to indicate habitual activity that is repeated and sporadic:

> *She's always breaking things.*
> *The car's always breaking down.*

What is happening happens very often, but it does not happen at set times. If there is reference to repeated points of time, indicating regularity, the non-progressive is used:

> *The car always breaks down when I start for home.*

We may contrast:

> *I always break the eggs first.*
> *I'm always breaking the crockery.*

The progressive carries with it too a hint of the speaker's disapproval, especially with adverbials such as *for ever* or *everlastingly.* Some more examples of this use, which is quite common, are:

> *I was continually falling ill.*
> *They were for ever leaving the gate open.*
> *He's always asking silly questions.*
> *He's for ever losing his money.*
> *They're always getting in the way.*
> *You're continually making poor excuses.*
> *She's been dropping things recently.*
> *He'd been continually stealing from his friends.*

In most of these examples there is no suggestion that the activity is continuous – the progressive is used because it is repeated and sporadic. But the activity may be both continuous (at every occasion) and repeated sporadically:

> *He's always grumbling.*
> *She's for ever writing letters.*

Indication of the sporadic nature or the speaker's disapproval of the activity may be carried by the intonation, by e.g., a high fall on the adverbial or by a 'stepping head' (the first stressed syllable on a high pitch, each succeeding one a step lower) and a low fall.

5.3. 'Non-progressive' verbs

There are some verbs that are commonly not used in the progressive form at all, even where they seem to indicate duration:

> *I forget his name.*
> *I see my brother over there.*
> *It contains sugar.*
> *They own a lot of property.*

These verbs differ from the other verbs of English in that they usually, even in the present tense, occur with the non-progressive. The non-progressive is, in fact, the norm, and progressive forms are used only where there is specific reference to duration or one of the special features indicated by the progressive. There are some fairly obvious reasons why these verbs are used with the non-progressive form, but the reasons apply to them *as a class* and are not valid on each occasion of use. This may be clearly shown by placing together the exactly comparable:

> *What are you doing?*
> *What do you see?*

In neither of these is there specific indication of duration nor is duration specifically excluded. In such circumstances most verbs occur in the progressive form, but the 'non-progressives' in the non-progressive.

There are some verbs such as READ, SLEEP, WORK that refer to non-momentary actions and sometimes occur in the non-progressive with adverbials that indicate duration (4.6.1.) and that in the progressive with future time reference indicate the duration of the activity rather than an intention as opposed to a decision (5.1.4.). These are, perhaps, marginally non-progressive verbs and deserve a separate mention, but they occur quite commonly in the progressive form, and for this reason are not treated in this section as 'non-progressive' verbs.

The verbs fall into two sub-classes – verbs of 'state' and 'private' verbs. The reason why these do not normally occur with the progressive is different for each sub-class.

5.3.1. *'Private' verbs.* Private verbs are those that refer to states or activities that the speaker alone is aware of. These are of two kinds, those that refer to mental activities and those that refer to sensations. Both commonly occur with non-progressive forms.

Examples of verbs referring to mental activities are:

THINK   *I think that's mine.*

IMAGINE   *I imagine he'll be there.*

HOPE   *I hope it's true.*

PLAN   *I plan to go to London tomorrow.*

FORGET   *I forget what you said.*

BELIEVE   *I believe that it's true.*

In all these examples the subject is *I*. But though it is common for the subject to be the first person this is not always so:

> *You think you're clever!*
>
> *Do you remember what he said?*

Examples of verbs referring to sensations are:

SEE   *I see my brother over there.*

SMELL   *I smell something burning.*

HEAR   *I hear music.*

TASTE   *I taste salt.*

FEEL   *I feel something hard.*

Once again these verbs are most common with the first person, but they may occur with other subjects:

> *He smells something burning.*
>
> *Do you see that tree over there?*

It must be noted here that these verbs very commonly occur with CAN, with no apparent difference in meaning – *I can see ..., I can smell ..., Can you feel ...?*, etc.

The frequent occurrence of these verbs with first person subjects gives a clue to the reason why they are so common in the non-progressive. For when these verbs are used, the speaker is in exactly the same position as the commentator – he is reporting something that is not perceived by the hearer (cf. 5.1.2.). Just as the radio commentator uses the non-progressive because his main aim is merely to report, so too the person who reports on his own mental activities or sensations is simply reporting and so uses the non-progressive form. As we have already seen, with most verbs we seldom need simply to report in the present. If we refer to a present activity it is only with reference to its duration, for there is no need to report what can be perceived by the hearer as well as the speaker. But the private verbs have the special characteristic that they refer to activities available for perception by the speaker only. He alone can report them and in so doing uses the appropriate form – the non-progressive.

The verbs can, of course, be used with second or third person subjects, but only to ask about the activity, or to report it at second hand or by inference. *Do you think* ... is looking for the answer *I think* ... while *He thinks* ... is either a report of *I think* ... or merely a guess. But in all these cases we are merely concerned with a bare statement; duration is not at issue.

The characteristics of the non-progressive verbs apply to them as a class, and, indeed, a class that is formally definable in terms of regular occurrence in the non-progressive. A verb that does not belong to the class will not occur in the non-progressive even if it is reporting a sensation. The verb SUFFER, for instance, does not belong to the class of non-progressive verbs at all – mainly, no doubt, because sufferings are so often observable by both speaker and hearer. Even when a purely private sensation is being reported, the progressive form is used:

> *I'm suffering from a headache.*

There are some other verbs which occur with little or no difference of meaning with progressive or non-progressive forms. These are to be regarded as optional members of the class, e.g., ACHE, ITCH:

> *My foot itches/is itching.*
> *My arm aches/is aching.*

5.3.2. *Verbs of 'state'.* There are many verbs which refer not to an activity but to a state or condition. The sense of duration is an integral part of the lexical meaning of the verb, and there is for this reason no need for a progressive form to indicate duration. Examples are:

CONTAIN	*It contains sugar.*
BELONG	*It belongs to me.*
MATTER	*It doesn't matter.*
DESERVE	*He deserves something better than that.*
CONSIST	*It consists of little but water and colouring.*
PLEASE	*It pleases me no end.*
DEPEND	*It depends on what you mean.*
OWN	*I own my own house.*

A rather special sub-group is that of the verbs which indicate the quality of creating sensations, those that may be treated as the intransitive forms of the verbs of sensation:

> *It smells sweet.*
> *It tastes nice.*
> *It feels soft.*

The verbs of sensation SEE and HEAR have no similar intransitive forms. The problem of these is dealt with in the section on homonyms (5.3.4.).

5.3.3. *Use in progressive forms.* The characteristic of the non-progressive verbs is that they are not normally used in progressive forms, i.e., that unless there is some specific reference to a feature marked by the progressive, the non-progressive is used. But they are used in certain circumstances with progressive forms. We may contrast the sentences at the beginning of the section with:

> *I'm forgetting names nowadays.*
> *I'm seeing things.*

The private verbs are used with the progressive where there is simply emphasis upon the duration:

> *I'm actually hearing his voice!*
> *He's seeing stars.*
> *She's hoping all the time that he'll come back.*

A more common use is to indicate habitual activity over a limited period (**5.2.1.**):

> *I'm feeling the cold these days.*
> *He's forgetting names nowadays.*
> *I'm thinking now that we ought perhaps to go.*

The progressive is also used for sporadic repetition (**5.2.2.**):

> *I'm continually forgetting names.*
> *He's always feeling ill.*
> *You're always imagining you'll win a prize.*

In other words, the private verbs function in very much the same way as the other verbs, with the sole exception that they are commonly used merely to report and in reporting occur in the non-progressive. But wherever there is specific indication of one of the features associated with the progressive, they too occur with progressive forms.

With the verbs of state the position is a little different. With them there is never emphasis on the duration and they cannot normally be said to have a habitual sense at all since they refer to permanent or semi-permanent states. Yet they are used with progressive forms where there is reference to limited duration, but it is not the limited duration of *habitual* activity:

> *He's looking better since his operation.*
> *I'm feeling all right now.*
> *We're living in London at the moment.*

We may contrast the last of these with:

> *We live in London.*

The progressive form suggests either that we have moved there recently, or that we intend to move soon, or both. The non-progressive indicates that London is our permanent home.

Similarly examples that indicate increasing or decreasing activity are to be found:

> *He's looking more and more like his father.*
> *It's mattering less and less now.*
> *It's tasting nastier and nastier.*

Again these differ from those dealt with previously only in that there can hardly be reference to *habitual* activity.

5.3.4. *Homonyms.* We have already seen that the verbs SMELL, FEEL and TASTE have two different uses, the one transitive with the sense of having the sensation, the other intransitive with the sense of having the quality to produce the sensation. The verbs are non-progressives in both their senses, but in one sense they belong to the private verbs, in the other to the verbs of state. There is yet a third use, with the meaning 'to act to achieve the sensation'. In this sense the verbs are not non-progressives. Examples of all three uses are:

> *I smell flowers.*
> *The flowers smell lovely.*
> *I'm smelling the flowers.*
> *I taste salt in the soup.*
> *The soup tastes salty.*
> *The cook is tasting the soup.*
> *I feel something rough.*
> *The cloth feels rough.*
> *I'm feeling the cloth.*

The verbs SEE and HEAR are not similarly used in three senses. In comparable senses different verbs are used:

	I see my brother.
(LOOK)	*He looks well.*
(LOOK AT)	*I'm looking at my brother.*
	I hear music.
(SOUND)	*It sounds beautiful.*
(LISTEN TO)	*I'm listening to the music.*

Diagrammatically we have:

(i)	(ii)	(iii)
SMELL	SMELL	SMELL
TASTE	TASTE	TASTE
FEEL	FEEL	FEEL
SEE	LOOK	LOOK AT
HEAR	SOUND	LISTEN TO

where (i) is a private verb with the sense of 'acquire the sensation', (ii) is a verb of state with the sense of 'produce the sensation', and (iii) is not a non-progressive verb with the sense of 'act to acquire the sensation'.

In view of the differences of the functions of the verbs and especially in view of the fact that the verbs SEE and HEAR are not used in all three senses, it is as well not to treat these as the same verb (lexeme) at all, but rather to speak of homonyms. It would, of course, be possible to handle them as a special class with a grammatical statement accounting for the three different uses (transitive non-progressive, intransitive non-progressive and transitive progressive). But SEE and HEAR would need to be included; *sound, listen to, look* and *look at* would have to be treated as forms of these verbs, not lexemes in their own right, in the way that *went* is a form of GO.

Treating these as homonyms (separate lexemes) avoids any suggestion that *I smell the flowers* and *I'm smelling the flowers* can be accounted for simply in terms of the durational characteristics of the progressive versus the non-progressive. For it is more than that. In the first SMELL belongs to the class of non-progressive verbs, in the second SMELL does not. But there are many other forms that raise problems. The difficulty arises from the fact that there are many contrasts of progressive and non-progressive forms in which there is clearly a difference of durational aspect, but in which this is not the only difference of meaning. With these there is reason for suggesting that we have again cases of homonymity; this accounts not only for the difference in the progressive/non-progressive category (for one only is a non-progressive verb), but also for the difference in meaning:

> *I imagine he'll come.*   (think)
> *You're imagining things.*   (having hallucinations)
> *I plan to go tomorrow.*   (intend)
> *I'm planning my holidays.* (making arrangements)
> *I think he'll come.*   (believe)
> *I'm thinking about it.*   (pondering)

It will obviously be difficult in some cases to decide whether to treat the differences of progressive and non-progressive in terms of verb classes (the non-progressives versus the rest) or to handle them purely in terms of the uses of the progressive/non-progressive category. In, for instance,

> *Now I'm remembering*

we might say that the progressive form is used because it emphasises the duration, or perhaps indicates limited duration. Alternatively we might argue that REMEMBER here has the meaning of 'make a conscious effort to remember' and that with this meaning it is not a non-progressive verb at all. We are at the borderline of lexis and grammar, and some of our decisions will have to be arbitrary.

5.4. More on the perfect

There are some special uses of the perfect and a potential ambiguity that are to be considered here.

5.4.1. *Special uses.* There are three special uses to note.
(i) Very recent activity is indicated by *just* with a perfect form:

> *I've just seen him.*
> *He's just gone.*
> *I've just been lecturing.*
> *I'd just been waving good-bye to him.*

The activity itself does not continue right up to the present moment, but as we have already seen this does not exclude the use of the perfect. We can suggest that *just* is essentially a present time adverb, and that it includes the present, but this is to add nothing to what is simply a fact, that *just* occurs with the perfect. In fact, since the activity is past one might equally expect the use of the non-perfect past, and though this is rarer in British English (perhaps not in American), it does occur:

> *He just went down the road.*
> *I just saw him.*

Where recent activity in the past is indicated the perfect is always used – *He had just gone*, etc., but as has already been explained, the past perfect is the past time analogue of both the present perfect and the past non-perfect (a 'past-past') (4.5.4.).
(ii) The perfect with nuclear stress on the auxiliary and usually with a fall rise intonation is used to refer to past experiences:

> *I ᵛhave read ₗOliver ₗTwist.*
> *She ᵛhas ₗvisited ₗParis.*

The use of the perfect is perhaps to be explained here on the grounds that past experiences are part of a person's present make-up – that reading 'Oliver Twist' is included among the experiences that make me what I am. But, as in the previous section, it is doubtful whether such an explanation has any value; the use is essentially 'idiomatic', in that it cannot be clearly predicted from what has already been said about the perfect.
(iii) The verb BE is used with a special meaning with the perfect and with the perfect alone occurs with *to*:

> *I've been to London.*
> *He'd been to my house.*

We will not attest, however:

>*I am to London (or *I was to London)
>*He was to my house.

With the perfect and followed by *to* the verb has the meaning of having gone and returned. There is a difference, then, between:

>He's gone to London,

and   He's been to London.

In the former he is still in London, in the latter, he has returned.

Quite commonly the verb occurs in the use mentioned in (ii), to refer to past experiences:

>I ᵛhave been to ₁London,   (but it was years ago).

5.4.2. *A potential ambiguity.* Where there is reference to habitual use, there is potentially at least an ambiguity. The following sentence has two possible meanings:

>Every time I've seen them, they've been bathing.

This might mean either that on each occasion they were actually bathing or that on each occasion they had (previously) been bathing. The ambiguity arises from the fact that the perfect may be used to refer either to the overall period of time that we are talking about, or in addition about each repeated period. The overall period of time is clearly shown by *Every time I've seen them* to be one that began in the past and continues up to the present moment. But the successive periods of time that are to be related to the series of points of time – my seeing them – may either be periods that simply overlap these points of time (non-perfect type), or they may be periods that began before and continued up to the points of time. This may be shown diagrammatically:

Overall period   *Now*

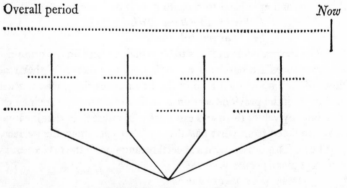

Every time I've seen them

In the majority of cases a sentence of the pattern *Whenever* ... or *Every time* ... followed by perfect forms in both clauses would be interpreted in the first of the two senses – the perfect being taken to refer only to the overall period of time – the activity on each occasion merely overlapping the points of time. This would be the more obvious interpretation of the sentence we have been considering.

The other sense would usually be indicated by some specific mark. Of course, if the dependent clause does not have a perfect form, then the perfect can only refer to series of periods of time:

> *Every time I see him, he's been bathing.*

This can only mean that he has already been bathing on each occasion. Similarly this use may be shown by *just* or *already*:

> *Whenever I've called, he's just/already been bathing.*

Intonation, too, can suggest the second rather than the first meaning, especially nuclear stress on *been*:

> *Whenever I've ⸝called, he's ˋbeen ₎working.*
> *Every time you've ⸝called, I've ˋbeen ₎mending the ₎car*
> (but you've never actually caught me at it).

There is similar ambiguity with a non-progressive perfect form:

> *Every time he's come, he's cut his finger.*

This may mean that he has cut his finger either before or after his arrival. Once again it depends on whether the perfect relates only to the overall period of time or to the series. If it refers only to the overall period, then we merely have a habitual statement in 'perfect' time corresponding to:

> *Every time he comes, he cuts his finger.*
> *When he came, he cut his finger.*

In these examples the non-progressive implies immediate succession – the cutting of the finger followed his arrival. But if the perfect also refers to each occasion, then the time relations are similar to those of:

> *Every time he comes, he's cut his finger.*
> *When he came, he had cut his finger.*

The finger-cutting took place in a period preceding, but continuing up to, the point(s) of time that are marked.

Once again there are features of the situations referred to that aid decision. Normally it would be assumed that the perfect related only to the overall period and that, therefore, the activity followed the points of time indicated by *whenever*, etc:

> *Whenever I've taken up carpentry, I've cut my finger.*

But it is more likely that the activity preceded each of the points of time in:

> *Whenever I've had to go to the doctor, I've cut my finger.*

Again, of course, the use of *just, already* would make clear the meaning: *Whenever I've called, he's just left.*

References

Page 81 **Habitual.** Cf. A. A. Hill, *Introduction to linguistic structures* (op. cit.), 207–11.

Page 93 **Limited duration.** Cf. W. F. Twaddell, *The English verb auxiliaries* (op. cit.), 8.

Page 95 **Private verbs.** M. Joos quoted by A. A. Hill in *Introduction to linguistic structures* (op. cit.), 207. Joos has now abandoned this term in *The English Verb* (op. cit.), 116, and calls all the non-progressive verbs 'status' verbs.

Chapter 6

The simple phrase: secondary pattern (1)

We now turn to consider the secondary pattern – the forms that include the secondary or modal auxiliaries.

6.1. The paradigms

The secondary pattern is an extension of the primary. In the place of each pair of present and past tense finite (word) forms in the primary pattern, there is an infinitive preceded by one of the secondary (modal) auxiliaries.

For the modal WILL the paradigm is:

(1)	*will*	*take*		
(2)	*would*	*take*		
(3)	*will*	*be*	*taking*	
(4)	*would*	*be*	*taking*	
(5)	*will*	*have*	*taken*	
(6)	*would*	*have*	*taken*	
(7)	*will*	*have*	*been*	*taking*
(8)	*would*	*have*	*been*	*taking*
(9)	*will*	*be*		*taken*
(10)	*would*	*be*		*taken*
(11)	*will*	*be*	*being*	*taken*
(12)	*would*	*be*	*being*	*taken*
(13)	*will*	*have*	*been*	*taken*
(14)	*would*	*have*	*been*	*taken*
(15)	*will*	*have*	*been*	*being* *taken* (?)
(16)	*would*	*have*	*been*	*being* *taken* (?)

Tense is still marked by the finite form, though this is now a modal auxiliary form; all the other categories are marked in exactly the same way as in the primary pattern. There is again, theoretically at least, a paradigm of sixteen forms.

There is only a 'basic' paradigm. With the secondary auxiliaries there are no participials, infinitivals or phrases containing imperatives (cf. **4.1.2.**). Participles, infinitives and imperatives are not included in the forms of the modal auxiliaries.

A similar statement may be made for the other secondary auxiliaries, except that for MUST, OUGHT, DARE and NEED there is no distinction of tense; there are, thus, only eight forms. On morphological grounds there is no reason to handle the eight forms as either present or past; the distinction of tense is not made. In their uses, moveover, though they commonly function like present tense forms they also fulfil some of the functions of past tense.

Numbers 15 and 16 are again marked with a question mark. If such forms are not to be found in the primary pattern, they will not exist in the secondary. Numbers 11 and 12 are rare, though not actually never attested. Where these might be expected (reference to duration of the activity), the corresponding non-progressives would be more usual. I personally should not normally say

> *He will be being examined while we are there,

but rather

> He will be examined while we are there.

But the progressive forms cannot be completely ruled out; they do occur in some people's speech, and I am not sure that I never use them myself (though I am clear that I can always use a non-progressive). Again H. E. Palmer marks them as 'wanting'.

The forms in the secondary pattern are not wholes in the way in which those of the primary pattern are. Their initial elements, the secondary auxiliaries, can be treated separately both in their syntax (always followed by an infinitive) and in their use (though there are special problems of tense). In this respect secondary pattern phrases partly resemble complex phrases, but they differ from them in that the secondary auxiliaries may occur initially only. We may contrast

	I want to begin ...
and	I begin to want ...
with	I ought to begin ...
but not	*I begin to ought ...

6.2. Problems of statement

The analysis of the modal auxiliaries is made difficult by two factors. First, the past tense forms do not often refer to past time. Secondly, there are a number of different uses of some of them (especially WILL and CAN) that are not wholly semantically distinct and that are not easily defined in formal terms. We begin, then, with some remarks on these two difficulties.

6.2.1. *The function of tense.* Four of the modal auxiliaries, WILL, SHALL, CAN and MAY, have (morphologically) present and past tense forms. But these are not regularly used to mark time relations; it is not the main function of the past tense forms to indicate past time. There is, for instance, no time difference in the following pairs:

> He may go.   He might go.
> I shall ask him. I should ask him.
> Can you help? Could you help?

But there is in some cases a difference in time:

> He can run ten miles with ease.
>
> When he was a boy he could run ten miles with ease.

In reported speech, moreover, the usual pattern *is* followed. With a past tense verb of reporting, a past tense form of the auxiliary is used where the original utterance had a present tense form (unless the statement is still held to be valid – **4.4.2.** and **7.1.5.**):

> He'll come.   He said he would come.
> He may come. He said he might come.

Yet a further complication is that, under certain circumstances, the modals that have only one tense form (MUST, OUGHT, DARE and NEED) may be used (in that one form) to refer to past time (**7.1.2.** and **7.1.5.**).

There is, of course, no real justification for handling WILL and SHALL as essentially the markers of the future, and none for referring to them in terms of 'future tense' (cf. **4.2.3.**). The most that need be said is that in one of their uses they do simply refer to future time. But it is a characteristic of all the modals that they may refer to the future and may be collocated with future time adverbials:

> He will/shall/can/may/must/ought to/daren't/needn't come
> tomorrow.

The simplest way of handling the problem is to consider all the present tense forms first, and state in detail their various uses. This takes us to the end of this chapter. Only positive forms will be considered, since negation provides some difficulties of its own (**7.5.**), except in the case of DARE and NEED, which function as auxiliaries only in negation or inversion (and the latter is not a convenient pattern for analysis). Secondly (in Chapter 7), the forms that are used to refer to past time will be dealt with; where there are no past tense forms we must consider whether there are other forms that are analogously used for past time reference (for instance, *had to* in relation to MUST). Next the other functions of tense will be dealt with. Finally we return to the problem of negation.

6.2.2. *The formal criteria of the various uses.* It is very obvious that some of the modals are used in a variety of senses. WILL, for instance, may be used to refer to the future or to habitual activities as in:

> *He'll come tomorrow.*
>
> *He'll come in at night and sit down without saying a word.*

Formally there are three types of criteria that may be used to distinguish these uses:

(a) Collocation with adverbials:

> *I can come tomorrow,*
>
> *She can be very unkind at times,*

(b) the possibility of the replacement of the modal by another modal, or by no modal (a secondary pattern form by a primary pattern form):

> *You can go now.*
>
> *You may go now.*

(c) Comparison with the analogous forms used for past time or negation:

> *I must go.*
>
> *I had to go.*
>
> *I needn't go.*

and (rarely – **6.5.1.**) with forms used to refer to future time;

(d) occurrence in conditional clauses (WILL only, see **6.3.1.**).

The third criterion means that we must, to some degree, anticipate a later part of the analysis.

There is one problem of terminology that must be settled here. It would be possible to talk about the 'past tense form' (e.g., *had to* of MUST), but it may be better to restrict this terminology to relations that are more obviously morphological (though in fact there is little difference between the *had to*/MUST relation and that of *went*/GO), and to talk of *had to* as the past time 'analogue' of *must*. *Needn't* is similarly the negative analogue of *must* (but *mustn't* the negative form of MUST). Where, however, confusion is unlikely there will be reference simply to 'past time' and 'negation' forms (as contrasted with past tense and negative forms).

6.3. WILL

We begin, then, with a consideration of the uses of the present tense forms, and in this section with the uses of *will*. There are three sets of criteria for the classification of the uses of *will*:

(a) the possibility of collocation with future time adverbials will distinguish between the future and the non-future uses (collocation with other adverbials (habitual and present time) permits further distinctions);

(b) in one use only (reference simply to the future) *will* is not used after *if* (in conditional clauses);

(c) in one use there is the possibility of the substitution of *will* by *shall* (in limited contexts) and in others of the verbal form by a form with no modal.

Six uses of *will* are suggested here:

  (i) Futurity (**6.3.1.**)

 (ii) Volition (**6.3.2.**)

(iii) Induction (**6.3.3.**)

(iv) Characteristic (**6.3.4.**)

 (v) Probability (**6.3.5.**)

(vi) Insistence (**6.3.6.**)

6.3.1. *Futurity. Will* is, of course, treated in many grammar books as the marker of future tense, together with *shall*. A complete sub-section is devoted to the problem of the relation between *will* and *shall* (**6.4.3.**). But it is clear that one of the uses of *will* is to refer simply to future time, and that in this use it is collocated with future time adverbials:

> *It'll rain tomorrow.*
> *The letters will arrive in a few days.*

In this use it does not occur after *if* (in conditional clauses). The form that is used analogously to *will* in a conditional clause is the non-modal (primary pattern) form:

> *He'll be ill tomorrow,*

but   *If he's ill tomorrow, ...*

This use of the non-modal form is not, however, to be regarded as merely the future use of the primary pattern forms (**5.1.4.**) as exemplified by *I'm going to London tomorrow* or *I start work tomorrow*. For these are limited to intentions and plans, and we shall not attest (or rarely):

> **It's raining tomorrow,*

or   **I'm ill tomorrow,*

whereas we shall attest:

> *If it's raining tomorrow, ...*
> *If I'm ill tomorrow, ...*

These are then the conditional analogues of:

> *It'll be raining tomorrow.*
> *I'll be ill tomorrow.*

With *I* and *we, shall* may be substituted for *will*:

> *I'll see him soon.*   *I shall see him soon.*
> *We'll be ill tomorrow.*   *We shall be ill tomorrow.*

But the traditional paradigm *I shall, you will*, etc. is misleading in that it suggests that *I will* is not used to refer simply to future time. Most commonly of course, it is the weak form [l] that is to be found:

> *I/We'll be ill tomorrow.*

But the strong form may occur (in this example) with nuclear stress:

> *I/we `will feel better tomorrow.*

In either case *shall* ([ʃəl] or [ʃæl]) could occur.

6.3.2. *Volition.* A second use that refers to the future (formally, with collocation with future time adverbials) suggests willingness or agreement. It is formally distinguished from the previous use in that in this use *will* does occur in conditional clauses:

> *If he'll come tomorrow*   (*He'll come tomorrow*),

which must be contrasted with (i)

> *If he comes tomorrow*   (*He'll come tomorrow*).

This use of *will* is very common, more common perhaps than the previous one, at least with all verbs that refer to activities that may be willed or agreed. With verbs of this kind plain future reference is more likely to be made by *going to* or by the use of the non-modal progressive, while the use of *will* especially in questions suggests a willingness (and in questions is an invitation). The following would, thus, usually be interpreted as asking the person addressed to do something, rather than asking whether he intended to do it:

> *Will you read a paper tomorrow?*
> *Will you come with us this evening?*

Questions requiring information rather than making an invitation would be:

> *Are you going to read a paper tomorrow?*
> *Are you coming with us this evening?*

Of course with other verbs the possibility of an invitation are ruled out by their meaning. With these *will* may be used in an enquiry:

> *Will you feel better tomorrow, do you think?*

The rarity of *Will you* in sense (i) is, however, related to the whole problem of *will* and *shall*, and is reconsidered in the next sub-section.

Will is also used in a future sense and with the possibility of occurrence in conditional clauses in such sentences as:

> *The books will all fit here.*
> *The board will easily bear his weight.*

Collocation with a future time adverbial is however, unlikely. But we cannot handle these sentences in terms of any of the other uses of *will* since they do not satisfy the criteria. They do not fit (i) in view of the possibility of the conditional:

> *If the books will all fit here,* ...

Nor can they be equated with (iii) and (iv) both of which would require the possibility of replacement by a non-modal form:

> *The books all fit here,*

nor with (v) which would require a parallel use of *will have*, nor with (vi) which requires nuclear stress. We must either then treat these sentences as examples of a different use, or treat them under the heading of volition, satisfying the major conditions of having future reference (formally shown not by collocation with adverbials, but only by the impossibility of substitution in a given context by a non-modal present time form) and occurrence after *if*.

6.3.3. *Induction. Will* is used for 'general' timeless truths, that may be proved inductively, of the kind illustrated by:

> *Oil will float on water.*
> *Pigs'll eat anything.*

In this sense there is no possibility of collocation with future time adverbials, and indeed it is only rarely that there would be collocation with any adverbials at all, though adverbials such as *always* might occur:

> *Oil will always float on water.*

More important, there is the possibility of the replacement here of the verbal form by non-modal simple form in its habitual use (though only for 'inductive' statements – see **5.1.3.**):

> *Pigs eat anything.*
> *Oil floats on water.*

(But we shall not find a similar use of *will* for the 'general truths' of the type *The sun rises in the east.*)

6.3.4. *Characteristic.* A very similar use is one that expresses characteristic activity. There is again no possibility of collocation with future time adverbials, and the possibility of occurrence after *if*.

> *She'll sit there for hours doing nothing.*
> (Don't listen to him.) *He'll tell you anything.*

This use is very similar to the previous one, except for the fact that it will always have 'personal' subjects. There will, however, never be collocation with *always*. The *will* form may often be replaceable by the non-modal form, though only in the sense of iterative activity. But the converse is not true. Not every non-modal form may be replaced by this *will* form; replacement is possible only when the activity is essentially characteristic. We cannot equate:

> *I go to work every morning,*

with   *I'll go to work every morning.*

A special point about this use is that it is very rare with *I* and *we*, not unnaturally, since it describes characteristic features, often with some disapproval, as in:

> *He'll come in and sit down without speaking.*
> *She'll keep talking so that no one else can get a word in.*

6.3.5. *Probability. Will* is used to indicate that something probably is happening. In this sense it may occur with adverbials of present time:

> *The French will be having a holiday today.*
> *He'll be at home now.*
> *That'll be the postman.*

The most important formal characteristic of this use is that its past time analogue is *will have* (cf. **7.1.3.**):

> *The French will have been having a holiday yesterday.*
> *He'll have been at home then.*
> *That'll have been the postman.*

A further point is that this use usually occurs only with progressive forms, except in the case of non-progressive verbs. It usually refers, that is to say, to activity or states continuing at the present moment. We may contrast:

> *She'll sit there for hours.* (**6.3.4.**)
> *She'll be sitting there now.*

We may add here:

> *That'll do.*

This is an idiomatic use of DO and might therefore be excluded from the general statement. But in the same sense we find:

> *That'll be enough.*
> *That'll suit me fine.*

This use of *will* may perhaps be handled here or under **6.3.2.** (last paragraph).

6.3.6. *Insistence.* Finally we may note a use of *will* that always has nuclear stress on the modal. In this sense it has the meaning of insisting upon acting:

> *You ˋwill do these things!*
> *If you ˋwill act the fool!*

Perhaps we may include here the familiar *Boys will be boys*, though this does not always have nuclear stress on *will*. But it does not fit easily into the other uses. It may then be handled here (though lacking the essential defining feature), or it may simply be treated on its own as idiomatic.

6.4. SHALL

Only two uses of *shall* may be noted. A third sub-section **6.4.3.** deals with *will* and *shall* together.

The two uses are:

 (i) Futurity (**6.4.1.**)
(ii) Promise (**6.4.2.**)

6.4.1. *Futurity*. With *I* and *we*, *shall* is used in exactly the same way as *will* (i). In this use it may be replaced by *will*, and like *will* does not occur after *if* (the analogous form being non-modal):

> *I shall be ill tomorrow.*
> *We shall be ill tomorrow.*
> Cf. *If we're ill tomorrow, ...*

It is worth noting, however, that *will* is the only form used with e.g., *John and I*, *you and I*, in spite of the fact that these are, in traditional terms, 'first person plural' like *we*. We shall find in colloquial speech only:

> *John and I will be there.*   (or, *I'll*)
> *You and I will find it amusing.*

6.4.2. *Promise*. The second use is what Jespersen calls 'obligational'. This covers a variety of meanings, but may be formally established by the fact that *shall* cannot, in this use, be replaced by *will*, and that it may occur in conditionals. In this use it is found with *I* and *we* in questions and with the other pronouns and nominal subjects in statements:

> *Shall I come?*
> *You shall have it tomorrow.*
> *He shall do it.*
> Cf. *If he shall do it, ...*

These seem to have a variety of meanings. The first is a question about the wish of the person addressed – 'Do you want me to come?' The second is a promise to act and the third is a promise to enforce action.

But what is, perhaps, common to them all is that the initiation of the activity is always *external* to the subject. But this too is best considered together with a consideration of *will*.

The distinction between the two uses of *shall* is most clearly made, formally, in terms of the substitutability of the first with *will* (in free variation in certain circumstances, but determined in others).

6.4.3. Shall *and* will *together*. It is reasonable to follow the traditional grammarians in treating the forms *will* and *shall* together. But, as we have already seen, we cannot re-establish the old 'future' paradigm *I shall, you will*, etc. But we must note:

(i) that both *will* and *shall* occur with *I* and *we* in what appears to be free variation (though *you and I, he and I* occur only with *will*);

(ii) that *I shall*, no less than *I will* is normally reported in reported speech as *he would*. Similarly *I should* might be the reported form of *he will* or *you will*, though *I would* would be more likely. The point is that the choice of *would* or *should* depends on the pronoun rather than on the occurrence of *will* and *shall* in the original utterance:

> He said he would come   (*I shall come* or *I'll come*),
> He said I should come   (*He'll come*),
> or   He said I'd come.

Yet this will not permit us simply to establish *will* and *shall* as alternants with *I* and *we* only, and *will* as the only form used to refer to future time with all other pronouns and with noun subjects. For this will ignore the fact that *Shall I ...?* and *Will you ...?* in spite of *I shall ...* and *I will ...* do not normally refer to the 'plain future' (the first being an offer, the second a request).

It might, perhaps, be possible to account for the uses of *will* and *shall* by considering first, those that are not 'plain future' but refer to action initiated by the speaker or the person addressed. We may suggest that *will* indicates internal initiation, by the subject of the verb (his willingness), but *shall* indicates external initiation, by someone else. It follows from this that since, in statements, the speaker will usually announce activity initiated by himself, he will say *I will* (internal – he initiates it, and he is the subject). On the other hand since, when he asks a question, he is concerned about activity initiated by the person addressed, he will say *Shall I ...?* (external since he does not initiate the activity) but *Will you ...?* (internal since the person addressed, the subject of the verb, initiates it). Whether the speaker or the person addressed initiates the

activity it will always be external with *he*, so we shall find both *He shall ...*
and *Shall he ...?* We therefore expect the paradigms:

I will.	*Shall I?*
You shall.	*Will you?*
He shall.	*Shall he?*
We will.	*Shall we?*
They shall.	*Shall they?*

By a further step we could postulate that the forms that refer to the
pure future are those forms that do *not* appear in the previous paradigms.
We expect:

I shall.	*Will I?*
You will.	*Shall you?*
He will.	*Will he?*
We shall.	*Will we?*
They will.	*Will they?*

This is indeed a familiar, traditional, picture. But it is not wholly correct.
Two minor modifications are needed:

(i) With *I* and *we*, *will* and *shall* are both used in the statement as well as
in the question.

(ii) *Shall you* is found in literature but not in colloquial English – at least
in my own speech. *Will you* may occur in its place.

An important point is that, in accordance with what was said in the
previous paragraph, *Shall I ...?* and *Will you ...?* must usually be interpreted as asking about the initiation of the activity (by the hearer), and
are not plain future questions (*provided* that the activity is of a kind that
can be initiated – if not, they may simply refer to the future):

> *Shall I come tomorrow?*
> *Will you come tomorrow?*

For pure future reference non-modal progressive forms would be used:

> *Am I coming tomorrow?*
> *Are you coming tomorrow?*

6.5. CAN

Six distinct uses of *can* may be noted. These are to be formally established
in terms of four sets of criteria:

(a) the possibility of reference to the future, and collocation with future
time adverbials, and where *can* is not used for future reference, what
form is used;

(b) collocation with other adverbials;

(c) the function of the analogous form *could*, whether it is used with past time reference (7.1.1.) or in a tentative use (7.2.1.) (if the latter, only *could have* will be used for past time reference – 7.2.3.);

(d) the possibility of the substitution of *may* for *can*.

The six uses are:

(i) Ability (**6.5.1.**)

(ii) Characteristic (**6.5.2.**)

(iii) Permission (**6.5.3.**)

(iv) Possibility (**6.5.4.**)

(v) Willingness (**6.5.5.**)

(vi) Sensation (**6.5.6.**)

6.5.1. *Ability*. The most familiar use of *can* (and one that grammarians often regard as basic) is to express ability to do something. In this sense it is not used with future time adverbials to refer to the future; future time is indicated by *will be able to*. *Could* refers to past time (but see **7.1.1.**):

> *He can lift a hundredweight.*
> *I can read Greek.*
> Cf. *When he's older he'll be able to lift a hundredweight.*
> (Not **When he's older he can lift a hundredweight*).
> *When he was young he could lift a hundredweight.*

6.5.2. *Characteristic*. Reference is to characteristic, though sporadic, patterns of behaviour, usually, but not always, in a derogatory sense. There is no analogous future time form; the nearest is *will* plus the simple form, though with the difference that *will* indicates regular characteristic behaviour, *can* sporadic behaviour. A very common collocation is with *at times*. *Could* is used to refer to past time (**7.1.1.**):

> *She can be very catty at times.*
> *He can tell awful lies.*
> Cf. *When she's older, she'll be very catty.*
> *When she was younger, she could be very catty.*

To be included here, though with inanimate subjects, are such as the following:

> *Carelessness can kill.*
> *That can do a lot of good.*

Again *at times* (and *sometimes*) are likely adverbials. Indeed both these sentences and the earlier ones differ little from sentences with a non-modal simple form with *at times* or *sometimes*. (*She's very catty at times. Carelessness sometimes kills.*)

6.5.3. *Permission.* Permission to act may be granted by using *can*. In this sense *can* may be replaced by *may*, though *may* is a little more formal. *Can* may refer to the future. There is no analogous form for simple past time reference, only a habitual *could* and a negative *couldn't* (**7.1.1.**) and *could* as a tentative form but usually only in request questions (**7.2.1.**):

>He can do as he likes.
>You can come tomorrow.
>You can go now.

Cf. >You may go now.
>Could I go now?

6.5.4. *Possibility.* *Can* is used to suggest that perhaps something may be. It is again replaceable by *may* and can refer to the future. Many English speakers would prefer *may* (except in questions – see below):

>He can be there now.
>He can be hiding.

Cf. >He may be hiding.

One clear formal distinction between this use and the previous one is that only in this use may reference to the past be made by *can have*:

>He can have been hiding,

but not >*He can have done as he liked.*

(though there is also a habitual *could* and a negative *couldn't* as in **6.5.3.**).

A second point is that *can* is not replaceable by *may* in questions (though it is in the use of **6.5.3.**):

>Can he be hiding?

but not >*May he be hiding?*

yet both >Can I go now?

and >May I go now?

We must perhaps handle here such sentences as:

>What can that mean?
>Whatever can he be doing?

Certainly the past time form is *can have*, not *could*. In the first example *may* would imply something different (see **6.6.2.**); with the second it would be unusual. A form with no modal could occur (*What does it mean?*), whereas the non-modal simple form in the earlier sentences (*He's there by now*) would produce a very different sentence. These differences may be accounted for in terms of the occurrence of *What* and *Whatever*, or alternatively we could recognise yet another use of *can*.

6.5.5. *Willingness.* *Can* is used in a sense very similar to that of *will* (ii), to ask a favour or to make an offer, and is replaceable by *will* but not by *may.* In this sense it always refers to the future and may be collocated with future time adverbials. *Could* is used as a tentative form:

> *Can you pass the salt?*
> *Can you help me tomorrow?*
> *I can do that for you.*
> Cf. *Could you pass the salt?*
> *Will you pass the salt?*

6.5.6. *Sensation. Can* is regularly used with verbs of sensation, without adding anything not implied by the simple verb (though the simple verb is much less common). It may be used to refer to the future (though with future reference there is often a sense of ability or permission). *Could* is used to refer to the past:

> *I can see the moon.*
> *I can hear music.*
> Cf. *I see the moon.*
> *If you come up here, you can see the moon.*
> *I could see the moon last night.*

6.6. MAY

Two uses only of *may* are to be noted:
 (i) Permission (6.6.1.)
(ii) Possibility (6.6.2.)
In both senses *may* can be replaced by *can* (in senses (iii) and (iv), permission and possibility). Only by reference to the past time analogues may the two uses be distinguished formally.

6.6.1. *Permission. May* is used to give permission. Reference may be to the present or future time. There is no past time analogue. *Might* is used as the analogous tentative form only in request-questions:

> *You may go.*
> *You may come tomorrow.*
> *May I come in?*
> Cf. *You can go.*
> *Might I come in?*
> but not *You might go.*

6.6.2. *Possibility.* In the sense of possibility, *may* is again used with reference to both present and future time. Only where it refers to the present is it usually replaceable by *can* (commonly only in questions).

Yet *may* in this use is not used in questions (*can* or *might* being used instead). *Might* is used in a tentative sense (**7.2.1.**) or for habitual past (**7.1.1.**); the past time analogue is *may have* (**7.1.3.**):

> *He may come.*
> *He may be there now.*

Cf. *He can be there now* but not *He can come,*
not **May he be there now?* but *Can ...? Might ...?*
> *He might come.*
> *He may have come yesterday.*

An idiomatic use, i.e., one that cannot be generalised, is that of:

> *What may that mean?*

This is used to ask (often with some sarcasm) the intended meaning of the previous speaker. It is equivalent to *What do you mean by that?* and thus different from *What can that mean?* which is not so limited in its use.

6.7. MUST

Two uses of *must* are to be recognised:
 (i) Obligation (**6.7.1.**)
(ii) Conclusion (**6.7.2.**)
They are to be formally distinguished with reference to the past time analogues, and to the forms used analogously for negation, and also by the fact that only one may be used with future reference.

6.7.1. *Obligation. Must* is used to express obligation, though in various degrees (it may be used, as the second example shows, to do a little more than offer an invitation). In this sense it may refer to the future. The analogous past time form is *had to* (**7.1.4.**) and the negation form, *needn't* (**7.5.**):

> *I must go now.*
> *You must come again.*
> *He must do as I say.*

Cf. *I had to go then.*
> *I needn't go now.*

6.7.2. *Conclusion. Must* also indicates a conclusion or near certainty. It is not used in this sense with future reference. In past time the analogous form is *must have* (**7.1.3.**) and in negation *can't.*

> *There must be a hundred people there.*
> *He must be mad to do that.*

Cf. *There must have been a hundred people there.*
> *There can't be a hundred people there.*

6.8. OUGHT

Only one sense of *ought* need be noted – to express duty:

> *I ought to go now.*
> *You ought to come again.*

Ought leaves open the possibility of non-action, while *must* does not. We may thus attest:

> *He ought to go, but he won't,*
> but not **He must go, but he won't.*

6.9. DARE and NEED

As we saw earlier, the positive forms of these, except with inversion, do not function as auxiliaries at all. In this chapter, therefore, we shall ignore these positive forms, and deal only with the negatives (this is of importance when we deal, in the next section, with past time reference, since for all the other auxiliaries only positive forms will be considered).

Only one use of each auxiliary need be recognised. These are difficult to paraphrase, though *daren't* is almost equivalent to *haven't the courage to*, and *needn't* may be interpreted in terms of lack of necessity, usefulness or obligation:

> *I daren't ask him about that.*
> *You needn't bother about that.*

6.10. Summary

The various uses and their main formal characteristics are, then, as follows:

WILL

  (i) Futurity

- (a) Not after *if* (replaced by non-modal form).
- (b) Replaceable by *shall* with *I* and *we*.
- (c) Collocation with future time adverbials.

  (ii) Volition

- (a) Occurs after *if*.
- (b) Not replaceable by *shall*.
- (c) Collocation with future time adverbials.

 (iii) Induction

- (a) Rarely collocated with adverbials and only with 'habitual' adverbials.
- (b) Replaceable by non-modal simple form.

 (iv) Characteristic

- (a) Not collocated with *always*.
- (b) Rarely replaceable by non-modal form (very rare with *I* and *we*).

  (v) Probability

- (a) Collocation with present time adverbials.
- (b) Replaceable by non-modal progressive form or simple form with non-progressive verbs.

| | (c) | *Will have* for past time. |
| (vi) Insistence | | Always nuclear stress on *will*. |

SHALL
(i) Futurity	(a)	Not after *if* (replaced by non-modal form).
	(b)	Replaceable by *will* with *I* and *we*.
(ii) Promise		Not replaceable by *will*.

CAN
(i) Ability	(a)	Replaceable by a form of BE ABLE TO in certain grammatical contexts.
	(b)	No collocation with future time adverbials.
	(c)	*Could* in past time.
(ii) Characteristic	(a)	No collocation with future time adverbials but with *at times*.
	(b)	*Could* in past time.
(iii) Permission	(a)	Replaceable by *may*.
	(b)	No analogous simple, positive, past time forms.
(iv) Possibility	(a)	Replaceable by *may* (except in questions).
	(b)	*Can have* for past time.
(v) Willingness	(a)	Replaceable by *will* (but not *may*).
	(b)	Collocation with future time adverbials.
(vi) Sensation		Replaceable by a non-modal form.

MAY
(i) Permission	(a)	Tentative form *might* only in questions.
	(b)	No past time analogue.
(ii) Possibility	(a)	Tentative form *might* in all sentences.
	(b)	Not used in questions.
	(c)	*May have* for past time, *might* habitual only.

MUST
(i) Obligation	(a)	Past time *had to*.
	(b)	Negation *needn't*.
(ii) Conclusion	(a)	Past time *must have*.
	(b)	Negation *can't*.

References

A detailed statement, in traditional notional terms, of the **modals** dealt with here in Chapters 6 and 7 is to be found in O. Jespersen, *A modern English grammar* (op. cit.), Part V.

Chapter 7

The simple phrase: secondary pattern (2)

In this chapter we deal with all the uses of the modals other than those of the present tense form to refer to present or future time.

7.1. Past time reference

In this section we shall deal not only with those forms that are used simply to indicate past time but also those that are used in reported speech with a past tense form of reporting. It was suggested in the parallel section on the primary pattern (4.4.) that these were very closely related. In the case of the modal auxiliaries, the secondary pattern, there is the complication that not all the past tense forms are used simply to refer to past time (though they are all used in reported speech); *should*, for instance, is used in reported speech but not as a past time form corresponding to *shall*. We may contrast the primary pattern *like* and *liked* with the secondary pattern *shall like* and *should like:*

Present time	*I like it*	*I shall like it*
Reported with past time verb	*I said I liked it*	*I said I should like it*
Past time	*I liked it*	—

Moreover, as was seen in the previous chapter, the forms used for past time reference, the past time analogues, may vary for one single modal in its different uses, and are certainly not always the past tense form. A further complication is that not all the modal auxiliaries have past tense forms. We must consider, then, what are the past time analogues (as well as the forms used in reported speech) for each use of the modal auxiliaries.

There are four possibilities:

(a) the past tense form is used (*would, should, could* and *might*),
(b) the present tense form is used,

(c) a form with *have* (perfect instead of past) is used,
(d) a different verb is used, or there is no past tense correlate at all.

We will consider these possibilities in turn, separately, and then what forms occur in reported speech.

7.1.1. *Past tense forms.* Very few of the past tense forms are used to refer to past time with exact parallelism with the present tense forms. Only four uses are clearly found with the past tense forms:

WILL
(vi) Insistence   *He ˋwould act the fool.*

CAN
 (i) Ability   *He could lift a hundredweight.*
 (ii) Characteristic *She could be very unkind.*
 (vi) Sensation   *I could hear music.*

The past tense forms, are, however, used widely to refer to *habitual* activity. This is especially true of *would*, which may refer to habitual activity of any kind, not merely in the restricted sense of WILL (iv):

                    She'd sit there for hours,
and   *I'd go to school every day.*

The analogous form of the first of these contains *will*, but not that of the second (but only a non-modal form):

                    She'll sit there for hours.
                    I go to school every day.

Another past time form analogous to the non-modal simple (habitual) is, of course, *used to:*

                    I used to go to school every day.

In spite of its habitual nature there is no past tense analogue of *will* (iii) (induction). But this is to be expected. Inductive statements are essentially present in an all-time sense, and would not be made with specific past time reference.

Similarly *could* and *might* may be used in past time, in a habitual sense of some of the uses:

CAN
(iii) Permission   *When I was a boy we could walk across these fields.*
(iv) Possibility   *We could go for a walk in the evenings.*
 (v) Willingness   *I could always help her out.*

MAY
 (ii) Possibility   *We might go for a walk in the evenings.*

In the first sense of WILL (futurity) *would* occurs only in a literary style:

> *He would die the following day.*

In speech this type of 'future in the past' is not generally made use of; *was to* is possible:

> *He was to die the following day.*

But normally the simple form *He died* (with no indication of the futurity) would be used.

In the second sense of WILL (volition), only the negative *wouldn't* occurs:

> *He wouldn't come.*

There is no analogous positive form. Either *He was willing* ... or *He agreed* ... would be used. Similarly the uses of CAN noted above may occur with negative past tense forms in non-habitual senses:

CAN

(iii) *He couldn't come.* (*His mother wouldn't allow him.*)

(iv) *It couldn't be in there, so we didn't look.*

 (v) (*She had to do it herself.*) *I couldn't do that.*

CAN in its first sense (Ability) provides one problem. We have noted *could* as a past time analogue but it must be added that *could* is never used to refer to a single successful achievement. We shall not attest:

> **I ran fast and so could catch the bus.*

Yet BE ABLE TO is so used:

> *I ran fast and so was able to catch the bus.*

In view of this it could be argued that even in its first use (Ability) CAN is used only for habitual activity in the past. But this is not wholly justifiable since in the present CAN does not refer to a single event. It is a non-linguistic point that is involved here – that ability in the past is often linked with achievement. BE ABLE TO is used to indicate the achievement; CAN is not. But naturally the negative (*couldn't*) implies non-success so we may well attest:

> *I ran fast, but still couldn't catch the bus.*

7.1.2. *Present tense forms.* Only one present tense form is used for past time reference – *daren't*:

> *He wanted to come, but he daren't.*

The form *didn't dare* would be more common here, but *daren't* is not impossible, even where there is collocation with a past time adverbial:

> *I daren't come yesterday.*

7.1.3. *Forms with* have. Past time reference is made with all of the modals in one of their uses with *have*:

WILL
  (v) Probability   *He'll have been there all day yesterday.*
CAN
  (iv) Possibility   *He can have been at home yesterday.*
MAY
  (ii) Possibility   *He may have come last week.*
MUST
  (ii) Conclusion   *They must have done it then.*
OUGHT   *You ought to have come with us yesterday.*
DARE   *I daren't have asked him when we met.*
NEED   *You needn't have said that when he asked.*

Every one of these forms, however, may also refer to a 'present perfect' period of time – a period that includes the present (see 7.4.).

For some of the uses the past time form seems to be past tense plus *have:*

WILL
  (ii) Volition   *He would have done that for you.*
CAN
  (iii) Permission   *He could have gone.* (No one stopped him.)
  (v) Willingness   *I could have done that for you.*

But these are 'impossible' forms (referring to events that did not happen); these are dealt with in 7.3.3.

7.1.4. *Other forms.* There is one verb only whose past time analogue is an entirely different verb – MUST (i) with HAVE TO:

> *I must go now.*
> *I had to go then.*

We may contrast the two uses of MUST. In use (ii) (Conclusion) the past time form is *must have.*

We must note here that HAVE TO is similarly used for reference to other time periods (see 7.4.).

All the other uses of the modals do not seem to have, strictly, any past time analogue, chiefly because they refer to future time. There are ways of expressing roughly similar senses in past time but only by paraphrasing:

WILL
  (i) *was about to*   *He was about to come.*
  (ii) *agreed to*   *He agreed to come.*
SHALL
  (i) *was about to*   *I was about to go.*
  (ii) *promised*   *He promised you should come.*

MAY

(ii) *permitted*   *He permitted him to go.*

7.1.5. *Reported speech.* For the verbs that have past tense forms, there is no difficulty at all. With a past tense verb of reporting the past tense forms of the verbs are used, in all their senses. One exceptional point only may be noted – that the occurrence of *would* and *should* with plain future reference is largely determined by the pronoun and not by the occurrence of *will* and *shall* in the original utterance. This has already been handled in **6.4.3.** We find then:

He said ...

WILL	(i)	... *it would rain tomorrow.*
	(ii)	... *he would come.*
	(iii)	... *oil would float on water.*
	(iv)	... *she'd sit there for hours.*
	(v)	... *he'd be there by now.*
	(vi)	... *they `would do that.*
SHALL	(i)	... *he would come.*
		(*I said I should come.*)
	(ii)	... *I should have it.*
CAN	(i)	... *he could lift a hundredweight.*
	(ii)	... *she could be very unkind.*
	(iii)	... *he could go.*
	(iv)	... *he could be hiding.*
	(v)	... *he could do that for her.*
	(vi)	... *he could hear music.*
MAY	(i)	... *he might go.*
	(ii)	... *he might be there.*

With OUGHT, DARE and NEED, the present tense forms *ought*, *needn't* and *daren't* are used regularly in reported speech, even with past time reference:

He said he ought to go.   (I ought to go.)

he daren't go.   (I daren't go.)

he needn't go.   (I needn't go.)

There is also the possibility of *didn't need/dare* – where the full verb DARE and NEED are used:

He said he didn't dare to go.

he didn't need to go.

Similar alternatives are to be found in the present too, of course – *I don't dare/need*, and it is therefore reasonable to regard the forms with *didn't* as the past time analogues of these and not of *daren't* and *needn't*.

MUST provides a little difficulty. In use (i) the form is *had to:*

> He said he had to go. (*I must go*).

But *must* is possible here:

> He said he must go.

(and this is not an example of the present being used to indicate the present validity of the original statement – see below). For use (ii) *must have* is found:

> He said there must have been a hundred people there.
> (*There must be ...*)

As with the primary pattern, present tense forms may be used with the past tense verbs of reporting, if the original statement is still valid (4.4.2.). We may attest, therefore:

> He said he will come.
> He said he can do it. etc.

With *must, ought, daren't* and *needn't*, of course, the validity at the present time of the original statement cannot be stated unambiguously since these forms are used as the regular 'sequence of tenses', forms with past tense verbs of reporting. Whereas, then, we shall not say:

> *He said he'll come, but he won't,

(for ... *he'll come* implies that the original statement is still true) we can say:

> He said he ought to come, but he oughtn't.

(for *he ought* is merely the form reporting 'I ought' and does not suggest that it is still valid).

Finally, what are the forms used to report, with a past tense verb of reporting, the past time forms? The answer is, in all cases but one, the same form as that used for past time reference:

> He said ...

... he would go there every day.	(*I would ...*)
... he could run ten miles.	(*I could ...*)
... he ought to have come.	(*I ought to have ...*) etc.

The only exception is with *had to* the past time analogue of *must*, where there is the possibility of *had had to* (though *had to* is equally possible, as with similar primary pattern forms – see 4.4.2.):

> He said he'd had to do it.
> (*I had to do it.*)
> He said he had to do it.

The second example may, of course, also report *I have to ...*

It is very important to note that *ought to have, daren't have* and *needn't have* are *not* used to report *ought, daren't* and *needn't*, in spite of the fact that they are the past time analogues of these forms. *Ought* reports *ought*, *ought to have* reports *ought to have* and so on:

> He said he ought to have gone.　　(*I ought to have gone only.*)
>
> He said he ought to go.　　(*I ought to go only.*)

7.1.6. *Summary.* It is now possible to tabulate the forms used to refer to past time and in reported speech that correspond to all the modals in their various uses. Round brackets are used to indicate 'impossible' past time forms and square brackets to indicate forms that could be used in paraphrase where there are no obvious past time analogues.

	Past time	Reported speech
WILL		
(i) Futurity	[*was about to*]	*would/should*
(ii) Volition	*would* (literary only)	
	wouldn't (negative only)	*would*
	(*would have*)	
	[*agreed*]	
(iii) Induction	–	*would*
(iv) Characteristic	*would*	*would*
(v) Insistence	*would*	*would*
(vi) Probability	*will have*	*would*
SHALL		
(i) Futurity	[*was about to*]	*should/would*
(ii) Promise	[*promised*]	*should*
CAN		
(i) Ability	*could* (not achievement)	*could*
	was able to (achievement)	
(ii) Characteristic	*could*	*could*
(iii) Permission	*could* (habitual)	*could*
	couldn't (negative)	
	(*could have*)	
(iv) Possibility	*can have*	*could*
	could (habitual)	
	couldn't (negative)	
(v) Willingness	*could* (habitual)	*could*
	couldn't (negative)	
	(*could have*)	
(vi) Sensation	*could*	*could*

MAY
  (i) Permission   *[permitted]*   *might*
  (ii) Possibility   *may have*   *might*
                     might (habitual)

MUST
  (i) Obligation   *had to*   *had to*
                                       must
  (ii) Conclusion   *must have*   *must have*

OUGHT
                     ought to have   *ought*

DARE
                     daren't   *daren't*
                     daren't have
          N.B. *didn't dare*   *didn't dare*

NEED
                     needn't have   *needn't*
          N.B. *didn't need*   *didn't need*

7.2. 'Tentative' use

We have already anticipated this section by noting earlier that some of the past tense forms are used in a 'tentative' sense – that they are less positive than the present tense forms. A similar, though rarer use of the past tense was noted for primary pattern forms (4.4.3.). *Should* raises some problems of its own and is dealt with in a separate sub-section.

7.2.1. WILL, CAN *and* MAY. Each of the forms *would*, *could* and *might* is found in one of the uses of the verb in a tentative sense, making either less positive statements, or more polite requests. Examples of less positive statements are:

WILL
  (v) Probability   *That would be the postman.*

CAN
  (iv) Possibility   *He could be there now.*

MAY
  (ii) Possibility   *He might be there now.*

The forms that are used in more polite requests are those that ask for permission or ask if the person addressed is willing to do something:

WILL
  (ii) Volition   *Would you pass the salt?*

CAN

(iii) Permission   *Could I go now?*

 (v) Willingness   *Could you pass the sugar?*

MAY

 (i) Permission   *Might I go now?*

It is to be noted that both CAN and MAY in their sense of permission have tentative past tense forms only in requests. In this use there are no tentative statements corresponding to *You can go* and *You may go*. This fact is one of the criteria for distinguishing the permission and possibility uses of these two auxiliaries (the main criterion being that for possibility alone do they have past time forms with *have*).

In all other uses the occurrence of one of these past time forms may be accounted for in terms of incomplete unreal conditionals (see 7.3.2.). This is shown by the following examples where an *if* clause would be possible (but it would not be, without a complete change of meaning, with the examples quoted above):

WILL

 (ii) Volition   *I would do that for you*   (if you asked me).

CAN

  (i) Ability   *I could lift that*   (if I tried).

(iv) Willingness   *I could do that for you*   (if you let me).

7.2.2. SHALL. *Should* is equally used with present time reference, in almost exactly the same sense as *ought to:*

> *You should do something about that.*
> *He should ask my permission first.*

We could treat this as a 'tentative' form of SHALL (ii), though it is much more widely used, and semantically there is far more difference between *shall* and *should*, than between the other pairs of forms. But it does fit into the pattern; there was a similar problem with *would* and its relation to WILL (iv) (7.1.1.).

A very special use of *should* is to be found in sentences of the type:

> *It is very odd that he should do that.*
> *It is lucky the weather should be so fine now.*
> *It was unfortunate he should be ill just then.*
> *That this should happen was a terrible blow.*

Should is used here with both present and past time reference. The forms may be replaced here by either present or past simple (non-modal) forms:

> *It is very odd that he does/did that.*
> *It is lucky that the weather is so fine now.*
> *It was unfortunate that he was ill just then.*
> *That this happened was a terrible blow.*

A similar use is to be found in:

> *Who should I see but Bob!*

This too may be used with either present or past time reference similar to:

> *Who do I see but Bob!*
> *Who did I see but Bob!*

In this use *should* is restricted to utterances that express surprise or some other kind of emotion. Formally the restriction is to subordinate noun clauses introduced by *that* or no conjunction, with a 'linking verb' (BE, SEEM, etc.) as the main verb of the sentence and to non-question utterances introduced by *who*, *which*, *what*, *when* or *where*.

Another very special use of *should* is noted with the conditionals (7.3.1.).

7.2.3. *Forms in past time.* Reference to past time is made with *have*:

WILL

(iv) Probability   *It would have been John who called.*

CAN

(iv) Possibility   *He could have been there then.*

MAY

(ii) Possibility   *He might have been there.*

With the other uses of the auxiliaries a past tense form plus *have* refers to an 'impossible' past time event – one that did not, in fact, take place. These are essentially the same as unreal past time conditionals (7.3.3.):

WILL

(ii) Volition   *I would have done that for you.*

CAN

(i) Ability   *I could have lifted that.*

(iv) Willingness   *I could have done that for you.*

Both CAN and MAY in their use for possibility may also refer to 'impossible' events:

> *He might/could have been killed*   (but he wasn't).

There is the possibility of contrast between present and past tense forms with *have* in view of:

> *He may/can have been killed.*

But this is not a contrast between 'impossible' and 'possible'. For, in the first place, as we have just seen, the past tense forms do not always refer to the 'impossible'. *He might have been killed* does not necessarily imply that he was not killed. More surprisingly, perhaps, the present tense forms, especially that of MAY, are used with *have* for 'impossible' statements:

> *You may/can have been killed.*   (Why did you do such a stupid thing?)

This is clearly contrary to the general pattern, but is nevertheless not uncommon.

For reported speech with a past tense verb of reporting, the usual pattern is simply that the same form is used as was used in the original utterance. So *could* reports *could* and *could have* reports *could have* (though *could* also reports *can*):

> *He said it could be there.*   (*It could be there*, or *It can be there.*)
>
> *He said it could have been there.*   (*It could have been there.*)

But forms with *have* are sometimes used to report forms without *have;* *could* might be reported by *could have* – the second example above could report *It could be there.*

7.3. Conditions and wishes

We have already dealt briefly with conditions (or conditional sentences) and wishes in the section on past tense with the primary pattern (4.4.3.). Rather more needs to be said about them with the modals.

7.3.1. *Real conditions.* Examples of real conditions are:

> *If he comes, I shall go.*
> *If he's here, he's probably working in the garden.*
> *If he did that, he was certainly very simple.*

In these the verbal pieces in both clauses, the main clause and the subordinate clause, are used with their normal time references (and regular collocation with adverbials) – with one exception. The exception is, as we have already seen, that *will* and *shall* are not used in the subordinate clause for plain future reference; the non-modal form is used instead. *If I go* is the analogue of both *I shall (will) go* and *I go.*

The time reference of the verbal forms in each clause is usually the same – in the examples above it is future, present and past respectively. But this is not necessarily so, as shown by:

> *If he did that, I shall not talk to him.*
> *If he was seen, he's probably still here.*
> *If he comes tomorrow, he understood what was said,*
> (or more commonly, but still with past time reference,
> ... *he must have understood*).

The tentative forms *would*, *should*, *could* and *might* occur in real conditions:

> *If he comes, he should tell me.*
> *If I ask him, would he agree?*
> *If I should go, you ought to too.*
> *If you could do that, it'll be fine.*
> *If he comes, I might tell him about it.*

A special use of *should* is found in:

> *If I should see him, I'll tell him.*

Moreover, *should* may occur with inversion and without *if* (the only other forms so used are *were* and *had* – see next sub-section):

> *Should I see him, I'll tell him.*

That this is a real condition, with *should* in a tentative use, is made clear by the present tense form of WILL in the main clause.

7.3.2. *Unreal conditions.* The use of the past tense to mark unreal conditions is illustrated quite clearly by the following pairs of examples:

> *If I come, he'll go.*
> *If I came, he'd go.*
> *If you can do that, so can I.*
> *If you could do that, so could I.*
> *If you'll only be quiet, I'll tell you.*
> *If you'd only be quiet, I'd tell you.*

But the difference between real and unreal conditions is not simply in terms of tense. Consider the following:

> *If you allow that, you are very foolish.*
> *If he comes, I go.*
> *If he's here, he's in the garden.*

The corresponding past tense forms are:

> *If you allowed that, you were very foolish.*
> *If he came, I went.*
> *If he was here, he was in the garden.*

Yet these are not unreal conditions, but past time real ones. The corresponding (but present time) unreal conditions contain *would* or *should*:

> *If you allowed that, you would be very foolish.*
> *If he came, I should go.*
> *If he was here, he would be in the garden.*

Formally this point may be shown in terms of collocation with adverbials:

> *If he was here yesterday, he was in the garden.* (real, past)
> *If he was here now, he would be in the garden.* (unreal, present)

10

With an unreal condition, then, the main clause will not contain a primary pattern (non-modal) form. If the real condition has a verbal form with no modal, *would* or *should* occurs in the corresponding unreal condition. *I should/would go, he would go* are, then, the unreal condition analogues of *I go, he goes* and also, of course, of *I shall/will go, he will go*:

> If it rains a lot, I go by car.
> If it rains tomorrow, I shall go by car.
> If it rained a lot, I should go by car.
> If it rained tomorrow, I should go by car.

WILL and SHALL thus have two strikingly different patterns in conditional sentences. In the main clause of an unreal condition *would* and *should* are required where there is no future reference. In the subordinate (*if*) clause almost the converse is true (for both real and unreal conditions); where there is plain future time reference *will, would, shall* do not occur (and *should* only in the use noted in 7.3.1.). But in both cases the distinction between a non-modal form and a form with WILL is 'neutralised'.

A form sometimes used in the subordinate clause of an unreal condition is *were to* or *was to* (see 4.4.3.):

> If I were to come, he'd go.
> If it was to rain tomorrow, I should go by car.

Reference is commonly, but not always, to future time. Present time is indicated in:

> If he was still to be here, I should be very angry.

Were to is used, though not commonly, with inversion and no *if*:

> Were you to do that, I should be angry.

Past tense modal forms other than *would* and *should* may occur in the main clause of unreal conditions (and *would* in senses other than plain futurity). But it is only in the uses in which there is the possibility of future time reference that they so occur:

WILL

(ii) Volition   *If you asked them, they would come.*

CAN

(i) Ability   *If you practised, you could run three miles.*
(iii) Permission   *If you answered the question, you could go.*
(v) Willingness   *If it was difficult, I could do it for you.*
(vi) Sensation   *If you came here, you could see it.*

MAY

(ii) Possibility   *If you asked me, I might tell you.*

Even *ought* is used:

> If he wanted to find out, he ought to ask me.

The forms analogous to *must, daren't* and *needn't* are, as might be expected from parallels elsewhere (see especially below 7.4.), *would have to, wouldn't dare to* and *wouldn't need to:*

> *If he comes, I must go.*
> *If he came, I would have to go.*
> *If he comes, you needn't go.*
> *If he came, you wouldn't need to go.*

There are no forms analogous to some of the present tense modals in some of their uses:

SHALL

(ii) Promise   *If you come, you shall have it.*

The corresponding unreal condition is *not:*

> *If you came, you should have it.*

The nearest in usage would be:

> *If you came, I should promise that you would have it,*

or   *If you came, you would have it, I promise.*

In the subordinate clause, the rule is simply that a past tense form occurs, where the real condition had a present tense form. Some of the forms in some of their uses are unlikely. *Must* is, of course, reflected by *had to;* and *daren't, needn't* by *didn't dare, didn't need,* though *daren't* is possible (cf. 7.1.2.):

> *If you must go, I shall go too.*
> *If you had to go, I should go too.*
> *If they daren't come, I shan't help them.*
> *If they didn't dare to/daren't come, I shouldn't help them.*

Ambiguity is possible when *would* or *could* occur in the main clause and a past tense form in the subordinate. The sentences may, then, either be past real or present unreal:

> *If he went to the circus, he would enjoy himself.*
> *If he practised, he could lift two hundredweight.*

The usual interpretation would be that these are unreal (referring to unlikely future events), but they might refer to actual events in the past (and could be distinguished formally in terms of collocation with adverbials).

For reported speech with past tense verbs of reporting, the position is the same as it is with reporting 'tentative' forms – that in general the forms are the same as in the original utterance, though occasional forms with *have* may be used to report forms without:

> *I would go, if she came.*
> *He said that he would go, if she came,*

rarely   *He said he would have gone, if she'd come.*

There are also unreal conditions with a relative pronoun but no *if*:

> *People who did that, would be foolish.*
> *Anyone who tried, would find himself in trouble.*
> *A man who behaved like that, ought to be punished.*

7.3.3. *Unreal conditions in past time.* Past time unreal conditions ('impossible' conditions) provide no patterns that have not yet been met. They are essentially 'past-past' – past for unreality and past for past time. In the main clause a past tense modal plus *have* occurs; in the subordinate clause either a past tense modal plus *have* or past perfect form is used (on the past perfect as a past-past, cf **4.4.2.** and **5.4.1.**):

> *If he'd come, I'd have gone.*
> *If you could have done it, I could have done it too.*

Had is quite commonly used with inversion and no *if*:

> *Had he come, I'd have gone.*

A very special form *If I'd have known* is dealt with in **8.2.5.**

In reported speech with past tense verbs of reporting the same forms are used – English has no 'past-past-past' forms.

7.3.4. *Wishes.* In wishes – forms introduced by e.g., *I wish, If only* – the position is similar to that in the *if* clause of unreal conditionals. For present time (or future time where the present tense form has future time reference) a past tense form is used; for past time a past perfect or a past tense modal plus *have* is used:

> *I wish I knew.*
> *I wish I was going with you tomorrow.*
> *I wish I could do that.*
> *I wish I had seen him.*
> *I wish I could have gone with you.*

But there is one very important difference. It is that a simple, non-modal, past tense form is not used to refer to the future, as the form corresponding elsewhere to a form with *will* or *shall*. Although we may relate:

> *It'll rain tomorrow,*

and   *If it rained tomorrow ...*

we shall not similarly attest:

> **I wish it rained tomorrow,*

(unless the statement form is

> *It rains tomorrow,*

i.e. tomorrow is the day of the week or year on which it always rains – a fixed pattern, cf. **5.1.4.**). Rather we shall attest:

> *I wish it would rain tomorrow.*

In many cases, however, the occurrence of *would* seems to be an example of the WILL of volition, not plain futurity:

> *I wish you would make up your mind.*
> *If only he would help!*

This could be argued even in the case of *I wish it would rain tomorrow* since we may attest:

> *If it'll rain tomorrow ...*

This, of course, must be the WILL of volition since for plain futurity we should find (**6.3.1.**):

> *If it rains ...*

A further point is that we shall not usually attest such sentences as:

> **I wish I should see him tomorrow,*

or **I wish I would see him tomorrow,*

but rather *I wish I was seeing him tomorrow,*

or *I wish I was going to see him tomorrow.*

The non-occurrence of **I wish I would/should* does suggest that WILL (and SHALL) do not occur in use (i) (plain futurity) in wishes. But plain futurity is not indicated, as it is in conditionals, by the simple non-modal form, but by some other form – especially the progressive or GOING TO. Yet the fact remains that *would* is very common after *I wish* and *If only*. It is not perhaps wholly feasible always to identify it as an example of the WILL of volition. Indeed we might decline to make the distinction between WILL (i) and WILL (ii) here altogether.

There is one other combination in which past tense forms occur – after *It's time*:

> *It's time we went.*
> *It's time you could.*   (In reply to *I can't.*)

7.4. Future and 'perfect' time reference

There are two points to note concerning the modals used for reference to the future and 'perfect' time (time beginning in the past but continuing up to, and including the present or a past point).

First, all the forms with *have* that refer to the past (**7.1.3.**) may equally refer to a 'present perfect' time – a period that includes the present. In other words with these forms the contrast between the non-perfect past and present perfect is not maintained. We may attest: *He will/can/may/ must/ought to/daren't/needn't/have arrived by now.*

Those that have future reference (or may have future reference) more-over may refer to a 'future perfect' period of time – a period preceding but going up to, a future point of time:

WILL

(i) Futurity   *I'll have it done tomorrow.*

SHALL

(i) Futurity   *I shall have seen him when I get there.*

MAY

(i) Possibility   *I may have finished later in the evening.*

OUGHT   *He ought to have done it by the time I come back.*

Less common, perhaps, are:

SHALL

(ii) Promise   *You shall have seen him before you leave.*

CAN

(i) Ability   *I can have finished it by tomorrow evening.*
(iii) Possibility   *He can have gone by then.*

NEED   *You needn't have written it all when I come back.*

Secondly we have already noted the use of a form of HAVE TO as a past time analogue of the *must* of obligation (7.1.4.) and of a form of BE ABLE TO as a past time analogue of the *can* of ability when there is indication of achievement as well as ability (7.1.1.). In fact forms of these verbs are also used for future and 'perfect' time reference as analogues of *must* and *can* in these uses:

> *He's had to go away.*
> *He'd had to get permission first.*
> *He'll have to finish it tomorrow.*
> *He's been able to do it for a long time.*
> *He'd been able to help.*
> *He'll be able to finish it.*

Similarly we find *will have had* and *will have been able to* for 'future perfect' time.

7.5. Negation

Much of what is to be said about negation has already been touched upon in establishing the various uses formally.

For most of the modals negation may simply be dealt with in terms of a negative form – *will/won't*, etc. But *mustn't*, *oughtn't* are the negative forms of MUST and OUGHT only in their morphology. In terms of wider

syntactical patterns, the form used in negation, the analogue of both
MUST (i) (Obligation) and OUGHT is *needn't*. Compare:

> *I can go, but John can't.*
> *Can I go? No, you can't.*
> *I must go, but John needn't.*
> *Must I go? No, you needn't.*
> *I ought to go, but John needn't.*
> *Ought I to go? No, you needn't.*

In semantic terms, *mustn't* and *oughtn't* do not negate the obligation
to act, but express a positive obligation not to act.

With CAN, there is a contrast between (**2.5.5.**):

> *You can't go,*

and   *You can`not go.* [juː kən `nɔt gou]

> (Do what you please ... *You can go, or you can `not go.*)

Here *can't* negates (semantically) the ability (or permission to act), while
can `not positively states ability (or permission) not to act. We find, then,
the following pattern:

Positive	*You can go*	*You must go*
Negative (i)	*You can't go*	*You needn't go*
Negative (ii)	*You can `not go*	*You mustn't go*

where (i) indicates (semantically) negation of the auxiliary and (ii)
negation of the following infinitive. With all other auxiliaries this distinction cannot be made; we cannot with WILL, for instance, differentiate
between denying the futurity of acting and stating the futurity of non-
acting.

For MUST (ii) (Conclusion) the negation form is *can't*:

> *He must be there.*
> *He can't be there.*

There are not two kinds of negation here. *Can't* implies a negative conclusion, *must* a positive one.

As we have seen, (**7.1.1.**) WILL (ii) and CAN (iii), (iv) and (v) have past
tense past time positive forms that are used only in a habitual sense, while
only the negative forms may refer to specific occasions.

Chapter 8

BE, HAVE and DO

So far we have considered BE, HAVE and DO only as primary auxiliaries. But forms that are identical with those of these verbs are found in quite different uses, and we must either say that these verbs do not occur only as primary auxiliaries or that there are other verbs BE, HAVE and DO (probably three other verbs BE, and five verbs HAVE). In varying degrees these have some of the characteristics of the primary auxiliaries.

8.1. BE

There are, it would appear, three other verbs BE, one a full verb, the others problematic.

8.1.1. *The full verb with anomalous finites.* BE is a full verb in English. We find such sentences as:

> *He is very sad.*
> *He was in the garden.*

In function the verbal forms are exactly paralleled by the forms in the following:

> *He seems very sad.*
> *He sat in the garden.*

Unless we have a completely new definition of 'auxiliary' BE is a full verb in these sentences. It is not followed by any other verb, and has no place at all in the tables that have already been set up. The full verb has the following characteristics of an auxiliary:

(i) it has all the finite and non-finite positive forms – *am, is, are, was, were, been* and *being,* all with the same function with regard to number and person as the auxiliary BE;

(ii) it has all the weak forms as in:

> *I'm sad.* [aim sæd]
> *He's sad.* [hiːz sæd]
> *We were sad.* [wiː wə sæd]   etc.

(iii) it occurs in negation, inversion, code and emphatic affirmation without DO:

> *He isn't sad.*
> *Is he sad?*
> *I am sad and so is he.*
> *He ˋis ˌsad.*

Not only do these forms occur without DO, but, with certain exceptions 8.1.2.) they cannot occur with DO. We shall not find:

> **He doesn't be sad.*
> **Does he be sad?*
> **I am sad and so does he.*
> **He ˋdoes be sad.*

It is because of these characteristics of BE, even when a full verb, that H. E. Palmer refers to the 'anomalous finites', which are not to be identified with the auxiliary verbs. The finite forms of BE are 'anomalous finites' whether they are forms of the full verb or as the auxiliary.

8.1.2. *With* DO. A characteristic of the auxiliaries and of BE as a full verb is that they do not occur with DO. But there are some forms of BE that do occur with DO.

(i) As we have already seen (2.3.2. and 4.1.2.), there is no imperative form **ben't*; instead *don't be* occurs. *Do be* is also found. But as these are characteristic of the primary auxiliaries, we need take no special note of them when occurring as forms of the full verb:

> *Do be at home when I call.*
> *Don't be too confident.*

(ii) There is no similar use of DO with the primary auxiliary, however, to its occurrence in:

> *If you don't be quick, you'll miss them.*
> *If he doesn't be a good boy, I shan't give him anything.*

The positive form is even more striking:

> *If you be quick, you'll see them.*

Here *be* occurs as a finite (present tense) form. In fact, we could equally use the 'regular' forms in these sentences:

> *If you aren't quick ...*
> *If he isn't a good boy ...*
> *If you're quick ...*

Moreover, the only positive form with the third person singular is:

>If he's a good boy ...

But there is a difference. *Be* is used to refer only to temporary states, the other forms may refer to permanent states. We may contrast:

>*If you be quick, you'll catch him.*
>*If you're quick, why do you take such a long time?*

There is a very similar use of a verb BE with a finite form *be*, in the sense of 'agree to play the part of':

>*If you be the queen, I'll be the king.*

Again there is a contrast:

>*If you're the queen, then I'm Julius Caesar!*
>(= *You're no more the queen than I am Julius Caesar.*)

We must recognise here another verb BE which has *be* as a finite form, as well as *am* and *are*. But there is no similar form to replace *is*, or to replace *was* and *were*. We might expect *[biːz] and *[biːd], and indeed I have attested both in the speech of children.

8.1.3. *With* to + *infinitive.* Forms of the verb BE, are also followed by *to* plus the infinitive (structure 2):

>*He's to come tomorrow.*
>*You are to be congratulated.*
>*They are to be married next week.*
>*They were to have come today.*

BE with *to* has a sense close to that of MUST or OUGHT (first two examples,) or of the WILL of futurity (the second two). It is very commonly used for the 'future in the past'. In this usage its forms occur without DO in negation, inversion, etc.:

>*He isn't to do that.*
>*Am I to understand that you are coming?*
>*He's to come and so are you.*
>*They `are to come.*

The simplest treatment of these forms is in terms of another verb BE, this time, perhaps, a modal (secondary) auxiliary. For it follows the pattern of the modals in having no infinitive – there is no *to be to ..., -ing* form or past participle. We shall not attest:

>*He will be to go.*
>*He is being to go.*
>*He has been to go.*

It does not occur, this means, in conjunction with other auxiliaries.

Like OUGHT it is followed by *to* + infinitive. But it differs in one respect from the modals, in that it has the finite form *am, is, are, was* and *were* (in contrast with *can, could,* etc.). In spite of this it is best treated as a modal; otherwise it can only be a very defective full verb.

Rather different are:

> *The house is to let.*
> *He is to blame.*

For in spite of the active form *to let* and *to blame,* the sense is passive. We may compare (with some difference of meaning but not in terms of that of active versus passive):

> *The house is to be let.*
> *He is to be blamed.*

These latter sentences do belong to the pattern discussed here. But *to let* and *to blame* must be treated as idioms; we shall not attest similar forms with other verbs:

> **The house is to paint.*
> **He is to punish.*

8.2. HAVE

There are, perhaps, five verbs HAVE, one a full verb, the others problematic.

8.2.1. *The full verb with anomalous finites.* Like BE, HAVE is a full verb:

> *He has plenty of money.*
> *He had a fever.*

These are completely paralleled by:

> *He earns plenty of money.*
> *He caught a fever.*

The full verb has the following characteristics of an auxiliary:

(i) it has the finite form *has* (which is quite 'irregular' as a form of a full verb);

(ii) it has weak forms as in:

> *He has a nice house.*　　[hiː həs]
> *They'd nothing to say.*　　[ðeid]
> *I've a good idea to ...*　　[aiv]

(iii) it occurs in negation, inversion, etc.:

> *I haven't anything.*
> *Have you a pencil?*
> *I've a pen and so has he.*
> *He ˋhas some.*

As in the case of BE the forms considered here are anomalous finites though not auxiliary verbs.

A common alternative to HAVE is HAVE GOT, morphologically the perfect of GET:

> *I've got sixpence.*
> *I haven't got sixpence.*
> *Have you got sixpence?*
> *I've got sixpence and so has he.*

8.2.2. *With* DO. There are some forms of HAVE which occur with DO even where an anomalous finite would be grammatically possible:

> *The village shop doesn't have ice-cream.*
> *Did you have a good time?*

These forms are not in free variation with the anomalous finites. The sentence

> *The village shop hasn't ice-cream* (or *any ice-cream*)

is a quite different sentence; the first sentence means that the shop does not stock ice-cream, the second that it has none in stock. We can say

> *The shop hasn't any ice-cream, because it doesn't have ice-cream,*

or even *The shop hasn't any ice-cream, but it does have it.*

But *Did you have a good time?*

cannot be similarly compared with

> **Had you a good time?*

The latter sentence is not possible in English.

We must, then, recognise another verb HAVE. Unlike our second full verb BE, the second full verb HAVE is used in a wide variety of collocations. Perhaps the simplest statement about the difference between the two verbs HAVE is to say that HAVE with the anomalous finites is used only to refer to actual possession, ownership, or characteristics at a given time, while the HAVE whose forms occur with DO is used in all other cases. With this latter verb it may, perhaps, be possible to distinguish yet again two usages, though they are certainly not wholly distinct:

(i) The verb is used in the general sense of TAKE, RECEIVE, GET, EXPERIENCE:

> *Did you have nice weather?*
> *We didn't have a good holiday.*
> *Did you have any trouble getting here?*
> *They had breakfast at ten and so did we.*
> *Did you have a letter from me this morning?*
> *What did she have – a boy or a girl?*

(ii) It is used to refer to habitual 'having', as in:

> *The village shop doesn't have ice-cream.*
>
> *Does he have money in his pocket when he goes to school?*

The picture is, however, complicated by the fact that even in the sense of 'to have in one's possession', HAVE may occur with DO in that:

(a) in the speech of many Americans, and to some degree in my own speech, such utterances as the following are perfectly normal:

> *I don't have any money.*
>
> *Do you have a match?*
>
> *He has a hat and so do I.*
>
> *I ⟍do have one.*

(b) the past tense *did + have* occurs often where *hadn't* might be expected, even in standard British speech:

> *He didn't have any money*   or *He hadn't any money.*
>
> *Did the shop have any ice-cream?*
>
> *John had a shilling and so did Mary* or *... so had Mary.*

In my own speech I find it is especially in the inverted form that *did* occurs and that sentences such as the following are most improbable:

> **Had the shop any ice-cream?*
>
> **Had John a shilling?*

Grammatically, then, we can distinguish a second verb HAVE that occurs with DO instead of having anomalous finites. But it is a far from simple task to distinguish between the two verbs semantically.

8.2.3. *With* to + *infinitive.* Forms of the verb HAVE are also followed by *to + infinitive* (structure 2):

> *I have to go now.*
>
> *They had to tell you that.*

In this usage HAVE expresses obligation or necessity, and is synonymous with MUST. The past tense form *had*, is, in fact, the past time analogue of *must* (7.1.4.).

The forms commonly occur with DO:

> *I don't have to go now.*
>
> *Did they have to tell you that?*
>
> *I had to do it and so did she.*
>
> *We ⟍do have to see them.*

But the anomalous finites are also possible, if less likely:

> *You haven't to go yet.*
> *Have I to see him?*
> *I have to and so have you.*
> *We ˋhave to go.*

It might seem possible to treat HAVE here either as a modal auxiliary or as a full verb since it follows both patterns. But, as a full verb, it is in no way defective (unlike the parallel BE). It has all the non-finite forms and can be classed with verbs of the model AGREE (9.2.2.):

> *He has had to be told.*
> *He is having to think again.*
> *He will have to go.*

The forms *had, having* and *had* here can only be regarded as forms of the full verb. The modal auxiliaries have no comparable forms. The simplest analysis is to treat HAVE here as a full verb. That some of its forms are anomalous finites is an exceptional feature but is wholly paralleled by the fact that the other full verb HAVE, as well as BE, follows the pattern of auxiliaries in this respect.

A further point to be noted, which strengthens the case for treating the verb here as a different verb, is that orthographic *have* is frequently phonetically [hæf] with a final voiceless consonant as in:

> [ai hæf tə gou nau]   *I have to go now.*

The auxiliary and the full verb that was dealt with in the previous section have the form [hæv] but not [hæf]:

> [ai hæv teikn it]   *I have taken it.*
> [ai hæv tuː]   *I have two.*

Finally, as with the first verb HAVE a common alternative is HAVE GOT (morphologically the perfect of GET).

> *I've got to go now.*

The past tense *had got* is possible but much rarer. We may attest:

> *I'd got to go,*

but more common would be:

> *I had to go.*

8.2.4. *With noun phrase + verbal form.* HAVE also occurs in such sentences as:

> *I'm having a new house built.*
> *He has his hair cut once a month.*

In these sentences it is a catenative of the type of LIKE (9.3.6.).

In this usage HAVE does not, as in the other usages, have an alternative in HAVE GOT. The second sentence above cannot be replaced by:

He's got his hair cut once a month.

Rather, in this usage HAVE and GET (not HAVE GOT) are equivalent. We may compare with the two sentences above:

I'm getting a new house built.

He gets his hair cut once a month.

HAVE in this use may be followed by an infinitive without to, an -ing form or a past participle (structures 1, 3 and 4). Examples are to be found in 9.3.6.

8.2.5. Had *with infinitive*. There are two uses of the form *had* in which it occurs with structure 1 (infinitive only). These are exemplified by:

I'd better stay at home.

If I'd have known, I wouldn't have gone.

The first of these is quite common (but see **2.5.3.**). The strong form of 'd is *had*:

Had I better stay at home?

If it were not for this the form would fit more easily into the general pattern by interpreting – 'd as the weak form of *would*, since WILL regularly occurs with structure (1) (whereas HAVE does not). But it would seem that we can only regard this as a limited use of HAVE always accompanied by *better* which is associated with this pattern. In this usage it follows exactly the pattern of the auxiliaries:

I hadn't better go.

Had I better go?

I'd better go and so had you.

I ⟍had better go.

It may even be identified as a modal auxiliary since:

(a) it is associated with structure 1 (not an absolute test – but most of them are associated with this pattern);

(b) it has no distinct –s form (this may be accounted for on the grounds that it is a past tense form, but the same is true, historically, of some of the modal auxiliaries, and if we treat *had* here as a distinct verb, we ought not to insist that it is past tense any more than *ought* is – synchronically at least).

The second of the usages (*If I'd have known*) is one that will be rejected in a normative grammar and will be interpreted as an error for *If I'd known*. But there can be no doubt that it is attested, and we cannot even exclude:

Had I have known ...

But the form is quite exceptional. Though it is followed by an infinitive, it is always the infinitive *have*, while the verb that follows is almost always KNOW (*known*). Such sentences as **If I'd have come ...* are sufficiently rare to be discounted.

8.3. DO

There is very little to say about DO apart from the auxiliary.

8.3.1. *The full verb.* DO is a full verb in:

> *He does a lot of work.*
> *I'll do my duty.*
> *He did nothing about it.*

Unlike BE and HAVE, there are no anomalous finites of DO as a full verb. We cannot say:

> **He doesn't a lot of work.*
> **Did he his duty?*

With negation and inversion, that is to say, we require the auxiliary DO:

> *He doesn't do a lot of work.*
> *Did he do his duty?*

Similarly with the emphatic affirmative the auxiliary is required:

> *He `did do a lot of work.*

With 'code' of course it is impossible to tell by the form whether we have the full verb or the auxiliary in:

> *He does a lot of work and so do I.*

The full verb DO has no weak forms, but there is no contrast in this respect between full verb and auxiliary since the weak forms of the auxiliary occur in a position in which the full verb cannot – initially with inversion. While we may not attest:

> **He does* [dəz] *a lot of work.*

we equally will not attest (in standard English):

> **He does* [dəz] *come.*

In one respect only does the full verb have a characteristic of an auxiliary – in that its *-s* (in speech) form is irregular:

> *do* [duː]   but *does* [dʌz] not **[duːz]*

There is, however, one other full verb in English, which has no parallel auxiliary, yet similarly has an irregular *-s* form – SAY (**3.2.**).

8.3.2. *The 'empty' verb.* In 'code' the auxiliary DO functions as what might be called an 'empty' or zero auxiliary – it occurs where an auxiliary is required by the grammatical rule and there is no auxiliary in comparable form. But it is not easy to interpret the following in this way:

> *If you want to go you can do so.*
> *They decided not to go. To do so would have made things*
> *very difficult.*

In the first of these CAN alone could function in 'code':

> *If you want to go, you can.*

DO is 'vicarious' in the sense that it refers back to, 'stands for', another verb, but takes the place of a full verb, not an auxiliary. In the second DO does not function as an auxiliary as is shown by what may follow:

> *Don't be reading when I come in.*

We cannot go on with

> **To be so ...*

but only

> *To be doing so ...*

The auxiliaries, that is to say, do not have 'code' function in their infinitive forms preceded by *to* (the question arises only of course for primary auxiliaries – the secondary auxiliaries have no infinitives). In *to do so* DO must be treated as an 'empty' full verb, rather than an 'empty' auxiliary.

Similarly DO is used in question forms with the catenatives (**9.1.2.** and **9.4.**):

> *What does he want to do?*
> *What do you like doing?*
> *What do you want them to do?*

Its occurrence here is a criterion of the catenatives.

Reference

Page 148 **Empty verb.** Cf. W. F. Twaddell, *The English verb auxiliaries* (op. cit.).

Chapter 9

The complex phrase

A complex phrase is defined as one containing more than one (form of a) full verb. The simplest kind of complex phrase is one that contains simply two full verbs, such as:

> *I like fishing,*
> *I want to go to London,*

but there is no theoretical limit on the number of verbs that may occur in a complex phrase. Examples of sentences with more than two are:

> *I got him to persuade her to ask him to change his mind,*
> *He kept on asking her to help him get it finished,*

and from a recent book on Linguistics:

> *I don't want to have to be forced to begin to try to make more money.*

The verbs that may be followed by other verbs in this way are all (apart from the auxiliaries) catenatives. Every verb in sequences such as those illustrated here, apart from the last one, must be (if it is not an auxiliary) a catenative.

9.1. Problems of statement

Apart from the task of classifying the variety of structures within the phrase, there is a fundamental problem of the theoretical status of the complex phrase and the more practical problem of distinguishing it from other types of structure.

9.1.1. *Types of structure.* The catenatives may be classified in terms of the structures suggested in **1.3.2**. The four structures were:

1. infinitive alone E.g. *He helped wash up.*
2. *to*+infinitive *He wants to go to London.*
3. *-ing* form *He keeps talking about it.*
4. past participle *He got hurt in the scramble.*

With structures 2 and 3, however, and to a limited degree structure 1, some of the verbs we shall deal with are followed not by single infinitives or *-ing* forms (single words), but by infinitivals or participials (consisting of several words):

> *He likes to be working in the morning.*
> *I want to have finished it soon.*
> *He needs to be told about it.*
> *I want to have been informed by six.*
> *He keeps being caught.*
> *I regret having said that.*

We shall need then to talk about the possibility of occurrence of progressive, perfect, passive, etc., participials and infinitivals.

In addition to these, however, we must also handle structures in which a noun phrase occurs between the two verb forms. Once again there are the four possible structures, though with a nominal phrase intervening:

1. *He made them finish the job.*
2. *He persuaded them to take a holiday.*
3. *He kept them talking a long time.*
4. *He had the prisoners shot.*

9.1.2. *Verbal nouns and adjectives.* Traditional grammatical analysis handles the non-finite forms in the structures we are considering as 'verbal nouns' or 'verbal adjectives'. The infinitive forms with or without *to* are nouns and the past participles, adjectives, while the *-ing* forms are either nouns (gerunds) or adjectives (the term 'participle' being restricted in this kind of analysis to the latter). *Prima facie* it is extremely plausible to compare:

> *I want to read*

with *I want a book,*
and *I like reading*
with *I like books,*

and to say that *to read* and *reading* are, like *a book* and *books*, noun forms having the nominal function of being the object of the sentence. Similarly we might compare:

> *He keeps reading*

with *He keeps quiet,*
and *He got hurt*
with *He got hot.*

By a similar argument the two participles here are adjectives, having the adjectival function of complement. In support of this type of analysis it may be noted that the forms have nominal or adjectival function elsewhere. The infinitive and the 'gerund' may function as subjects of the sentence (though the infinitive is rare in this function), while the 'participle' may modify a noun:

> *To err is human.*
> *Reading is a very pleasant occupation.*
> *A sleeping child.*
> *A hurt child.*

A fundamental objection to this kind of analysis is that some of the verbal nouns and adjectives must be allowed to have objects. This establishes them as a very unusual kind of noun or adjective, so unusual indeed that there would seem little point in calling them nouns and adjectives at all. We find:

> *I want to read a novel,*
> *I like reading novels,*
> *He kept reading novels,*

and similarly

> *To read novels is a waste of time,*
> *Reading novels is a waste of time,*
> *Children eating biscuits.*

It will, moreover, even be necessary on such an analysis to allow that a verbal noun can have a subject, in for instance:

> *I want John to read a novel.*

Here presumably *John* is the subject of *to read*. But it is only in this pattern that there is need to establish a subject of the verbal noun. We shall not find the whole piece *John to read a novel* occurring in any other potentially nominal function. We shall not, for instance, attest:

> **John to read a novel is a very good idea.*

Even if we allow that verbal adjectives and nouns may, in view of their 'verbal' nature, have both subjects and objects there are still difficulties in the way of such an analysis.

(a) There are cases where it would be difficult to decide whether the *-ing* form is a noun or an adjective, for instance:

> *He keeps talking.*

It might seem plausible to compare this with:

> *He keeps quiet*

rather than with *He keeps a dog.*
But on the other hand we find;

> *He continued talking,*

but not

> **He continued quiet.*

Yet we do find   *He continued the lesson.*

Similarly we find

> *He stopped talking,*

but not   **He stopped quiet.*

Yet we also find *He kept them talking,*

> *He stopped them talking,*

but not   **He continued them talking.*

This is not to deny that *He kept talking* and *He continued talking* are different (see **9.2.3.**), but merely suggests that analysis in terms of adjective versus noun is not very helpful.

(b) There are a number of verbs (lexemes) in English which do not normally have objects yet are followed by infinitives or *-ing* forms, especially by infinitives. For instance, GO, DECIDE, INTEND:

> *I'm going to talk to him.*
> *He decided to go.*
> *I intend to come.*
> *I intend coming.*

There would seem little point in treating the infinitives and *-ing* forms here as nouns if these verbs do not normally have objects at all.

(c) The structure that follows any particular verb can only be stated lexically for the verb itself. In spite of the possibility of:

> *He began talking,*

and   *He began to talk,*

and   *He continued talking,*

and   *He continued to talk,*

we shall find only

> *He stopped talking,*

and   *He kept talking,*

but not   **He stopped to talk*   (except in an entirely different sense with a different structure),

and   **He kept to talk.*

The verb, that is, 'selects' the construction, rather like a verb of Latin 'selects' the case of the noun it governs. This is not, of course, an overriding objection to the analysis; but it does provide English with a type of government that has never yet been suggested.

(d) The question form that corresponds to many of the declarative forms with infinitives or *-ing* forms are not of the kind:

> *What do you want?*
> *What does he keep?*

but   *What do you want to do?*

> *What does he keep doing?*

With a catenative, that is to say, another verbal form is obligatory. If no other verb is required lexically, a form of the 'empty' verb DO (8.3.2.) occurs. There is potential ambiguity in:

> *I like boxing.*

This may mean either that I like to box or that I like other people boxing. But the questions are, respectively:

> *What do you like doing?*
>
> *What do you like?*

In the second meaning, *boxing* is clearly to be treated as a noun, the object of *like*, parallel with *football* and *ice-cream* in:

> *I like football.*
>
> *I like ice-cream.*

There is an obvious advantage in stating that with the other meaning *boxing* is *not* a noun, *not* the object of *like*, but that we have a structure of a different kind.

(e) It is not at all clear what would be the most appropriate analysis of:

> *I don't like him reading novels.*

We could on the one hand treat *reading* as a noun, the object of the sentence (with its own subject and object). Alternatively we could state that *him* is the object of the sentence and that *reading novels* is an adjectival clause modifying it. In support of the first analysis we would compare:

> *I don't like him to read novels,*

and in support of the second:

> *I don't like coffee hot.*

The problem is even more complicated by the possibility of:

> *I don't like his reading novels.*

Here *reading* is presumably a noun and the sentence is like:

> *I don't like his hat.*

Again we may question whether there is any value in an analysis that forces decision in terms of noun and adjective. But see below (9.3.6.).

(f) Traditional analysis would certainly recognise a 'participle' rather than a 'gerund', an adjective, in:

> *I saw them beating him.*

Indeed there would be no apparent problem about treating *beating him* as an adjectival modifier of *them*. This interpretation is supported by the fact that we can also find:

> *I saw them beaten.*

Here, obviously, one would assume the participle functions as an adjective. But there is great difficulty if we also introduce:

> *I saw them beat him.*

For here we presumably have in *beat* an infinitive, a noun, but it would seem ridiculous to treat this sentence as being of a different structure from the other two. The only way out of the difficulty, if one insists upon interpretation in terms of nouns and adjectives, is to say that *beat* also is a participle (a non-progressive form of *beating*); yet this interpretation has not commended itself to any of the traditional grammarians. For the problem of the three forms here see below (**9.3.4.**).

9.1.3. *The structure of the phrase.* The most sophisticated analysis of the traditional kind would state that in:

> *I don't like John doing that,*

the object of *like* is not *John* or *doing* but *John doing that*. This would involve a hierarchical statement for:

> *I got him to persuade her to ask him to change his mind,*

in which the object of *got* is *him to persuade her to ask him to change his mind*, the object of *persuade* is *her to ask him to change his mind*, the object of *ask* is *him to change his mind* and the object of *change* is *his mind*.

Diagrammatically we have

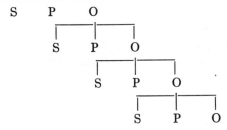

This analysis involves 'downgrading' or 'rank-shifting' in which a clause containing subject, predicator and object itself functions as a single clause element – the object of the main clause.

The hierarchical approach is clearly appropriate here but not the interpretation in terms of sentence elements whereby we are forced to say that the downgraded clause is the *object* of the previous verb. For this involves us in precisely the same problem as the gerund/participle distinction. For we shall have to decide whether *John doing that* is the object in:

> *He keeps John doing that,*

and whether *doing that* is the object in:

> *He keeps doing that.*

Or is it an (adjectival) complement?

There is no need for becoming involved in controversies of this kind. All that is required is a hierarchical analysis in which the downgraded clause is quite deliberately not assigned status as a clause element, object or complement. This is better shown diagrammatically by brackets than by a tree:

$$S \ P \ (S \ P \ ((S \ P \ (((S \ P \ O))) \ )) \ )$$

On this analysis we can still regard *him* as the subject of *persuade*, *her* as the subject of *ask* and so on, but are not forced to establish the status, as a clause element, of the following downgraded clause.

It may be useful to illustrate the structure in a transformational way in which:

> *He got her to do it*

is derived from

> *He got + She does it.*

There are two further modifications to the statement. First we must distinguish between:

> *He keeps waiting*

and
> *He keeps him waiting.*

It must further be stated that the subject of the two verbs is the same in the first sentence but different in the second. This could be shown by subscript numerals – $S_1 \ P \ (S_1 P)$, $S_1 \ P \ (S_2 \ P)$

> *He $_1$ keeps + He $_1$ waits*
> *He $_1$ keeps + He $_2$ waits*

It is clearly necessary to distinguish in terms of voice:

> *He keeps hitting*

and
> *He gets hit.*

This could be handled in a transformational statement of the type:

> *He keeps + He hits*

and
> *He gets + He is hit.*

This kind of analysis is even more important when dealing with a sentence of the type:

> *He wants watching,*

which is very different from:

> *He wants to watch.*

Clearly *watching* is, in some sense, passive and *to watch* active. This is not notional grammar; we have here important grammatical relations. Consider, for instance:

> *The car keeps back-firing*

and
> *The car needs cleaning.*

Yet we shall not find:

> **The car needs back-firing*

nor
> **The car keeps cleaning.*

This is, of course, to be associated with the fact that CAR collocates with BACK-FIRE as the subject of the active verb, but it does not collocate with CLEAN as the subject of the active verb, but only as its object, or as the subject of the passive verb:

> *The car back-fires*

and   *The car is cleaned,*

or   *Mr. Brown cleans the car.*

There are two possible ways of handling:

> *The car needs cleaning.*

We may say either that *cleaning* is passive and that its subject (as in other similar structures) is *the car* or that *cleaning* is active and that *the car* is its object. These two analyses are in effect saying the same thing. We do not really need the subject/object and active/passive distinctions at all here, these being less appropriate for downgraded clauses of this kind. The distinction could be avoided by talking simply of 'actor' and 'goal', the actor being the subject of an active verb and the 'agent 'of a passive one, the goal being the object of the active verb and the subject of the passive. *Car* would be thus the goal of *cleaning* but the actor of *back-firing*. This solution is not adopted. It is simpler to treat *cleaning* as passive (though only in one function, not in form) since this permits us to say as with all other similar structures that the subject of the first (finite) verb is also the subject of the second.

9.1.4. *Analysis of the structures.* From what has already been said it will be clear that no section in this chapter will deal with a complete structure of the verbal phrase, but with the structures as we have defined them, with the syntactical relations, that is, between pairs of verbal forms in the phrase, the entire phrase being built up by sequences of structures of this kind.

It would be perfectly possible to do no more than to give a list of the verbs of the language associated with each of the four structures. We could simply note, for instance, that HELP is associated with structure 1, WANT and HOPE with structure 2, KEEP and STOP with structure 3, and GET with structure 4. But this alone would not be very informative for the following reasons.

(a) Some verbs may appear with only one structure, others with more than one. We may find for instance:

> *He likes to talk,*
> *He likes talking,*

but only   *He keeps talking.*

(b) Two verbs may both occur with two structures, yet in the one case there would seem to be very little difference in the meaning and in the other a very great deal of difference. We may contrast, for instance:

	I intended to come
and	*I intended coming*
with	*I remembered to come*
and	*I remembered coming.*

The first two sentences have almost, if not exactly, the same meaning, whereas the second two are very different.

(c) There are relations of a transformational kind. An important one is that involving active and passive which was dealt with in the last subsection. Another kind of active/passive relation is shown by:

	He kept them talking
and	*He liked them talking,*

since in the passive we find:

	They were kept talking,
but not	**They were liked talking.*

The analysis that follows attempts to handle together the verbs that occur with the same structures. But the classification of the verbs in terms of the structure without noun phrase is different from (and more complicated than) the classification in terms of the structures with noun phrase. For instance we find:

	I like to go,
	I like going,
	I like them to go,
	I like them going.
	I intend to go,
	I intend going,
	I intend them to go,
yet not	**I intend them going.*
	I started talking,
	I started to talk,
	I started them talking,
yet not	**I started them to talk.*

For this reason the structures with and without noun phrase are handled separately.

9.1.5. *Negation in the complex phrase.* The finite verb may, of course, be negated in the usual way (2.2.1.). The non-finite forms are negated by a preceding *not*:

> *He agreed not to do anything.*
> *I like not having a television set.*
> *He asked them not to come.*

Not is rare with structures 1 and 4 but is not impossible as shown by:

> *Have you ever known him not come?*
> *I don't like children not taught road safety.*

There are restrictions on its occurrence but they seem to be explicable in terms of semantic non-compatibility. We shall not find (except perhaps jocularly):

> **He helped not wash up.*
> **He failed not to come.*
> **She kept not reading the book.*
> **He got not hurt in the accident.*

In some cases *not* may be used but an alternative form may be preferred. More likely than:

> *The car needs not cleaning for a month*

is
> *The car needs not to be cleaned for a month,*

and instead of:

> *He keeps not answering*

we might expect (**10.7.**):

> *He keeps on not answering.*

But these are lexical rather than grammatical restrictions and are not dealt with in detail here.

9.2. Structures without noun phrase

In terms of these structures the verbs fall into seven main classes:

(a) Structure 1 only, e.g. HELP
(b) Structure 2 only, e.g. AGREE
(c) Structure 3 only, e.g. KEEP
(d) Structures 2 and 3 with little difference in usage, e.g. LIKE
(e) Structures 2 and 3 with a marked difference in usage, e.g. REMEMBER
(f) Structures 2 and 3 involving a difference in voice, e.g. NEED
(g) Structure 4 only, GET

9.2.1. *Model* HELP. The sequence verb+infinitive without *to*, with no intervening noun phrase is very rare. It is to be considered under three headings.

(i) The verb HELP is the only verb in the language which is freely followed by any other verb in this structure:

> *Can I help wash up?*
> *You can help put the books away.*
> *You can help push the car.*

(ii) There are several combinations which are essentially fixed phrases or idioms where the two verbs are limited collocationally. Among these are LET GO, LET FLY, LET DRIVE, MAKE DO:

> *He let fly with his foot.*
> *We have to make do with soup this evening.*

LET LIVE occurs only in the saying:

> *Live and let live.*

HEAR TELL and HEAR SAY also occur, though they are possibly more American than British:

> *I heard tell that he's coming today.*

(iii) A problem is provided by LET FALL and LET SLIP, as in:

> *He let fall that he would be coming.*
> *We must not let such an opportunity slip.*

We may similarly note LET GO:

> *He let go the rope.*
> *He let the rope go.*

The second of each of these pairs is obviously verb structure 1 with an intervening noun phrase. Are we to analyse the first of each pair in the same way, though with a different sequence of the noun phrase and the verb? What is important is to note that the alternative sequence is not possible with all combinations of LET + a verb. In spite of:

> *He let the people walk on the grass*

we cannot possibly attest:

> **He let walk the people on the grass.*

It is reasonable, therefore, to treat LET SLIP, LET FALL and LET GO, when followed by a noun phrase, as examples of this structure 1, though noting that they are essentially 'fixed phrases'.

9.2.2. *Model* AGREE. There are many verbs that occur with structure 2 only. It is not easy to sub-divide the structures and the verbs that are associated with them. We can, however, establish four main patterns, though there are a few verbs that do not conveniently fit in to any of these four.

(a) With many verbs there is always reference to a future event, and the possibility of collocation with an adverbial of future time:

> *I hope to see him tomorrow.*
> *I promise to come tomorrow.*
> *I want to talk to you.*
> *I intend to see him tomorrow.*

The most common verbs that appear in this pattern are AGREE, AIM, ARRANGE, ASK, ASPIRE, BEG, CHOOSE, CONDESCEND, CONSENT, DECIDE, DECLINE, DESERVE, ELECT, EXPECT, HESITATE, HOPE,

LONG, MEAN, OFFER, PREPARE, PROMISE, REFUSE, SCORN, STAND, SWEAR, THREATEN, UNDERTAKE, WANT, WISH, and in a negative form (*don't*) CARE. We may add here MAKE in the colloquial:

> *He made to open the door,*

and also HAVE (8.2.3.). Verbs in this class are followed not merely by the simple infinitive, but by infinitivals marking the categories of progressive/non-progressive, perfect/non-perfect and voice:

> *I hope   to come*
> > *to be reading*
> > *to have finished*
> > *to have been reading*
> > *to be told*
> > *to be being helped*
> > *to have been informed*

Many of these verbs occur with the same structure with an intervening noun phrase (9.3.3.).

(b) There are a number of verbs which might be described as 'adverbial' or as verbs of 'manner' in that they could be replaced by an adverbial phrase and the second verb used in a finite form:

> *He came to see.*
> Cf. *He saw at last.*
> *He hastened to say.*
> Cf. *He said in haste.*

Some of the verbs here are used negatively:

> *He failed to come.*
> *He neglected to come.*

Both of them, of course, imply that he did not come. Verbs used in this pattern are APPEAR, CHANCE, COME, HAPPEN, HASTEN, MANAGE, PROCEED, SEEM, TEND, negatively FAIL, NEGLECT, OMIT. These verbs may also be followed by the infinitival, not merely the simple infinitive (though the simple infinitive is probably much the more common). They do not occur with any other structure (including structures with noun phrase) except CHANCE with a rather different meaning (9.2.3. and 9.3.7.).

(c) We might also wish to treat together ATTEMPT, STRIVE and TRY – the 'verbs of effort'. Perhaps we might even add LEARN. All of them suggest looking towards an end:

> *He is attempting to climb the mountain.*
> *He is learning to swim.*
> *He is striving to achieve something.*
> *He is trying to help.*

These verbs are usually followed only by the infinitive though a passive infinitival is possible:

> *He is trying to be noticed.*

There is one special point about TRY; alongside *try to* we find *try and*:

> *Try to come,*
> *Try and come,*
> *I'll try to do it.*
> *I'll try and do it.*

But this is restricted to the form *try* – we shall not find:

> **He tries and comes.*
> **He tried and came.*

TRY also occurs, but in a different sense, with structure 3 (9.2.3.).

(d) A more miscellaneous group is that of MAKE, SAY, SERVE, STAND (some of them clearly colloquial):

> *He made to open the door.*
> *He said to remain here till he returned.*
> *It only serves to keep the rain off.*
> *I stand to lose a lot of money.*

9.2.3. *Model* KEEP. There are verbs that occur with structure 3 only.

(a) Three common verbs are FINISH, KEEP, STOP. They are followed only by an *-ing* form or a passive (non-perfect, non-progressive) participial:

> *He kept talking.*
> *He kept being caught.*
> *He stopped talking.*

These verbs also occur with a noun phrase:

> *He kept them talking.*
> *He stopped them talking.*

They may also have passives:

> *They were kept talking.*
> *They were stopped talking.*

Nevertheless, if we take together verbs of continuing, beginning and stopping, they do not all function in the same way (see **9.2.4.** and **9.3.5.**). We find, for instance, that we can say:

> *He started to talk*

as well as   *He started talking,*

not   **He kept to talk,*

and there is no   **He continued them talking,*

and also it is probably unlikely that we shall find:

They were begun talking

in spite of   *They were started talking.*

(b) Perhaps this is the best place to handle:

He went fishing.

This is almost equivalent to:

He went and fished.

Here GO, rather like KEEP, is almost 'adverbial'. The activity indicated by
the second verb took place – he fished. GO collocates with verbs that
imply movement – FISH, HUNT, LOOK FOR, etc., but is followed only by
the simple -*ing* form (not any of the participials).

(c) We may add CHANCE, RISK and TRY (in the sense of experimentation):

I risked going there.
I tried switching on the light.

The second sentence is very different from:

I tried to switch on the light.

In the first of these it is clear that the action was performed. In the second
there was an attempt to perform the action; it may or may not have been
successful. It would seem that the only way to handle the distinction is in
terms of two different functions of TRY with two different lexical meanings. We must, of course, contrast here the behaviour of ATTEMPT,
STRIVE and LEARN (9.2.2.). With ATTEMPT structure 3 is rare and seems
to have very little difference in meaning from 2:

He attempted to climb the mountain.
He attempted climbing the mountain.

With STRIVE there is no possibility of structure 3; we cannot say:

*He strove finishing it.

With LEARN we may attest both:

He learnt to swim

and   *He learnt swimming.*

But here *swimming* is presumably to be treated exactly as a noun like
football or *tennis*. We shall not, for instance, attest:

*The child learnt walking

in spite of   *The child learnt to walk.*

(d) A miscellaneous group is AVOID, CONSIDER, DENY, ENJOY,
MISS, POSTPONE, PRACTISE, (*don't*) FANCY, (*don't*) MIND as in:

I avoided/considered/denied/enjoyed/missed/postponed
didn't fancy/didn't mind/coming,

and   *I practised playing the piano.*

It might be possible to treat these as merely verbs plus object (and not catenatives) in view of:

> *I avoided the blow.*
> *I practised the music.*

But one test of a catenative is whether the related question is of the type:

> *What did you avoid?*

or

> *What did you avoid doing?*

With these verbs questions of either kind are possible (see **9.4.2.**).

9.2.4. *Model* LIKE. The verbs that occur with structures 2 and 3 are of three kinds.

(a) There are a large number of verbs of liking and disliking with which the infinitive or *-ing* form occurs and has a function very similar to that of a noun as the object of a verb:

> *I like to do that.*
> *I love to swim in the summer.*
> *I like doing that.*
> *I love swimming in the summer.*

With these verbs it is quite easy to understand traditional analysis **in** terms of a verbal noun. There are indeed two characteristics of the patterns we are considering here that would support an analysis in terms of a verb+an object. First there is the fact that either the infinitive or the *-ing* form (=gerund) may occur. Secondly, all the verbs are ordinary transitive verbs in English; that is to say, they regularly occur in what is to be treated as a S.P.O. (=Subject, Predicator, Object) structure:

> *I like ice-cream.*
> *I love the Italian Alps.*

Verbs to be included here are DETEST, DISLIKE, DREAD, HATE, LIKE, LOATHE, LOVE, PREFER, (*can't*) AFFORD, (*can't*) BEAR, (*can't*) STAND. These are commonly followed by all the infinitivals and participials:

> *I like* *to come*   *coming*
>   *to be reading*
>   *to have finished*   *having finished*
>   *to have been reading* *having been reading*
>   *to be told*   *being told*
>   *to be being helped*
>   *to have been informed* *having been informed*

A common form is:

> *I should have liked to have gone,*

which the purists insist is wrong since it is doubly perfect; they would prefer:

> *I should like to have gone*
>
> or   *I should have liked to go.*

With the verbs of disliking, that is all the verbs above except LIKE and LOVE, structure 2 is often used to refer to a specific future action:

> *I hate to tell you this but ...* (and the speaker goes on to tell the hearer the very thing that he hates to tell him).

In contrast:

> *I hate doing this*

would normally be used not to refer to a specific action but to suggest that I often do it. There is, however, no complete clear-cut contrast here; both structures may be used for either purpose. We may note for instance:

> *I hate telling you this but ...*
>
> and   *I hate to swim in the sea.*

But there is a greater likelihood of structure 2 where there is reference to a specific action in the future. The same point is not true of LIKE and LOVE. We cannot in a similar way say:

> *I like to tell you this ...*

On the other hand, *should like* and *should love* are used to refer to a specific action, and indeed there is a possibility of collocation with an adverbial of future time:

> *I should like to do that tomorrow.*

There are some verbs of similar meaning that occur with structure 3 only (or very rarely with 2) – ENJOY, FANCY, (*don't*) MIND.

(b) There are a number of verbs that refer to beginning, ending or continuance of an action, BEGIN, CEASE, CONTINUE and START, and (more colloquial) GET. These are, like the verbs considered in the previous paragraph, all transitive verbs. They are usually followed only by the simple infinitive or *-ing* form (or the passive infinitival or participial).

> *He continued to talk.*
>
> *He began to talk.*
>
> *I got to think that ...*
>
> *He continued talking.*
>
> *He began talking.*
>
> *I got thinking that ...*
>
> Cf.   *He continued the lesson.*
>
> *He began the lesson.*

Yet these four verbs behave differently in other structures. BEGIN,

GET and START alone may be followed by a noun phrase (**9.3.5.** and
9.3.8.):

> *He began/started them talking.*

We shall not attest:

> **He ceased/continued them talking.*

START alone, moreover, is the only verb that occurs in the passive form:

> *They were started talking.*

(c) There are a few verbs that are used to refer to a single action in the
future, notably INTEND, PLAN, PROPOSE:

> *I intend going/to go tomorow.*
>
> *I plan going/to go tomorrow.*

There is no obvious difference in meaning between the alternatives.
Generally, of course, the infinitive, structure 2, is used to refer to a single
action in the future (**9.2.2.**).

9.2.5. *Model* REMEMBER. With structure 2 REMEMBER and FORGET
have an 'adverbial' use as in **9.2.2.** The action is shown to have taken
place or not to have taken place. Any form but the simple infinitive
would be very rare after these verbs:

> *I remembered to go.*   (I went.)
>
> *I forgot to go.*   (I didn't go.)

With structure 3 they are used to refer to a past action:

> *I remembered going.*

This is equivalent to:

> *I remembered that I went.*

FORGET is used only in such expressions as:

> *I shall never forget seeing her*

but not   **I forgot seeing her.*

All the infinitivals may occur. The use of a perfect form is not, however,
very different from that of a non-perfect. There is often no difference
between:

> *I remembered going ...*

and   *I remembered having gone ...*

(though it may be argued that the first may imply that I remembered the
act of going, the second that I remembered only the fact that I went).
FORGET is rare in this use, but REGRET occurs with a similar meaning:

> *I regret going.*
>
> *I regret that I went.*

With structure 2 REGRET refers to an immediate future action, like
HATE in **9.2.4.**:

> *I regret to say ...*

RECOLLECT in spite of its similarity in meaning occurs only with
structure 3:

> *I recollected doing it.*

9.2.6. *Model* NEED. With NEED, WANT and less commonly DESERVE
and REQUIRE, a following infinitive (structure 2) is active, an *-ing* form
(structure 3) is passive:

> *The man wants watching.*
> *The man wants to watch.*

The first of these may be replaced by a form with a passive infinitival:

> *The man wants to be watched.*

Similarly we have:

> *The car needs cleaning.*
> *The car needs to be cleaned.*

In this construction the infinitive and the *-ing* form, though both formally (in terms of the morphology of the phrase) active, differ in respects
that are elsewhere to be treated as differences of voice, and indeed the *-ing*
form is equivalent to (and replaceable by) a passive infinitival. It should
be noted, however, that WANT+the infinitive is used in two different
ways – that lexically WANT has two meanings here. It may refer to a
desire or it may refer to a need. *He wants to watch* may mean either that he
desires to watch or that it would be a good thing for him to watch. With
the *-ing* form WANT is used in only the second of these two senses, but
generally WANT+the infinitive would be interpreted in the first. With
NEED, however, there is no possibility of these two different uses:

> *He needs to watch*

and

> *He needs watching*

are exactly comparable, excepted that *watching* is replaceable by *to be
watched*.

9.2.7. GET. Structure 4 is found only with GET:

> *He gets punished regularly.*
> *He got killed.*

GET here functions in a manner very similar to BE in the primary paradigm:

> *He is punished regularly,*
> *He was killed,*

but in spite of the similarity of their usage it must be noted that GET is,
unlike BE, not an auxiliary verb. We shall not attest:

> **Gets he punished regularly?*
> **He gotn't killed.*

Prima facie there might seem reason to include here LOOK, BECOME, FEEL, in view of:

> *He looked excited.*
> *He became irritated.*
> *He felt deceived.*

But in these cases we may treat the final word as an adjective functioning simply as the complement of the verb. This is shown quite clearly by its co-occurrence with *very:*

> *He looked very excited.*
> *He became very irritated.*
> *He felt very deceived.*

Equally we shall not find:

> **He looked killed.*
> **He became killed.*
> **He felt killed.*

In other words, while every past participle may occur after GET only those participles which function in the language as adjectives occur after LOOK, BECOME and FEEL, and there is no need to recognise with them a complex verbal phrase.

9.3. Structures with noun phrase

We now consider those structures which have a noun phrase between the two verbs and in which the noun phrase is the subject of the second verb. There are, of course, four possible structures exemplified by:

1. *I saw them come.*
2. *I advised them to come.*
3. *I saw them coming.*
4. *I saw them beaten.*

In dealing with these four structures we must not simply consider the four structures themselves, but also note that there are passive transformations of some of them. Obvious examples are:

2. *They were advised to come.*
3. *They were seen coming.*

There is, however, no possibility of:

1. **They were seen come.*

The passive form here follows the pattern of structure 2 in that the infinitive is preceded by *to:*

> *They were seen to come.*

With a catenative in the passive, that is to say, structure 2 corresponds to both structure 1 and structure 2 with a verb in the active. There is not normally a passive transformation of structure 4. We shall not normally attest, though perhaps we cannot altogether exclude the possibility of:

4. *They were seen beaten.*

In terms of their function in these four structures and their passive transformations the vast majority of the verbs in English fall into eight main classes.

(a) Structure 1, or structures 1 and 2; with passive, e.g. HELP
(b) Structure 1, or structures 1 and 2; no passive, e.g. LET
(c) Structure 1 only; with passive, e.g. ASK
(d) Structures 1 and 3; with passive, e.g. SEE
(e) Structure 3 only; with passive, e.g. KEEP
(f) Structures 2, 3 and 4, or 3 and 4; no passive, e.g. LIKE
(g) Structure 3 only; no passive, e.g. REMEMBER
(h) GET occurs with structures 2, 3 and 4 and has passives.

9.3.1. *Model* HELP. HELP occurs with structure 1 as well as structure 2 (though, of course, the passive only with structure 2):

> *He helped them do it.*
> *He helped them to do it.*
> *They were helped to do it.*

There is no obvious difference between structures 1 and 2 here. KNOW similarly occurs with 1 and 2:

> *Have you ever known them come on time?*
> *Have you ever known them to come on time?*
> *Have they ever been known to come on time?*

Its occurrence is confined to questions with *ever* or to statements with *never* or other semi-negatives. MAKE occurs with structure 1 and with a passive (structure 2, of course):

> *He made the boy finish his homework.*
> *The boy was made to finish his homework.*

9.3.2. *Model* LET. LET and HAVE occur with structure 1 and have no passive (except for the idiom LET GO):

> *I let them stay a while.*
> *I'll have you know I did it myself.*

9.3.3. *Model* ASK. There are very many verbs which occur with structure 2 that also occur in the passive:

> *She asked him to write a letter.*
> *He was asked to write a letter.*

Verbs of this class are ADVISE, ALLOW, ASK, BEG, CAUSE, CHALLENGE, COMMAND, COMPEL, DARE, DIRECT, DRIVE, EXPECT, FORCE, INTEND, INVITE, LEAD, MEAN, MOTION, OBLIGE, ORDER, PRESS, REMIND, TEACH, TELL, TEMPT, TROUBLE, TRUST, URGE, WARN. GIVE occurs with UNDERSTAND only:

> *He gave me to understand that ...*

Most of these are followed by the various infinitivals as well as (and most commonly) the simple infinitive. Some of these occur without an intervening noun phrase (see 9.2.2.). All are essentially 'causatives' in their meaning. The subject of the first verb is in some way instrumental in influencing the action of the subject of the second. But not all 'causative' verbs are in the class – cf. also 9.3.6.

9.3.4. *Model* SEE. In this section we deal with the verbs of sensation (5.3.1.). In fact they do not strictly form a single group in terms of the structure with which they are associated, but they must be handled together because of their characteristic distinction of usage with structures 1 and 3:

> *I saw him come up the street.*
> *I saw him coming up the street.*
> *I heard him walk into the house.*
> *I heard him walking into the house.*

The difference is essentially that of the non-progressive and the progressive. This is clearly shown where the distinction is between an incomplete (progressive) and a complete (non-progressive) action:

> *I saw them crossing the river.*   (I don't know if they reached the other side.)
> *I saw them cross the river.* (I saw them reach the other side.)

The sentences may be analysed in terms of:

> *I saw* + *He came up the street*
> *I saw* + *He was coming up the street*
> *I heard* + *He walked into the house*
> *I heard* + *He was walking into the house*

The verbs of which this is true are the verbs of sensation SEE, HEAR, FEEL and SMELL (but not TASTE), and WATCH and NOTICE:

> *We watched him come in.*
> *We watched him coming in.*

SEE and HEAR occur in the passive, though with structures 2 and 3:

> *He was seen to come up the street.*
> *He was seen coming up the street.*

SMELL does not occur in the passive and neither do WATCH and NOTICE (or very rarely). A passive of FEEL is possible but not very likely:

> *Something was felt to move.*
> *Something was felt moving.*

We must add here CATCH, FIND, OBSERVE, PERCEIVE. Although they occur only with structure 3 (not with 1), this too is to be treated as a progressive. CATCH and FIND occur in the passive too:

> *He caught them stealing.*
> *They were caught stealing.*

SEE and WATCH also occur with structure 4:

> *He saw his team beaten.*
> *He watched his team beaten.*

This is equivalent to structure 1 with a passive infinitival:

> *He saw his team be beaten.*

This (non-progressive) passive form is rare (structure 4 is used instead), but the participial (there is no alternative) is common:

> *He saw his team being beaten.*

9.3.5. *Model* KEEP. There are some verbs which occur only with structure 3 and have passives. They are normally followed only by the simple *-ing* form:

> *He started them talking.*
> *They were started talking.*
> *He left them standing near the gate.*
> *They were left standing near the gate.*

Verbs in this pattern are KEEP, LEAVE, SET, START and STOP. We should also add SEND, but only in the restricted collocations SEND FLYING, SEND PACKING:

> *The boy sent the book flying across the room.*
> *She sent her unwelcome guests packing.*

But we must note that in the pattern without noun phrase (9.2.3.) only KEEP and STOP are associated with structure 3 only.

9.3.6. *Model* LIKE. There are a few verbs that occur with structure 2 (rarely), structure 3 and structure 4, and have no passives. It is the absence of a passive that distinguishes these verbs from the verbs of the previous section and indeed it is this feature that is probably at the basis of the traditional participle/gerund distinction:

> *I hate them to stand outside.*
> *I hate them standing outside.*
> *I hate music played like that.*

Those that occur in this class are DETEST, DISLIKE, ENJOY, FANCY, HATE, LIKE, LOATHE, LOVE, PREFER, RESENT, WANT and the negatives (*can't*) AFFORD, (*don't*) MIND, (*can't*) STAND. Of these only LIKE and WANT commonly occur with structure 2. The structure may occasionally be found with DETEST, DISLIKE, LOVE and PREFER. These verbs are followed (with varying degrees of probability) by all the infinitivals and participials (cf. 9.2.4.) with structures 2 and 3. We must add here PREVENT since there is no passive form, even though semantically it would seem to belong to 9.3.5. The passive is always accompanied by *from*:

> *He prevented them crossing over the field.*
> *They were prevented from crossing over the field.*

One characteristic of many of the verbs of this class is that there is an alternative pattern to structure 3. Alongside:

> *I don't like him coming here*

we shall find   *I don't like his coming here.*

In other words instead of the pronoun *him* we find the possessive *his*. This is the so-called 'half-gerund'. In my own speech, however, this is not very common. Alongside this many of the books quote the possibility of a noun phrase with possessive -'s occurring before the -*ing* form as well as a noun phrase without it, that is to say, we can attest:

> *I don't like the boy doing that.*
> *I don't like the boy's doing that.*

In my own speech, however, this is very rare indeed. A little less rare perhaps is a proper noun with -'s:

> *I don't like John's doing that.*

But even this is very much less likely for me than:

> *I don't like John doing that.*

If we may allow that there are two possible structures it is very often in principle impossible to distinguish between them in speech. We cannot, for instance, differentiate between the two structures in:

> *I don't like her doing that,*

since *her* may here either be the object form of the pronoun or the possessive. Similarly there is no possibility of distinguishing in speech the two forms that can be distinguished in writing:

> *To prevent the ladies leaving us.*
> *To prevent the ladies' leaving us.*

In view of the fact that these two structures are so little different in their usage, and are so often indistinguishable, it is obviously utterly unprofitable to interpret the one in terms of a possessive + a gerund and the other in terms of a pronoun + a participle.

Another verb that should go in is HAVE (see **8.2.4.**), especially in the negative form, *can't have* or *won't have*. It differs, however, from the other verbs considered in this section in that it is associated not with structure 2 but with structure 1 (as well as structures 3 and 4):

> *I had him tell me about it.*
> *I had them writing another essay.*
> *I'm having a house built.*
> *I can't have you do that.*
> *I won't have him waiting for me.*
> *I can't have it done that way.*

9.3.7. *Model* REMEMBER. REMEMBER, FORGET and REGRET also occur with structure 3 and have no passive:

> *I remember him saying something about that.*
> *I'd forgotten them doing that.*
> *I regret them taking sides on this matter.*

With these verbs there is a reference to a past action. These sentences are almost equivalent to:

> *I remember that he said something about that.*
> *I'd forgotten that they did that.*
> *I regret that they took sides on this matter.*

The verbs may be followed by all the participials. The perfect forms, however, differ little in function from the non-perfect one (cf. **9.2.5.**). With FORGET, in fact, a sentence of this second kind is more likely. As with the verbs dealt with in the previous section these verbs may be followed by a possessive pronoun or (rarely) by a noun + possessive -'*s*:

> *I remember his saying something about that.*
> *I regret John's taking sides on this matter.*

We should also include here perhaps CHANCE and RISK:

> *I risked them coming/their coming.*

Here, though, reference is to a possible future action:

> *I risked the possibility that they would come.*

9.3.8. GET. GET is idiosyncratic in that it occurs with structures 2, 3 and 4, and has a passive with all three:

> *I got him to go.*
> *He got the car moving.*
> *He got his car started.*
> *He was got to go.*
> *The car was got moving.*
> *The car was got started.*

The last of these may possibly be sub-standard. More likely in standard English is:

> *The car was started.*

9.4. Contrasting structures

There are some sequences of verb + infinitive or -*ing* form that are not to be handled at all in the complex verbal phrase as analysed here. We shall not, for instance, handle:

> *I ran to catch the train*

with
> *I wanted to catch the train,*

or
> *The car hit the boy running across the street*

with
> *The man saw the boy running across the street.*

We must, then, contrast with the complex verbal phrase certain combinations of verb plus the infinitive, the -*ing* form or the past participle. The infinitive always occurs with *to;* there is, thus, no contrast with structure 1.

9.4.1. *Verb + infinitive.* There are several types of construction that we must consider.

(a) We must exclude from the complex phrase a verb + an 'infinitive of purpose'. Examples are:

> *I ran to catch a train.*
> *People have to work to earn a living.*

The reason for excluding these is simply that there is no restriction on the co-occurrence of one of these with any particular preceding verb. There is therefore no need for a grammatical statement in terms of classes of verbs and structures.

There is potentially, but only potentially, a difference in juncture between one of these independent infinitives and an infinitive in a complex verbal phrase. We may compare, for instance:

> *I want to catch the train.*

Here it would be very unusual to have a juncture ('single-bar' juncture) between *want* and *to catch,* while there would usually be a juncture between *ran* and *to catch.* We can make a contrast between:

> *I promise to make you happy*

and
> *I promise, to make you happy*

In the written form of these two examples the comma indicates the difference. With the comma the infinitive of purpose is indicated, and there would be greater possibility of the juncture. On the other hand, the utterance:

> *I'm going to tell him*

might, without any difference in the articulation, mean either that I shall in the future tell him, or that I am going in order to tell him. The infinitive of purpose may also occur in a different position – at the beginning of a sentence:

> *To do that you'll have to work harder.*

A verb that provides a little difficulty is WAIT. It is not clear whether we must analyse differently:

> *I am waiting to hear your answer*

and   *I am waiting, to hear your answer*

(in speech the difference being one of juncture). In other words can we consider that with WAIT we have the contrast of complex verbal phrase and verb + the infinitive of purpose? We may certainly note also:

> *I've been waiting a long time to hear your answer.*

It is impossible to reach a clear-cut decision regarding the status of WAIT + the infinitive form, but there is a case for contrasting the complex verbal phrase with the verb + the infinitive of purpose.

There is a similar contrast when there is a noun phrase between the two verbal forms. Ambiguity is possible, for instance, in:

> *I got them to eat.*

This could mean, of course, either that I made them eat or that I got them so that I could eat them. There is, however, little likelihood of ambiguity in:

> *I got the children to eat.*
> *I got the apples to eat.*

The first is an example of a complex phrase, the second of a verb + an infinitive of purpose. There is potentially a difference of juncture once again, the single-bar juncture being much more likely in the second example. But it is, of course, clear from collocation that in the first *the children* is the subject of *eat*, whereas in the second *the apples* is the object of *eat*, the subject being *I*. We must compare for this:

> *Children eat ...*

and   *... eat apples.*

This difference is always maintained in the two contrasting constructions. In the complex verbal phrase the intervening noun phrase is the subject of the following verb, whereas in the construction verb + infinitive of purpose, the subject of the sentence is the subject of the second verb.

(b) We must also exclude a verb + an 'infinitive of result':

> *I ran all the way to find that he had gone.*

Once again there is potentially a difference of juncture and a difference in terms of subject and object. The subject of the second verb is in all cases the subject of the sentence. This infinitive of result is, however, occasionally very restricted. FIND is the only verb that commonly occurs in the second verb position. It is, moreover, especially found co-occurring with WAKE:

> *He woke to find that he was alone.*

We ought, perhaps, to include here:

> *He lived to be ninety.*
> *He lived to see his grandchildren.*

Here, of course, the second verb is not FIND, but the first verb is always LIVE. It would, however, be possible to treat LIVE amongst the verbs that occur in complex verb phrases (9.2.2.). But we must contrast:

> *He came to see that he was wrong*   (9.2.2.)

and   *He came, to find that I was out.*   ('result')

The infinitive is very frequently preceded by *only* or by *never:*

> *He arrived at last, only to see that the others had all left.*
> *He went away, never to return.*

Here, of course, there is no possibility of ambiguity. The occurrence of *only* and *never* illustrates quite clearly that this is an infinitive of result.

There is a problem with STOP in:

> *He stopped to talk.*

This is, after all, very little different from:

> *He stopped and talked.*

It would be perfectly possible to regard *to talk* here as being an infinitive of result. It is quite clearly not an infinitive of purpose since there is a considerable difference in:

> *He stopped in order to talk.*

(c) With verbs that express emotion the infinitive is often found, as in:

> *He rejoiced to hear that he was going free,*
> *I grieve to tell you this,*

and in the nursery rhyme:

> *The little dog laughed to see such fun.*

It is equally found where there is a noun phrase after the first verb:

> *It pleased him to hear this.*

In this use the infinitive is found even more commonly with adjectives, as in:

> *I am glad/happy/delighted/sorry/ashamed*, etc., *to hear this.*

There is, of course, the possibility of contrast between this use of the infinitive and the infinitive of purpose. The line in the nursery rhyme might have read:

> *The little dog laughed, to make her cry.*

It would be perfectly possible to handle this type of use in terms of a complex verbal phrase, merely noting that the infinitive was used with verbs of the class GRIEVE, LAUGH, REJOICE, SMILE. Certainly there is not normally any juncture between the verb and the infinitive, but since this use is not widely generalisable it is best dealt with here.

9.4.2. *Verb+ -ing form.* We shall obviously not handle in the complex verbal phrase sentences of the type:

> *He arrived puffing and panting.*
> *I reached it, standing on the chair.*

Here the *-ing* form obviously modifies the subject of the sentence. Less obvious, however, is the status of:

> *She sat talking.*
> *We stood talking.*

SIT and STAND could be regarded as catenatives on the model of KEEP, (and regularly collocated with TALK). The only argument against this is the possibility of:

> *She sat in the chair talking.*
> *We stood in the street talking.*

An *-ing* form may also be a noun and the object of the verb (see **9.1.2.**):

> *We watched boxing on the television.*

We may compare:

> *We watched football on the television.*

9.4.3. *Verb+past participle.* We shall obviously exclude from the complex phrase:

> *He escaped, pursued by the warders,*

and we shall also exclude (though with less obvious justification):

> *He stood amazed.*

It would be possible to treat STAND as a verb associated in the complex phrase with structure 4 (cf. **9.2.7.**).

Where there is an intervening noun phrase there are, in theory at least, four possibilities as in the previous section. Examples with the same lexical items are not easily found. We have:

(a) Complex phrase:

> *He saw the children beaten.*

(b) Participle modifying the subject (with juncture):

> *He finished his work, driven on by ambition.*

(c) Participle modifying the object (defining):
> *He visited the house damaged by the flood.*

(d) Participle modifying the object (non-defining, with juncture):
> *We climbed the mountain, covered in snow.*

There are three interpretations – (a), (c) and (d) for:
> *He found the car (,) smashed to pieces.*

9.5. Other structures

There are a few other structures that might have been handled in this chapter but are not dealt with here in detail since they do not entirely fit the general pattern.

(a) Similar to the pattern of **9.3.3.** are:
> *I don't intend there to be any trouble.*
> *He meant there to be no argument.*
> *I want there to be a discussion on this.*

The characteristic features of this are first, that the place of the noun phrase is occupied by *there*, and secondly, that the following verb is always BE. They are, of course, to be related to the sentences of the structure:
> *There is/was trouble.*
> *There is/was no argument.*

Not all the verbs of **9.3.3.** occur with the structure considered here (e.g. CHALLENGE), while some of the verbs of **9.3.6.** do (e.g. WANT).

(b) With verbs of 'mental states' (opinion, knowledge, etc.) a structure of the type noun phrase+infinitive with *to* occurs but again only with BE:
> *I considered him to be a fool.*
> *He knew it to be true.*

These again could have been dealt with in **9.3.3.** but are best omitted because of their close relation with other structures that are not within the analysis of the complex phrase, those of:

(i)   *I considered him a fool.*

(ii)   *I considered that he was a fool.*

With some verbs both of these alternative structures are possible, with others they are not. We shall attest:
> *He knew (that) it was true*

but not   **He knew it true.*

(c) Some verbs are followed by 'conjunctives' and an infinitive with *to*, either with or without an intervening noun phrase:
> *He knew how to do it.*
> *He told him where to go.*

Once again there is a good case for treating these within the complex verbal phrase. An important point is that the actor of the infinitive form is, as in all the other structures considered in the complex phrase, to be identified with the subject of the finite verb where there is no intervening noun phrase and with the noun phrase itself where there is one. These relations are illustrated by (cf. a similar analysis in 9.1.3.):

> He $_1$ knew + how + He $_1$ does it
> He $_1$ told + where + He $_2$ goes

These structures are closely related to, and paraphrasable by, structures of the type:

> *He knew how he should do it.*
> *He told him where he should go.*

They **are** probably best handled along with them.

References

Page 151 **Nouns and adjectives.** H. E. Palmer and F. G. Blandford, *A grammar of spoken English* (op. cit.), 166 ff.
Page 172 **Half gerund.** Ibid, 170.

Chapter 10

Phrasal verbs and prepositional verbs

Finally we will briefly consider such items as GIVE IN, LOOK AFTER, MAKE UP and PUT UP WITH, in such sentences as:

> *The enemy finally gave in.*
> *He looked after his aged father.*
> *She made up the whole story.*
> *I can't put up with her.*

There are reasons for treating these as single units in the grammar:

(a) There are severe collocational restrictions. We can *give up* but not *give down*. We can *look after* someone but not *look before* him. We can *make up* a story but not *make down* a story. We can *put up with* discomfort but not *put down with* it.

(b) They are obviously semantic units. GIVE IN equals YIELD. LOOK AFTER may be replaced by the literary TEND. MAKE UP has the meaning of INVENT, PUT UP WITH of TOLERATE.

(c) All except one type, which is intransitive (exemplified by GIVE IN), have corresponding passives:

> *His father was looked after.*
> *The whole story was made up.*
> *She's a person who can't be put up with.*

10.1. Problems of classification

We are here concerned with combinations of verb and another element or elements that may provisionally be termed 'particles'. The problem is to establish under what conditions such combinations are in some sense single linguistic units.

Two kinds of classification are appropriate. The forms may be distin-

guished grammatically, first, in terms of the adverbial versus the prepositional nature of the particles. Secondly, they may be distinguished in
terms of idiom, some of the combinations being idiomatic, others not. The
two types of classification must be kept distinct. It is often not clear
whether the term 'phrasal verb' is defined in terms of the first, the second,
or both.

10.1.1. *Preposition and adverb.* An often-quoted pair of sentences is:
> *He ran up a hill.*
> *He ran up a bill.*

We leave aside in this section the question of the idiom but can establish
two grammatically different items, both RUN UP. The distinction can be
most simply made in terms of the traditional preposition and adverb,
UP being in the one case a preposition and in the other an adverb. This
is not to accept traditional word classes; it is merely necessary to show
that UP has two quite distinct functions and the terms 'preposition' and
'adverb' are adequate labels for our (limited) purpose. The grammatical
distinction is shown in three ways:

(a) In addition to the sentences quoted we may find, with a difference in
the sequence of the elements:
> *He ran a bill up.*

But we shall never attest:
> **He ran a hill up.*

(b) Where instead of, e.g., *a hill, a bill* there is a pronoun *it*, the sequence
of the pronoun and particle is fixed and contrastive. We shall attest only:
> *He ran up it.*   (a hill)
> *He ran it up.*   (a bill)

(c) Where the particle is final in the sentence there is usually a difference
of stress. The particle is final in, for instance, a relative clause, and we
may contrast:
> *The hills I ＼ran up.*
> *The bills I ran ＼up.*

In the first there is nuclear stress on *ran*, in the second on *up*. Admittedly
this contrast is not always maintained. It is possible to find a context in
which there would be nuclear stress on *up* in:
> *The hills I ran ＼up.*

This would be possible if there were contrast with *The hills I ran down.*
But clearly this is rare and in order to define the adverb versus preposition with maximum rigour we need merely exclude sentences in which
there is contrast of this kind.

To distinguish then between the adverb and the preposition we may say:

(a) Where there is a noun phrase with a noun as its head (*a bill, a hill*), the preposition occurs only before it, the adverb occurs either before or after.

(b) Where there is a noun phrase consisting of a pronoun, the preposition precedes, the adverb follows (with no alternative position).

(c) When in final position, the preposition does not have nuclear stress (except in contrast) whereas the adverb always has nuclear stress.

We may make similar contrasts with FLY IN and LOOK OVER:

(a)	*The passenger flew in the plane,*
	The pilot flew in the plane,
but not	**The passenger flew the plane in,*
yet	*The pilot flew the plane in.*
(b)	*The passenger flew in it.*
	The pilot flew it in.
(c)	*This is the plane the passenger ˊflew in.*
	This is the plane the pilot flew ˋin.
(a)	*The spectator looked over my shoulder,*
	The doctor looked over my shoulder,
but not	**The spectator looked my shoulder over,*
yet	*The doctor looked my shoulder over.*
(b)	*The spectator looked over it.*
	The doctor looked it over.
(c)	*This is the shoulder the spectator ˋlooked over.*
	This is the shoulder the doctor looked ˋover.

There is also a likelihood, though by no means a certainty, that the preposition will have no stress at all when in medial position, whereas the adverb will have full stress. Certainly we may often contrast:

	He ˈran up a ˋhill,
and	*He ˈran ˈup a ˋbill,*
	The ˈpassenger ˈflew in the ˋplane,
and	*The ˈpilot ˈflew ˈin the ˋplane.*

But this difference is not always maintained; it is only a potential difference. Both as prepositions and adverbs *up* and *in* may also occur in such utterances without stress.

Where there is no noun at all following the verb we must, of course, have verb plus adverb, since by definition a preposition will always be followed by a noun phrase. Therefore we have adverbs in:

> *The tree blew down.*
> *The injured man came to.*

Where there are two elements following the verb, the first will always be an adverb, and the second a preposition, as in *put up with*. We shall find, therefore, that we have four types of unit to deal with:

1. verb + adverb without noun phrase
2. verb + preposition with noun phrase
3. verb + adverb with noun phrase
4. verb + adverb + preposition with noun phrase

10.1.2. *Idioms.* All four kinds of the combination that we considered at the end of the last section may or may not be 'idiomatic', i.e. that there may or may not be severe collocational restriction coupled with semantic unity on the whole sequence. We may contrast:

1. GIVE IN with COME IN   *The enemy gave in.*
                            The guests came in.
2. TAKE TO with GO TO   *I didn't take to him.*
                            I didn't go to London.
3. MAKE UP with BRING UP   *She made up the whole story.*
                            She brought up a book. (to a child in bed)

Or PUT DOWN in two different meanings

The ruler put the rebellion down.
The teacher put the book down.

4. Here there are three possibilities: that the whole combination is an idiom, or that the first two elements only are an idiom, or that it is not idiomatic at all. We may contrast, as these three possibilities, PUT UP WITH, GIVE UP WITH, and WALK UP WITH:

I can't put up with that woman.
The soldiers gave up with their arms.
She walked up with her brother to visit us.

One test of the unity of the combination verb plus particle that has been suggested is the possibility of substitution of these combinations by a single word. Thus COME TO may be replaced by RECOVER, LOOK AFTER by TEND, MAKE UP by INVENT, PUT UP WITH by TOLERATE. Whatever substitution there is, is in terms of the whole combination and not parts of it. The advantage of this is that it would appear to be formal whereas the test of an idiom is largely semantic. This test will not, however, work very well. It will sometimes give us too much, sometimes too little. There would be some difficulty for instance in:

She went for him in a big way.

Here undoubtedly GO FOR is a semantic unit. But there seems to be no single verb that can be substituted for GO FOR yet there is a verb that may be substituted here for GO, viz., FALL:

>*She fell for him in a big way.*

So the substitution test would exclude GO FOR. On the other side we should have to include such combinations as GO INTO, in *He went into the house*, in view of the substitution of GO INTO here by ENTER, *He entered the house*. Similarly, of course, we can replace GO UP by ASCEND, GO DOWN by DESCEND, and so on. But there seems to be little point in treating these as single units linguistically.

10.1.3. *The four classes.* It would seem reasonable to make use of both criteria, both that of preposition versus adverb and that of idiom. We shall limit our attention to those combinations that are idiomatic and use the preposition versus adverb distinction to differentiate prepositional and phrasal verbs. The non-idiomatic combinations, which are not included, are distinguished from these as 'verbs + preposition' and 'verbs + adverb'. Among the prepositional and phrasal verbs there are four possible types:

1. phrasal verbs without object
2. phrasal verbs with object
3. prepositional verbs
4. phrasal prepositional verbs

10.2. Phrasal verbs without object

There are a very large number of combinations of verb + adverb without object; some of these are idiomatic, others are not. With GO none appear to be idiomatic, GO IN, GO OUT, GO UP, GO DOWN, GO ACROSS, etc., Most of the combinations with GET are equally not idiomatic, GET IN, GET OUT, GET UP, GET DOWN, GET ACROSS, but GET ON may or may not be idiomatic:

>*Before you can ride a bicycle you have to get on.* (on the bicycle)
>
>*In business most people want to get on.* (succeed)

It is interesting to compare pairs of phrasal verbs whose adverbial particles are in their other (purely adverbial) use, opposite in meaning:

BREAK UP/DOWN *We break up next Wednesday.* (the school term finishes on Wednesday)
>*She broke down when she heard the news.* (burst into tears)

GIVE IN/OUT *I give in!* (yield)
>*The engine gave out.* (failed)

BLOW UP is an idiom in the sense of EXPLODE.

The bomb blew up.

But BLOW DOWN is not:

The chimney pot blew down.

There is, of course, also the famous story of the foreigner in the train who was told to look out. Instead of realising that LOOK OUT was a phrasal verb meaning TAKE CARE, he took it as a literal combination of LOOK+OUT and put his head further out of the window with disastrous consequences.

Apart from their semantic unity and the collocational restrictions on the occurrence of verb and the particle, there is nothing that will establish which are phrasal verbs and which are not. There are some other characteristics of combinations of this kind, but they do not lead to any clearcut criterion for establishing the phrasal verb.

(a) Some of the combinations may be used transitively as well as intransitively, e.g. BLOW UP and BLOW DOWN:

The house blew up.

They blew up the house.

The chimney pot blew down.

The wind blew the chimney pot down.

The fact that some of these combinations may be used both intransitively and transitively (with transformational relations of the kind associated with active and passive voice – see 4.3.5.) does not give any further criterion for the phrasal verb. Both phrasal verbs and verbs+adverb occur in this pattern.

There are similar features involving different lexemes, e.g. BRING versus COME. But again the pattern does not differ for phrasal verbs and verbs+adverb:

He brought about his own downfall.

His downfall came about.

He brought in his friend.

His friend came in.

(b) There is a *prima facie* similar relation between transitive and intransitive verbs, but involving merely the presence or absence of an object, not as in the previous section transformational relations of the kind associated with active and passive. We may note:

They carried on.

They carried on the business.

He turned over.

He turned over the page.

13—L.S.

But this feature too does not lead to any criterion for distinguishing between phrasal verb and verb + adverb.

(c) In many cases the adverb may be replaced by a prepositional phrase:

He got across.
He got across the river.
He came down.
He came down the hill.

Even here, however, we cannot make the distinction between phrasal verb and verb + adverb, since we may note also:

He hung about.
He hung about the place.

We should, presumably, want to consider GET ACROSS and COME DOWN as non-idiomatic and therefore not as phrasal verbs, but to treat HANG ABOUT as an idiom and therefore a phrasal verb. But it must be allowed that most of the combinations with this characteristic are not idiomatic, not phrasal verbs.

(d) With some of the combinations we have the possibility of a difference of order:

He went away.
Away he went.

And we may note here the use of this order in what is a semi-imperative:

Back you get.
Out she goes.
In you go.

We can at least be certain that the phrasal verb will not have this order, in spite of *Down he came* (*He came down*) we shall not find *Down he broke (*He broke down*), nor shall we find *About he hung. But while this possibility allows us to establish some combinations as verb + adverb and not phrasal verbs, it will not allow us to establish them all. It will not allow us to establish, for instance, LOOK OUT in its literal sense. For we shall not attest:

**Out he looked.*

Yet it would seem reasonable to treat LOOK OUT as a verb + adverb in its literal sense and as a phrasal verb in the sense of PAY ATTENTION.

There is one adverb that is used only in a phrasal verb – TO. Except in COME TO (=RECOVER) and in the corresponding transitive form BRING TO, TO is always a preposition:

He came to after a few minutes.
They brought her to with smelling salts.

Cf.   *He came to London.*
They brought it to me.

10.3. Phrasal verbs with object

Verbs of this type are, of course, very common especially with certain verbs like TAKE and PUT. We may:

>*Put about a rumour.*
>*Put back the clocks.*
>*Put down a rebellion.*
>*Put up a candidate.*
>*Put in an application.*
>*Put out a pamphlet.*
>*Put over an idea.*
>*Put off a meeting.*

It would be difficult to decide which of these were idiomatic and which were not, and difficult therefore to draw the line between phrasal verbs and verb + adverb. Some of the phrasal verbs of this kind have more than a single meaning. A woman may make up her face, her mind, a fire, a four at bridge. A rather interesting contrast across the Atlantic is the use in Britain of FILL IN, and in America of FILL OUT. In Britain we *fill in* a form, in America a form is *filled out*.

With some combinations the adverb occurs only after the object:

>*He ordered the men about,*

not
>**He ordered about the men.*
>*He saw the children across,*

not
>**He saw across the children.*
>*He kept his subjects under,*

not
>**He kept under his subjects.*
>*He drove the car past,*

not
>**He drove past the car.*   (or at least not with the same meaning)

Once again, however, this will not provide a useful test of phrasal verb versus verb + adverb. For if we consider the examples above, some of these are idiomatic and some are not. The point is, perhaps, made more clearly by TAKE IN, which is used in at least three different senses:

>*She takes washing in.*
>*She took the homeless children in.*
>*The conjuror took the audience in.*

Arranged in order of decreasing probability in my own speech are:

>*She takes in washing.*
>*The conjuror took in the audience.*
>*She took in the homeless children.*

But it is the last of these three that would seem to be most literal.

With BRING TO, where TO is certainly adverbial and where we have clearly a phrasal verb, there is only the possibility of:

>*They brought the man to,*

and not   **They brought to the man.*

If TO precedes the noun it is always a preposition.

10.4. Prepositional verbs

There are not very many combinations of verb and preposition that are idiomatic, and therefore prepositional verbs. Most obvious ones are LOOK AFTER, LOOK FOR, TAKE TO, GO FOR:

>*He looked after his old father.*
>*I'm looking for my glasses.*
>*I didn't take to him.*
>*She went for him in a big way.*

Not all of these have passives. We shall attest:

>*His aged father was looked after.*
>*My glasses are being looked for.*

Yet we shall not find:

>**He wasn't taken to.*
>**He was gone for in a big way.*

The test of a passive transformation does not then help to establish what is a prepositional verb as opposed to a verb + preposition. Indeed there are some verbs + preposition that nevertheless have passives, for instance SLEEP IN, SIT ON:

>*She slept in the bed.*
>*The bed was slept in.*
>*They sat on the chair.*
>*The chair's been sat on.*

Yet there would seem little feasibility in treating SLEEP IN and SIT ON as single units, as prepositional verbs, rather than as verbs + preposition. A major objection to using the possibility of the passive transformation is that it yields a very vague dividing line. Some combinations like SLEEP IN are commonly found in the passive. Others like GO TO are never found in the passive. We cannot say:

>**The city was gone to.*

With others, passives are possible in varying degrees. An example is WORK IN:

>*They worked in this office.*
>*This office has been worked in.*

This second structure is certainly not impossible, but not very probable. Similarly it is not certain whether we can reject:—

> *The hill's been run down (by a lot of people).*
> *The house has been gone into (by a burglar).*

Some of the prepositional verbs are used in specific collocations such that the whole combination of the verb + the following prepositional phrase is idiomatic, as in:

> *He came off his high horse.*
> *She went for him hammer and tongs.*

We have to establish here as idiomatic units COME OFF (ONE'S) HIGH HORSE and GO FOR (SOMEONE) HAMMER AND TONGS.

10.5. Phrasal prepositional verbs

A phrasal prepositional verb is, of course, one with two particles, one adverbial the other prepositional, the whole combination being idiomatic. The most famous of all the phrasal prepositional verbs is PUT UP WITH:

> *I can't put up with that woman.*

Another is DO AWAY WITH:

> *He did away with his wife.*

Phrasal prepositional verbs may be contrasted not only with verbs + adverb + preposition, but also with phrasal verbs + preposition. PUT UP WITH may be either a prepositional phrasal verb (as above) or a phrasal verb + preposition (where it equals STAY WITH):

> *You can always put up with Mrs. Brown when you come to Bristol.*

An example of a verb + adverb + preposition is WALK UP WITH:

> *She walked up with her brother to visit us.*

The phrasal prepositional verbs have passives:

> *This woman cannot be put up with.*
> *The wife was done away with by her husband.*

The others, the phrasal verb + preposition and the verb + adverb + preposition do not. We shall not attest:

> **Mrs. Brown can be put up with by you when you go to Bristol.*
> **Her brother was walked up with ...*

10.6. Other verbal combinations

There are other word sequences that are reasonably to be treated as single units, e.g. TAKE CARE OF, SET FIRE TO, GET RID OF. All except the last seem to be combinations of verb, noun and preposition (RID is usually an adjective):

> *He took care of the matter.*
> *The men set fire to the house.*
> *He got rid of his old car.*

All have passives:

> *The matter was taken care of.*
> *The house was set fire to.*
> *The old car was got rid of.*

TAKE CARE OF, however, follows the more regular pattern of verb + noun + preposition in that CARE may (a) be modified by an adjective, (b) be the subject of the passive:

> *He took great care of the matter.*
> *Care was taken of the matter.*

10.7. Phrasal verbs as catenatives

Some phrasal verbs function as catenatives, though only in a few of the catenative classes. Examples are COME ON (cf. **9.2.2.**):

> *It came on to rain.*
> *He went on to say ...*

GIVE UP, KEEP ON, LEAVE OFF (cf. **9.2.3.**):

> *He gave up smoking.*
> *It left off raining.*

GO ON – used with either structure 2 or 3, but in a different sense:

> *He went on to talk about it.*
> *He went on talking about it.*

These are paraphrasable by:

> *He continued by talking about it.*
> *He continued talking about it.*

LISTEN TO, LOOK AT (cf. **9.3.4.**):

> *I listen to him playing the piano.*
> *He looked at the men working in the garden.*

There are other verbal combinations that function as catenatives, e.g. HAVE A GOOD MIND, MAKE UP ONE'S MIND, TAKE CARE. These all function like the catenatives of **9.2.2.**

Many verbs plus preposition may, of course, be followed by an *-ing* form:

> *I thought about coming.*

But the *-ing* form may be regarded here as a verbal noun, (it functions like any other noun phrase) without analysis in terms of a complex phrase.

References

Prepositional verbs, phrasal verbs, prepositional phrasal verbs. Cf. B. M. H. Strang, *Modern English structure*, Edward Arnold Ltd., London 1962, 156–9; and T. F. Mitchell, 'Syntagmatic relations in linguistic analysis', *Transactions of the Philological Society*, 1958, 101–18.

Verb index

References are only to those pages on which the verbs in question are dealt with specifically. The phrasal verbs, etc., of Chapter 10 are not listed separately but under the heading of the verb only, but some important words or word combinations that are not strictly single verbs are listed here.

ACHE, 97
ADVISE, 170
AFFORD, 164, 172
AGREE, 159-60
AIM, 160
ALLOW, 170
APPEAR, 161
ARRANGE, 160
ASK, 160, 169
ASPIRE, 160
ATTEMPT, 161, 163
AVOID, 163

BE, 19–37, 53, 55–104, 140–3
— + TO, 134, 142–3
BE ABLE, 124, 138
BEAR, 52, 164
BEAT, 48–9
BECOME, 50, 168
BEG, 160, 170
BEGIN, 49, 89, 165–6
BELIEVE, 96
BELONG, 97
BEND, 47–8
BESEECH, 53
BET, 48
BETTER, 40, 147
BID, 52
BIND, 49
BITE, 52
BLEED, 49
BLOW, 52, 68, 185
BREAK, 51, 184
BREED, 49
BRING, 53, 183–6, 188
BUILD, 48
BURN, 47
BURST, 48
BUY, 51

CAN, 19–37, 42–3, 96, 115–19, 122–139
CARE, 161
CAST, 48
CATCH, 53, 171
CAUSE, 170
CEASE, 165–6
CHALLENGE, 170
CHANCE, 161, 163, 173
CHOOSE, 52, 160
CLING, 49
COME, 50, 161, 183, 185–6, 189–90
COMMAND, 170
COMPEL, 170
CONDESCEND, 160
CONSENT, 160
CONSIDER, 163
CONSIST, 97
CONTAIN, 97
CONTINUE, 152–3, 165–6
COST, 48
CREEP, 50
CUT, 48

DARE, 19–39, 41, 107, 120, 124–9, 135, 170
DEAL, 51
DECIDE, 153, 160
DECLINE, 160
DENY, 163
DEPEND, 97
DESERVE, 97, 160, 167
DETEST, 164, 172
DIG, 49
DIRECT, 170
DISLIKE, 164, 172
DO, 19–44, 53, 56, 58–9, 112, 141–2, 144–5, 148–9, 189
DRAW, 52

DREAD, 164
DREAM, 51
DRINK, 49
DRIVE, 51, 170, 187
DWELL, 47

EAT, 52
ELECT, 160
END, 89
ENJOY, 163, 165, 172
EQUAL, 66
EXPECT, 160, 170

FAIL, 161
FALL, 52
FANCY, 163, 165, 172
FEED, 49
FEEL, 51, 96–100, 168, 170–1
FIGHT, 50
FILL, 187
FINISH, 89, 162
FIND, 49, 171, 176
FLEE, 50
FLING, 49
FLY, 51, 182
FORBID, 52
FORCE, 170
FORGET, 52, 96, 166, 173
FORGIVE, 52
FORSAKE, 52
FREEZE, 51

GET, 49, 144, 146–7, 157, 159, 165,
    167, 169, 173–5, 184
— RID OF, 189
GIRD, 48
GIVE, 52, 170, 180, 183–4, 190
GO, 24, 53, 153, 163, 183–4, 188–90
GOING TO, 40, 63
GRIEVE, 177
GRIND, 49
GROW, 52

HANG, 49, 186
HAPPEN, 161
HASTEN, 161
HATE, 164–5, 172
HAVE, 19–37, 53, 55–63, 66, 68,
    72–7, 101–4, 124–5, 127–9, 136,
    143–8, 169, 173
— + TO, 125, 138, 145–6
HEAR, 50, 96, 99–100, 160, 170
HELP, 157, 159, 169

HESITATE, 160
HEW, 48
HIDE, 52
HIT, 48
HOLD, 50
HOPE, 96, 157, 160
HURT, 48

IMAGINE, 96, 100
INTEND, 153, 166, 170
INVITE, 170
ITCH, 97

KEEP, 50, 157, 159, 162, 169, 171,
    187, 190
KNEEL, 51
KNOW, 52, 169

LAUGH, 177
LEAD, 49, 170
LEAN, 51
LEAP, 50
LEARN, 47, 161, 163
LEAVE, 51, 171, 190
LEND, 48
LET, 48, 160, 169
LET'S, 40
LIE, 52
LIGHT, 49
LIKE, 159, 164–5, 169, 171–2
LISTEN TO, 99, 190
LIVE, 176
LOATHE, 164, 172
LONG, 161
LOOK, 99–100, 168, 180, 182, 185–
    186, 188
— AT, 99, 190
LOSE, 51
LOVE, 164–5, 172

MAKE, 53, 160–2, 169, 180, 183
MANAGE, 161
MARRY, 66
MATTER, 97
MAY, 19–37, 107, 118–19, 122–39
MEAN, 51, 161, 170
MEET, 49
MIND, 163, 165, 172
MISS, 163
MOTION, 170
MUST, 19–37, 107–8, 119, 125, 127,
    129, 135, 138–9

NEED, 19–39, 41, 107–8, 120, 125–129, 135, 138, 159, 156
NEGLECT, 161
NOTICE, 170

OBLIGE, 170
OBSERVE, 171
OFFER, 161
OMIT, 161
ORDER, 170, 187
OUGHT, 19–37, 107, 120, 125–30, 134, 138–9, 142
OWN, 97

PERCEIVE, 171
PLAN, 96, 100, 166
PLEASE, 97
POSTPONE, 163
PRACTISE, 163
PREFER, 164, 172
PREPARE, 161
PRESS, 170
PREVENT, 172
PROCEED, 161
PROMISE, 125, 161, 174
PROPOSE, 166
PUT, 48, 180, 183, 187, 189

QUIT, 48

READ, 49, 77, 90, 95
RECOLLECT, 167
REFUSE, 161
REGRET, 166, 173
REJOICE, 177
REMEMBER, 100–1, 159, 166, 169, 173
REMIND, 170
REND, 48
REQUIRE, 167
RESEMBLE, 66, 68
RESENT, 172
RID, 48
RIDE, 51
RING, 49, 68
RISE, 51
RISK, 163, 173
RUN, 50, 67, 181

SAY, 46, 50, 148, 162
SCORN, 161
SEE, 52, 96, 99, 169, 170–1, 187
SEEK, 53

SEEM, 131, 161
SELL, 50
SEND, 48, 171
SERVE, 162
SET, 48, 171
— FIRE TO, 189
SEW, 48
SHAKE, 52
SHALL, 19–37, 62–3, 107, 109–10, 113–15, 126, 130–1, 138
SHED, 48
SHINE, 50
SHOE, 50
SHOOT, 50
SHOW, 48
SHRINK, 49
SHUT, 48
SING, 49
SINK, 49
SIT, 49, 177, 188
SLAY, 52
SLEEP, 50, 77, 95, 188
SLIDE, 49
SLING, 49
SLIT, 48
SMELL, 47, 96–7, 99–101, 170–1
SMILE, 177
SMITE, 51
SOUND, 68, 99
SOW, 48
SPEAK, 51
SPEED, 49
SPELL, 47
SPEND, 48
SPILL, 47
SPIN, 49
SPIT, 49
SPLIT, 48
SPOIL, 47
SPREAD, 48
SPRING, 49
STAND, 53, 161–2, 164, 172, 177
START, 89, 165–6, 171
STEAL, 51
STICK, 49
STING, 49
STINK, 49
STOP, 157, 162, 171, 176
STRIDE, 51
STRIKE, 50
STRING, 49
STRIVE, 51, 161, 163
SUFFER, 97

SWEAR, 52, 161
SWEEP, 50
SWELL, 52
SWIM, 49
SWING, 49

TAKE, 52, 183, 187
— CARE OF, 189–90
TALK, 177
TASTE, 96–7, 99–101, 170
TEACH, 53, 170
TEAR, 52
TELL, 50, 170
TEMPT, 170
TEND, 161
THINK, 53, 96, 100
THREATEN, 161
THROW, 52
THRUST, 48
TREAD, 52
TROUBLE, 170
TRUST, 170
TRY, 161, 163

UNDERSTAND, 53, 170
UNDERTAKE, 161
UPSET, 48
URGE, 170
USED, 19–40, 123

WAIT, 175
WAKE, 51, 176
WANT, 157, 161, 167, 172
WARN, 170
WATCH, 170–1
WEAVE, 51
WEEP, 50
WET, 48
WILL, 19–37, 42–3, 63, 105–15, 122–
    139, 147
WIN, 49
WIND, 49
WISH, 161
WORK, 77, 90, 95
WRING, 49
WRITE, 51

Subject index

Ability, 9, 116, 121, 123, 128, 130–1, 138–9
Actor, 62, 65, 157
Adverb, 181–8
Adverbial, 69–70, 72–3, 75, 77–8, 84, 90–2, 108–19, 133, 160, 165
'Adverbial' use, 161, 163, 166
Ambiguity, 83, 88–9, 91, 102–4, 135, 154, 175
Analogue, 108–19, 122–8, 138–9
Animate, 65
Anomalous finites, 140–6, 148
Aspect, 59
Auxiliary, 14–15, 19–44, 55–139, 142, 146

Category, 59–60
Catenative, 15, 150–79
Causative, 170
Characteristic, 111–12, 116, 120–1, 123, 128
'Code', 15, 21, 24–5, 30, 38, 141, 148–9
Collocation, 64, 107–18, 160, 177
Colloquial, 24, 39, 161–2, 165
Commentary, 83
Complement, 16–17, 168
Completion, 79, 83
Complex phrase, 13, 17, 150–79
Conclusion, 119, 121, 125, 139
Concord, 13
Condition, 72, 108, 132–6
Continuous, 59
Current relevance, 73–6

Decision, 89
Demonstration, 83
Dependent, 13
Dialect, 27
Disapproval, 94
Discontinuity, 23
Downgrading, 155
Duration, 61, 77–8, 93–5, 98

Effort, 161
Emotion, 176–7

Emphatic affirmation, 15, 21, 25–6, 38, 58–9, 141
Empty verb, 148–9, 154
Eternal truth, 86–7
Experimentation, 163
Exponent, 5, 10, 30

Finite, 12–13, 19–20, 140
Form, 11–13, passim
Formal grammar, 6–9
Full verb, 14–15, 20, 45–54, 140–6
Future, 2, 60, 62–3, 69, 81–2, 87–92, 107–10, 113–17, 134, 160
Future in the past, 63, 87–92, 142
Future perfect, 137–8
Futurity, 109–10, 113, 120–1, 128, 138

Gerund, 17, 151–5, 164, 171–2
Goal, 157

Habitual, 59, 60–1, 69, 81–7, 92–5, 99, 111, 117, 119, 123–4
Hierarchy, 16, 155
Historic present, 69
Homorganic, 34–5
Homonym, 99–101

Idiom, 119, 160, 169, 181, 183–9
Imperative, 13, 55, 58–9, 106
Impossible, 125, 128, 131–2, 136
Induction, 86, 111, 120, 128
Infinitival, 13, 55, 58–9, 106, 151, 161–162, 164–7, 170–2
Infinitive, 13, 16, 142, 145, 150–5, 159–70, 174–7
Inflexion, 1, 33
-ing forms, 12–14, 45–7, 151–5, 162–7, 171–4, 177
Insistence, 112–13, 121, 123, 128
Intention, 89–90
Intonation, 3–6, 23, 41–2, 87–8, 91–2
Inversion, 15, 21, 23–4, 37–9, 141, 143

Juncture, 3–4, 6, 174–7

Lexeme, 11
Limited duration, 93–4, 98

Manner, 161
Meaning, 6–9, 158, 166–7
Modal, 8, 13, 15, 21, 105–39
Morpheme, 8, 10
Morphology, 14, 27–35, 45–54
Motion, 88

Negation, negative, 3, 14–15, 21–3,
    28–9, 37–9, 42–3, 58–9, 77, 107–8,
    117, 119–21, 124, 138–9, 141, 158–9,
    161, 173
Neutralisation, 134
Non-finite, see Finite.
Non-habitual, see Habitual.
Non-perfect, see Perfect.
Non-progressive, see Progressive.
Non-progressive verbs, 95–101
Notional, 7, 156
Noun phrase, 13, 151, 159–60, 166,
    168–79, 182

Object, 62, 64, 151–3, 155–7, 163–4,
    177, 184, 187–8
Obligation, 113, 119, 121, 129, 139
Orthography, 28–9, 46

Paradigm, 55–60, 105–6
Paraphrase, 125–6
Participial, 13, 20, 55, 58–9, 105, 151,
    165
Participle, 17, 106, 151–5, 171
Particle, 180
Passive, 151, 156–8, 162, 167–73, 180,
    see also Voice.
Past participle, 13–14, 45–53, 59, 68–9,
    151, 167–8, 177–8
Past-past, 71, 76–7, 101, 136
Past tense, 13–14, 28, 35–6, 123–4,
    see also Tense.
Past time, 116–17, 122–9, 173
Perfect, 59–62, 72–7, 101–4, 125, 151,
    161, 173
Permission, 117–18, 121, 123–5, 128–
    130, 134, 139
Person, 13, 55
Phonetics, 4, 32, 45–6
Phrasal prepositional verb, 66, 184, 189
Phrasal verb, 180–91
Phrase, 11, 14, 16–17, 55
Plural, 6–7, 9–10, 13–14
Possession, 144
Possibility, 116–19, 123–5, 128–9, 131,
    134, 138

Predicator, 155
Preposition, 66–7, 181–3, 188–9
Prepositional verb, 66, 180, 184, 188–
    189
Present participle, 13, 151–5
Present tense, 122, 124, see also Tense.
Primary pattern, 14–15, 17, 20, 36–7,
    55–104
'Private' verbs, 95–100
Probability, 112, 120, 125, 128–9, 131
Progressive, 59, 61, 66, 77–9, 93–101,
    106, 112, 161, 170–1
Promise, 113–14, 121, 128, 138
Pronoun, 181–2
Purpose, 174–5

Question, 23–4, 113–15, 117–18

Rankshifting, 155
Real conditions, 132–3
Regular, 3, 14, 29, 48, 50, 141
Reported speech, 70–1, 107, 122, 126–
    129
Results, 73–6, 175–6

-s form, 12–14, 45–7, 148
Secondary pattern, 15, 17, 20, 36–7,
    105–39
Selection, 17, 153
Semantics, 6–9
Semi-negative, 24, 39, 41–2
Sensation, 9, 97–100, 118, 123, 128,
    134, 170–1
Sequence of tenses, 69
Simple form, 12–14
Simple phrase, 17, 19, 55–139
Simple present, 82–5
Singular, 6–7, 13–14, 55
Speech, 2–3, 172
Sporadic repetition, 93–5, 98
'State', verbs of, 97–100
Stress, 3–6, 25–7, 87–8, 111–13, 182
Strong forms, 27–8, 43
Structure, 15, 36, 150–79
Subject, 23, 62, 64–5, 152, 155–7, 170,
    175, 177
Suppletion, 53
Syllabic, 29–35

Tag, 41–2
Tense, 2, 5, 12–14, 20, 59–63, 69–72,
    105–8
Tentative, 71–2, 116–19, 129–32

Time, 61–3, 69–70, 81–2, 84, 107–8
Traditional grammar, 151–5
Transformation, 64–7, 158, 168–9
Transitive, 68, 164, 185

Unreal conditions, 133–6
Unreality, 71–2, *see also* Condition, Tentative, Wish.
Use, *passim esp.* 60–3, 81–92, 108

Verbal noun, 151–9, 164

Voice, 59, 62, 64–9, 161
Volition, 109–11, 120, 124–5, 128–31, 134

Weak forms, 29–35, 43, 141, 143
Willingness, 116–18, 123, 125, 128, 130, 134
Wish, 72, 136–7
Word, 1–2, 10–11, 56–7, 151
Writing, 2–3, 29